# Sisters *in the* Wilderness

# SISTERS
## *in the*
# WILDERNESS

## The Challenge of Womanist God-Talk

### DELORES S. WILLIAMS

ORBIS BOOKS
Maryknoll, New York 10545

ORBIS BOOKS
**Maryknoll, New York 10545**

Fathers and Brothers
**MARYKNOLL**™

Founded in 1970, Orbis Books endeavors to publish works that enlighten the mind, nourish the spirit, and challenge the conscience. The publishing arm of the Maryknoll Fathers and Brothers, Orbis seeks to explore the global dimensions of the Christian faith and mission, to invite dialogue with diverse cultures and religious traditions, and to serve the cause of reconciliation and peace. The books published reflect the views of their authors and do not represent the official position of the Maryknoll Society. To learn more about Maryknoll and Orbis Books, please visit our website at www.maryknollsociety.org.

Manufactured in the United States of America

**Library of Congress Cataloguing-in-Publication Data**
Williams, Delores S.
   Sisters in the Wilderness: the challenge of womanist God-talk / Delores S. Williams.
     p. cm.
   Includes bibliographical references and index.
   ISBN 978-1-62698-038-9
   1. Feminist theology. 2. Black theology. 3. Afro-American women—Religious life. I. Title.
BT83.55.W55 1993
230'.082-dc20
                     93-10654

# CONTENTS

# PART II: WOMANIST GOD-TALK

# FOREWORD TO
## THE 20TH ANNIVERSARY EDITION

Twenty years ago in 1993, when Delores S. Williams published her book, *Sisters in the Wilderness: The Challenge of Womanist God-Talk,* few African-American women who self-identify as womanist theologians were aware of the centrality of this text in relation to the metamorphoses taking place both within and around black women's existential context. That was a year when African-American women ripped historical seams and changed traditional patterns, a fact that can now be seen not only with the hindsight of religious scholars looking back over two decades of theological discourse but also from diverse perspectives across our multi-stranded, thickly-textured body politic.

For instance, in 1993 some of us celebrated Thelma D. Adair who, as the co-chairperson of the U.S. Committee on the Ecumenical Decade of Churches in Solidarity with Women, served as one of the planners and participants in the Reimagining Conference held in Minneapolis; Evelyn Brooks Higginbotham, who published her historical analysis of the social, political, and ethical contributions of women in the African-American Baptist church in *Righteous Discontent: The Women's Movement in the Black Baptist Church, 1880–1920*; and Toni Morrison, who won the Nobel Prize in Literature for her novel, *Beloved*.

Other readers may appreciate how in 1993 Maya Angelou read her poem, "On the Pulse of Morning" at the inauguration of the forty-second president of the United States; Mary Frances Berry, a founding member of the Free South Africa Movement, was appointed the first African-American woman to chair the Civil Rights Commission; Eleanor Holmes Norton, who serves the District of Columbia as delegate to the U.S. House of Representatives, and who continues to fight for D.C. statehood on behalf of its residents, gained the right to vote in the House of Representatives; and Carol Moseley Braun became the first African-American woman on the Senate Finance Committee. Her maiden speech to the Senate, delivered January 26, 1993, was a eulogy to Supreme Court Justice Thurgood Marshall.

And still again, a few among us may recall the mean-spirited character assaults against Black women in 1993 when Lani Guinier, a first-rate professor, one of this nation's leading legal scholars and civil rights advocates, was caricatured by a *New York Post* columnist as a "Quota Queen"; and in this same time-frame, Joycelyn Elders, the first African-American woman to hold the position of U.S. surgeon general, faced controversy over her opinions on issues such as sex education, the legalization of narcotics, procreative choice, and conservatives quickly dubbed her the "Condom Queen."

Some of us may remember that 1993 brought us a surprising gift from the world of hip-hop—Queen Latifah issued *Black Reign*, her most popular album, featuring her single "U.N.I.T.Y.," which won a Grammy Award for Best Solo Rap Performance.

With confidence, competence and conviction Delores Williams claimed her place among this cloud of progressive soul-sisters in 1993, by publishing this groundbreaking book, *Sisters in the Wilderness*. The contextual antecedents for this theological accomplishment are the living spaces carved-out by womanist theologians who were in sync with the liberation wisdom of 1985. At that time, Cheryl Townsend Gilkes, as the first national convener of the Womanist Approach to Religion and Society Group, presented African-American women who were members of the AAR/SBL with a laudable goal—the crafting of programmatic strategies that would ensure lasting participation in bringing our education, talents, and imagination to bear in the wider world.

Shawn M. Copeland sums up the womanist theological agenda as differentiating the experiences (e.g., religious, personal, cultural, social, psychological and biological) of African-American women in the hermeneutical circle of theological inquiry and research, reflection, and judgment. Before 1993, two womanist monographs were published, my Black Womanist Ethics (1988) and Jacquelyn Grant's *White Women's Christ, Black Women's Jesus: Feminist Christology and Womanist Response* (1989). Since the publication of *Sisters in the Wilderness* in 1993, womanists have published more than two dozen books, documenting the claim that rigorous inquiry and open communication of, by, and for Black women are essential as we rethink the content and method of theology, ethics, and biblical exegesis.

Still, critics from within the academy and outside it may ask what is the significance of the wilderness metaphor to people who teach and preach in a twenty-first century globalized world, a world that moves at break-neck speed within interlocking economies, cultures, governmental policies, military affairs and political movements. In the context of religious scholarship, Williams's answer is clear. Using the cautionary tale of Hagar, the Egyptian woman in the Book of Genesis, Chapter 16, the handmaid of Sarah, who is cast out into the wilderness, Williams exposes realistic details of the painful limits set against Black existence in U.S. society.

The heart of Williams's thesis acknowledges the joys and sorrows, ups and downs, gains and losses of Black women searching for meaning in an unjust world. With this book, Williams launched an interdisciplinary, inter-textual womanist conversation. She examined Hagar's legacies and myths via biblical exegesis and literary criticism and artfully wove together the threads of these two interpretive tools through nuanced African-American cultural history, in order to bring us to the contemporary understanding of what it means to refer to and identify African-Americans as Aunt Hagar's children—women, men and children who feel ostracized, alienated, and cast out into modern-day deserts. In other words, stories about our identity as Aunt Hagar's children exemplify how truth-claims about the bygone days of slavery are linked to our God-consciousness and survivalist intentions as descendents of freed people living in these contemporary times.

Writing metaphorically about the biblical understanding of wilderness, Williams responds to the question raised by critics in this way: Hagar's experience in the wilderness of Beersheba serves as a symbolic counterpart to the living reality of numerous African-American women and children who live in conditions of vast, bewildering peril, here and now. Pulling no punches, Delores Williams elaborates in graphic detail on the exorbitant price women in the African Diaspora pay with our embodied social-selves when forced into exploitative motherhood and coercive surrogacy.

Notably, for those of us who have been reading and teaching *Sisters in the Wilderness* since 1993, and who, as theological educators, will continue to use this book as a required text for decades to come, we accept Williams's invitation to join her in wrestling with Hagar's God, a God who sees and hears. She contends that theologians need to think seriously about the real-life consequences of redemptive suffering, God-talk that equates the acceptance of pain, misery, and abuse as the way for true believers to live as authentic Christian disciples. Those who spew such false teaching and warped preaching must cease and desist.

This twentieth-anniversary edition of *Sisters in the Wilderness: The Challenge of Womanist God-Talk* is a key theological source for womanist scholarship far beyond the traditional parameters of the American Academy of Religion and Society of Biblical Literature. With each passing year, Black women theologians continue to dispel the notion of patriarchal, androcentric, value-free objectivity by publishing our radically relativized, contextualized truth. We devote a great deal of time to interdisciplinary, cross-cultural, non-dualistic divides in our writing and teaching.

As progressively thinking African-American women, we are mindful of the various ways that our very presence creates cognitive dissonance in customary communities of power. Thus, Sisters in the Wilderness is a revealing window that encourages us to look to the margins, rather than the central spaces for the divine presence in women's real-world liberation struggles. By wrapping our minds around the complexities embedded in wilderness-living, womanists and all others who cast their lot with us, appreciate the way Williams brings into sharp focus the need for us to eradicate race, sex, class and gender oppression as well as Eurocentric imperialistic thinking embedded in the faith claims of church and society.

*Katie G. Cannon*

# PREFACE

I have come to believe that theologians, in their attempt to talk to and about religious communities, ought to give readers some sense of their autobiographies. This can help an audience discern what leads the theologian to do the kind of theology she does. What has been the character of her faith journey? What lessons has this journey taught? What kind of faith inspires her to continue writing and rewriting, living and reliving theology in a highly secular white-and-black world paying little or no attention to what theologians are saying?

These questions posed within the context of my life history remind me of a form of community sharing in the black church called testifying. Many times, as a little girl, I sat in the church pew with my mother or grandmother and heard the black believers, mostly women, testify about "how far they had come by faith." They expressed their belief that God was involved in their history, that God helped them make a way out of no way. As they shared their trials, tribulations and blessings, they asked the other communicants to pray for them. Their testimonies suggested they believed their lives were about more than white people's oppression of black people.

Now years later, after my participation in the civil rights movement of the 1960s; after the births of my four children; after my college training, late seminary education, Ph.D. studies; after the sudden death of my husband and my resulting single-parent status; I find myself testifying. Faith, hard won, has taught me how to value the gains, losses, stand-offs and victories in my life. Many times the painful moments would not have been healed were it not for the road I traveled to faith—learning to trust the righteousness of God in spite of trouble and injustice; learning to trust women of many colors regardless of sexism, racism, classism and homophobia in our society; learning to believe in the sanctuary power of family defined in many ways in addition to nuclear; discovering love in a variety of forms that heal, but also believing serious political action is absolutely necessary for justice to prevail in the world of my four black children and other mothers' children.

Faith has taught me to see the miraculous in everyday life: the miracle of ordinary black women resisting and rising above evil forces in society, where forces work to destroy and subvert the creative power and energy my mother and grandmother taught me God gave black women.[1] Ordinary black women doing what they always do: holding the family and church together; working for the white folks or teaching school; enduring whatever they must so their children can reach for the stars; keeping hope alive in the family and community when money is scarce and white folks get mean and ugly. I discovered that this miraculous "resisting and rising above" has *for generations* been many black women's contribution of faith, love and hope to the black family, to the church and to the black community in North America.

Growing up in an African-American community in the urban South in the late forties and fifties, I learned early to recognize the forces bent on conquering black women's power to resist and rise above obstacles. There were some white people's intentions of ending the lives of black women's children and demeaning black women. Most children in my neighborhood knew the lore about the lynching of the black man by white people on the lawn of the white hotel around the corner where white people lived. Many children knew a white man raped a black woman and nearly killed her when she resisted. Black people had no legal recourse in either case.

There were also some black men's intentions of conquering black women's power of resisting and rising above trouble. I remember hearing the bloodcurdling screams of the woman in the house next to ours when her husband beat her for acting uppity—showing off her education, he said. She had been a school teacher. She packed her clothes, took her child and went to her mamma's house. She never returned to her husband. I remember the man living in an alley house at the rear of my grandmother's property. One night, when I was ten years old, I saw him beat his wife unmercifully. She had hidden her day-work money and would not give it to him. She left the next day and never came back.

Physical violence done to black women was matched by emotional and psychological pressure put upon them. School principals and preachers also tried to put impediments in black women's way of resisting and rising above oppression. During the days of segregation in my native land of Kentucky, when black males were in charge of selecting the black females to fill teaching positions and were in charge of administering procedures to make divorced black fathers pay child support, many of these males in charge tried to put the distribution of jobs and services to women on the basis of whether the women would have illicit affairs with them. Racism and male supremacy in the courts, on the school boards and in the social service offices gave black women no legal recourse. Too often some of the preachers—to whom black women turned for support—were as involved in propositioning black women as were the other males. Nobody in the community did anything to stop this oppression of black women.

But in spite of antagonisms, ordinary spiritual black women continued their struggle to resist and rise above the forces seeking to destroy their lives and spirits. More often than not, they accounted for their perseverance on the basis of their faith in God who helped them "make a way out of no way."[2] The courage and perseverance of these everyday black women shaped a model of faith and social behavior passed down to generations of women in the community and church. These ordinary women celebrated their lives in the social sense of church basket meetings, family reunions, children's graduations, their own graduations, community organization, children's successes and church festivals in which they invested great care and preparation.

In the midst of testifying about my own faith and marveling at the faith and courage of female progenitors, I reflect upon what it means to take seriously (as a primary theological source) the faith, thought and life-struggle of African-American women. I am in the throes of what the ancient African theologian Augustine and the European theologian Anselm termed "faith seeking understanding." By understanding I mean exploring faith so that I provide theological responses to issues confronting African-American women and the black community trying to survive in today's world. "Faith seeking understanding" from an oppressed black female's perspective means affirming the necessity of political and spiritual "works" —affirming these for the salvation of one's self and for the salvation of the black family, of the homeless, of the destitute, of the young black people lost in the drug culture in North America.

Yet my female faith seeking understanding asks questions. Given what looks like genocidal impulses in American culture directed toward black people (male and female), what kind of "works" can stem from black women's belief in a God who helps them "make a way out of no way"? How do I shape a theology that is at once committed to black women's issues and life struggles and simultaneously addresses the black community's historic struggle to survive and develop a positive, productive quality of life in the face of death?

How do I design theological language and devise theological methods that not only speak in the academy but also speak to African-American women and the African-American community in a language they can understand? How does my black female theological voice join the chorus of non-black women's voices and male voices in theology without compromising black women's faith? How do we black female theologians speak with all our strength when some white female and some black male scholars work together to crowd out our voices or take control of our words?

I realize my theological preoccupation with faith seeking understanding cannot romanticize black women's Christian faith. I cannot ignore how this faith has also been shaped by a process in black and white communities that I recognize as "colonization of female mind and culture."[3] Nor can I ignore the fact that the African-American denominational churches, in their patriarchally and androcentrically biased liturgy and leadership, have been primary agents of this mind-culture colonization with regard to black women.[4] Yet the churches have also been psycho-social places where black women could find some relief from the terrible burdens in their lives—whether these burdens came from low self-esteem, from negative experience in love relations, from early deaths in the family, from loss of children to street and drug culture or from white racism and economic oppression. The African-American denominational churches told black women they were "somebody" in a society that hated their race and spurned their womanhood. However, there is no doubt in my mind that some male preachers take advantage of the great emotional needs some black women bring to the churches.

Historically, however, the African-American denominational churches have also been places where black women, aside from venting their pain in emotional response, have come for decidedly theological reasons. They love God and the spirit, and they come to church to celebrate the great work of the spirit that brings and sustains whatever is positive in their lives. Hence the shouting and rhythm in churches are part of black women's faith statement, celebrating and giving thanks to God and the spirit for working in their hearts and lives.

This means, then, that the African-American denominational churches function like two-edged swords. They sustain black women emotionally and provide "theological space" for black women's faith expressions. But they suppress and help to make invisible black women's thought and culture. Through their uncritical use of the Bible and through their patriarchal theology, many of the African-American denominational churches prohibit black women from asking many critical questions about women's oppression and about the support and reinforcement of that oppression by the Bible and by the Christian church in all its male-dominated forms.

Today a theological corrective is developing that has considerable potential for bringing black women's experience into theology so that black women will see the need to transform the sexist character of the churches and their theology. The corrective—emerging among black female theologians, ethicists, biblical scholars, ministers and laywomen—is called womanist theology.[5] This theology is beginning to provide real insight for my concern with faith seeking understanding. As I see it, womanist theology is a prophetic voice reminding African-American denominational churches of their mission to seek justice and voice for all their people, of which black women are the overwhelming majority in their congregations. Yet this prophetic voice is concerned about the well-being of the entire African-American community, female and male, adults and children.

A little more than ten years old, womanist theology emerged from what many of us saw as characteristic of black women's experiences of relation, loss, gain, faith, hope, celebration and defiance.[6] While its aim is discourse and work with black women in the churches, it also brings black women's experience into the discourse of *all* Christian theology, from which it has previously been excluded. Womanist theology attempts to help black women see, affirm and have confidence in the importance of their experience and faith for determining the character of the Christian religion in the African-American community. Womanist theology challenges all oppressive forces impeding black women's struggle for survival and for the development of a positive, productive quality of life conducive to women's and the family's freedom and well-being. Womanist theology opposes all oppression based on race, sex, class, sexual preference, physical disability and caste.[7]

Like black male liberation theology, womanist theology assumes the necessity of responsible freedom for all human beings. But womanist theology especially concerns itself with the faith, survival and freedom-struggle of African-American women. Thus womanist theology identifies and critiques black male oppression of black females while it also critiques white racism that oppresses all African Americans, female and male. Like white feminist theology, womanist theology affirms the full humanity of women.[8] But womanist theology also critiques white feminist participation in the perpetuation of white supremacy, which continues to dehumanize black women. Yet womanist theology is organically related to black male liberation theology and feminist theology in its various expressions (including African women's, Mujerista, Jewish and Asian women's theology).

Womanist theology, however, also branches off in its own direction, introducing new issues and constructing new analytical categories needed to interpret simultaneously black women's and the black community's experience in the context of theology.[9] Nonetheless, womanist theology is usually non-separatist and dialogical. It welcomes discourse with a variety of theological voices—liberation, white feminist, Mujerista, Jewish, Asian, African, classical and contemporary "male-stream," as well as non-feminist, non-womanist female voices. Womanist theology considers one of its primary tasks to dialogue with the church and with other disciplines.

Given all the testimony, observations, descriptions and questions raised above, my task at this point is to tell the reader how I, a womanist theologian, come to do the god-talk in this book. The following Introduction is a proper place to begin. But first I must express my gratitude to people who helped along the way. Tom Driver, Beverly Harrison, Carter Heyward, Cheryl Townsend Gilkes, Susan Thistlethwaite, Anne Elliott, JoAnne Terrell, the late Norman Wilkerson and James Cone read very early versions of this manuscript. Colleen Kristula and my daughter Rita A. Seay are due special thanks for their painstaking preparation of some of the earlier manuscripts. Yalini Senathirajah provided immeasurable support as she put portions of the final version of this book on the computer. Betty Bolden is due more appreciation than I can ever give. Her assistance to me in the Burke Library at Union Theological Seminary was invaluable. I can never forget her faith in my work and her encouragement when all my simultaneous roles—as mother, wife, student, poet, scholar, teacher—weighed most heavily upon me. I also am greatly appreciative of Beverly Harrison, a true friend, who often provided so much comfort as I dealt with and tried to work through the stress of multi-role demands. Seth Kasten and Drew Kadel, research librarians at Union's Burke Library, helped me work through research problems. I am grateful to both of them. I thank my children, Rita, Celeste, Steven and Leslie, for the advice they have given me over the years "to keep trucking, Mamma." Also, my late husband, Robert C. Williams, is appreciated for the patience and encouragement he gave as I plowed through transformations of faith, spirit and consciousness. And my mother, Gladys Carter, must be thanked for the great model of courage and perseverance she has been for her children. She, an African-American church woman, has always been there for us as "a mighty pleasant help in the time of trouble."

My very last words of preface are these: I *pray* this book will also speak in a meaningful way to those African-American women who struggle by faith to bring dignity, hope, spiritual sustenance, economic well-being and educational advancement to the everyday lives of black people and to the African-American churches. But my hope is that these black women, in all their giving, take Alice Walker's advice seriously and remember to *love themselves*. Regardless.

*Delores S. Williams*

# INTRODUCTION

Where would I begin in order to construct Christian theology (or god-talk) from the point of view of African-American women? I pondered this question for over a year. Then one day my professor responded to my complaint about the absence of black women's experience from all Christian theology (black liberation and feminist theologies included). He suggested that my anxiety might lessen if my exploration of African-American cultural sources was consciously informed by the statement "I am a black WOMAN." He was right. I had not realized before that I read African-American sources from a black male perspective. I assumed black women were included. I had not noticed that what the sources presented as "black experience" was really black male experience. At that time, the mid-seventies, not many black women's writings were available. The Schomburg series of nineteenth-century black women's writings edited by Henry Louis Gates, Jr., had not appeared. Neither had the series *Black Women in United States History*, edited by Darlene Clark Hine.

Nevertheless, when I began reading available black female and black male sources with my female identity fixed firmly in my consciousness, I made a startling discovery. I discovered that even though black liberation theologians used biblical paradigms supporting an androcentric bias in their theological statements, the African-American community had used the Bible quite differently. For over a hundred years, the community had appropriated the Bible in such a way that black women's experience figured just as eminently as black men's in the community's memory, in its self-understanding and in its understanding of God's relation to its life. As I read deeper in black American sources from my female perspective, I began to see that it was possible to identify at least two traditions of African-American biblical appropriation that were useful for the construction of black theology in North America.[1]

One of these traditions of biblical appropriation emphasized liberation

1

of the oppressed and showed God relating to men in the liberation struggles. In some African-American spiritual songs, in slave narratives and in sermons by black preachers reference was made to biblical stories and personalities who were involved in liberation struggle. Moses, Jesus/God, Paul and Silas delivered from jail, Shadrak, Meshack and Abednego delivered from the fiery furnace and "My God delivered Daniel and why not every man"—all of these references appeared in the deposits of African-American culture. Black male theologians had reflected upon these sources and also had been inspired by the liberation emphasis in the 1960s black cultural and political revolution. So they produced black liberation theology. Their validating biblical paradigm in the Hebrew testament was the exodus event when God delivered the oppressed Hebrew slaves from their oppressors in Egypt. Their Christian testament paradigm was Luke 4, when Jesus described his mission and ministry in terms of liberation. Their normative claim for biblical interpretation was "God the liberator of the poor and oppressed." I reasoned that it is possible, then, to name this tradition the *liberation tradition of African-American biblical appropriation.*

My discovery of the second tradition of African-American biblical appropriation excited me greatly. This tradition emphasized female activity and de-emphasized male authority. It lifted up from the Bible the story of a female slave of African descent who was forced to be a surrogate mother, reproducing a child by her slave master because the slave master's wife was barren. For more than a hundred years Hagar—the African slave of the Hebrew woman Sarah—has appeared in the deposits of African-American culture. Sculptors, writers, poets, scholars, preachers and just plain folks have passed along the biblical figure Hagar to generation after generation of black folks.[2]

As I encountered Hagar again and again in African-American sources, I reread her story in the Hebrew testament and Paul's reference to her in the Christian testament. I slowly realized there were striking similarities between Hagar's story and the story of African-American women. Hagar's heritage was African as was black women's. Hagar was a slave. Black American women had emerged from a slave heritage and still lived in light of it. Hagar was brutalized by her slave owner, the Hebrew woman Sarah. The slave narratives of African-American women and some of the narratives of contemporary day-workers tell of the brutal or cruel treatment black women have received from the wives of slave masters and from contemporary white female employers. Hagar had no control over her body. It belonged to her slave owner, whose husband, Abraham, ravished Hagar. A child Ishmael was born; mother and child were eventually cast out of Abraham's and Sarah's home without resources for survival. The bodies of African-American slave women were owned by their masters. Time after time they were raped by their owners and bore children whom the masters seldom claimed—children who were slaves—children and their mothers whom slave-master fathers often cast out by selling them to other slave holders. Hagar resisted the brutalities of slavery by running away. Black American women have a long resistance history that includes running away from slavery in the antebellum era. Like Hagar and her child Ishmael, African-American female slaves and their children, after slavery, were expelled from the homes of many slave holders and given no resources for survival. Hagar, like many women throughout African-American women's history, was a single parent. But she had serious personal and salvific encounters with God—encounters which aided Hagar in the survival struggle of herself and her son. Over and over again, black women in the churches have testified about their serious personal and salvific encounters with God, encounters that helped them and their families survive.

I realized I had stumbled upon the beginning of an answer to my question: Where was I to begin in my effort to construct theology from the point of view of black women's experience? I was to begin with the black community (composed of females and males) and its understanding of God's historic relation to black female life. And, inasmuch as Hagar's story had been appropriated so extensively and for such a long time by the African-American community, I reasoned that her story must be the community's analogue for African-American women's historic experience. My reasoning was supported, I thought, by the striking similarities between Hagar's story and African-American women's history in North America. But what would I name this Hagar-centered tradition of African-American biblical appropriation? I did not feel that it belonged to the liberation tradition of African-American biblical appropriation. My exposure to feminist studies had convinced me that women must claim their experience, which has for so long been submerged by the overlay of oppressive, patriarchal cultural forms. And one way to claim experience is to name it. Naming also establishes some permanence and visibility for women's experience in history.

At this point, my effort to name the women-centered tradition was facilitated by the work of anthropologist Lawrence Levine. He concluded that African Americans (especially during slavery) did not accommodate themselves to the Bible. Rather, they accommodated the Bible to the urgent necessities of their lives.[3] But in this business of accommodating the Bible to life, I knew that the black American religious community had not traditionally put final emphasis upon the hopelessness of the painful aspects of black history, whether paralleled in the Bible or not. Rather, black people used the Bible to put primary emphasis upon God's response to the community's situations of pain and bondage. So I asked myself: What was God's response to Hagar's predicament? Were her pain and God's response to it congruent with African-American women's predicament and their understanding of God's response to black women's suffering? Perhaps by answering these questions I could arrive at a name for this Hagar-centered tradition of African-American biblical appropriation.

A very superficial reading of Genesis 16:1–16 and 21:9–21 in the Hebrew testament revealed that Hagar's predicament involved slavery, poverty, ethnicity, sexual and economic exploitation, surrogacy, rape, domestic violence, homelessness, motherhood, single-parenting and radical encounters with God. Another aspect of Hagar's predicament was made clear in the Christian testament when Paul (Galatians 4:21–5:1) relegated her and her progeny to a position outside of and antagonistic to the great promise Paul says Christ brought to humankind. Thus in Paul's text Hagar bears only negative relation to the new creation Christ represents.[4] In the Christian context of Paul, then, Hagar and her descendants represent the outsider position par excellence. So alienation is also part of the predicament of Hagar and her progeny.

God's response to Hagar's story in the Hebrew testament is not liberation. Rather, God participates in Hagar's and her child's survival on two occasions. When she was a run-away slave, God met her in the wilderness and told her to resubmit herself to her oppressor Sarah, that is, to return to bondage. Latin American biblical scholar Elsa Tamez may be correct when she interprets God's action here to be on behalf of the survival of Hagar and child. Hagar could not give birth in the wilderness. Perhaps neither she nor the child could survive such an ordeal. Perhaps the best resources for assuring the life of mother and child were in the home of Abraham and Sarah. Then, when Hagar and her child were finally cast out of the home of their oppressors and were not given proper resources for survival, God provided Hagar with a resource. God gave her new vision to see survival resources where she had seen none before. Liberation in the Hagar stories is not given by God; it finds its source in human initiative. Finally, in Hagar's story there is the suggestion that God will be instrumental in the development of Ishmael's and Hagar's quality of life, for "God was with the boy. He grew

up and made his home in the desert [wilderness], and he became an archer"
(Genesis 21:20).

Thus it seemed to me that God's response to Hagar's (and her child's)
situation was survival and involvement in their development of an appropriate quality of life, that is, appropriate to their situation and their heritage.
Because they would finally live in the wilderness without the protection of
a larger social unit, it was perhaps to their advantage that Ishmael be skillful
with the bow. He could protect himself and his mother. The fact that Hagar
took a wife for Ishmael "from the land of Egypt" suggests that Hagar wanted
to perpetuate her own cultural heritage, which was Egyptian, and not that of
her oppressors Abraham and Sarah.

Even today, most of Hagar's situation is congruent with many African-
American women's predicament of poverty, sexual and economic exploitation, surrogacy, domestic violence, homelessness, rape, motherhood, single-
parenting, ethnicity and meetings with God. Many black women have testified that "God helped them make a way out of no way."[5] They believe God is
involved not only in their survival struggle, but that God also supports their
struggle for quality of life, which "making a way" suggests.[6]

I concluded, then, that the female-centered tradition of African-American biblical appropriation could be named the *survival/quality-of-life tradition of African-American biblical appropriation*. This naming was consistent
with the black American community's way of appropriating the Bible so that
emphasis is put upon God's response to black people's situation rather than
upon what would appear to be hopeless aspects of African-American people's
existence in North America. In black consciousness, God's response of survival and quality of life to Hagar is God's response of survival and quality of
life to African-American women and mothers of slave descent struggling to
sustain their families with God's help.

Several black scholars have suggested a bond in black American heritage
between the survival/quality-of-life struggle and the community's belief in
God's presence in the struggle. Historian John Blassingame points to this
reality in the slave community when he claims that

> one of the primary reasons the slaves were able to survive the cruelty
> they faced was that their behavior was not totally dependent on their
> masters. . . . In religion, a slave exercised his own independence of con-
> science. Convinced that God watches over him, the slave bore his [and
> her] earthly afflictions, in order to earn a heavenly reward. Often he
> disobeyed his earthly master's rules to keep his heavenly master's com-

mandments. . . . Religious faith gave an ultimate purpose to his life, a sense of communal fellowship and personal worth. . . . In short religion helped him preserve his mental health. Trust in God was conducive to psychic health insofar as it excluded all anxiety-producing preoccupations by the recognition of a loving providence.[7]

Church historian Gayraud S. Wilmore, in his discussion of the slaves' survival efforts, also suggests the inextricable relation between survival/quality-of-life and the slave's religious faith, which of course presupposed God's presence in the struggle:

> If whites thought they were dealing with children who could not discern the difference between white theology and white behavior they were sadly mistaken. As John Lovell, Jr., has observed, "The slave relied upon religion, not primarily because he felt himself converted; but because he recognized the power inherent in religious things." That power had to do, first of all, with the necessity of survival—with the creation of an alternative reality system that could keep the slave alive and possessed of some modicum of sanity. The protest and resistance elements we find in early forms of black folk religions in the Caribbean and in the southeastern United States express the determination to survive against all odds.[8]

The slaves' effort to create an alternative value system represents a struggle to achieve a positive quality of life. With their syncretized African-American religion (syncretized by elements of African traditional religions) they believed in God's presence with them. This belief, connecting with the survival/quality-of-life struggle, gave hope to the slaves' daily lives of oppression and toil.

Affirming the similarities between Hagar's predicament and African-American women's historic predicament (as well as affirming the congruence of the two understandings of God's response to these situations), the survival/quality-of-life tradition of African-American biblical appropriation showed me more clearly what was involved in constructing womanist god-talk.[9]

The first step was to provide black people with a deeper understanding of Hagar's story than the account in the Hebrew testament. This meant exploring social and cultural realities relevant to the biblical account. Thus Chapter 1 of *Sisters in the Wilderness*—entitled "Hagar's Story: A Route to Black Women's Issues" —rereads Hagar's story in the Hebrew testament taking seriously some of the Hebraic, Egyptian and nomadic social and cultural forces that could have had an impact upon Hagar's situation.

My rereading is a method of biblical interpretation shaped by the Latin American feminist way of viewing Hagar's story from the perspective of poor, oppressed women.[10] What this means is attempting to see the Hagar-Sarah texts in the Bible from the position of the slave woman Hagar rather than from the perspective of slave owners (Abraham and Sarah) and their culture. For the purposes of *Sisters in the Wilderness* this method is suitable because the African-American community in North America has already appropriated the story with Hagar as the central human figure rather that Sarah or Abraham.

Rereading does not mean changing the text as it appears in the Bible or adding "characters" to the Hagar-Sarah stories that do not appear in the biblical accounts.[11] Within the context of African-American interpretation, rereading can mean bringing in more nontraditional sources to aid in the interpretation than have been used by such leading Western exegetes as Gerhard von Rad, E. A. Speiser, Claus Westermann, Phyllis Trible, Elsa Tamez and others. For instance, the "rereader," conscious of the African-American tradition of appropriating Hagar and her story and trying to see the story from Hagar's position, might be interested in enlarging interpretation by focusing on some aspects of African (Egyptian) culture that might have affected Hagar's behavior on some occasions. Some Egyptian customs that might have affected Hagar, are described in Chapter 1. This attention to African heritage relative to Hagar's story resonates with African-American Christians' long attempt to uncover African residuals in their culture and religious experience and to discover as much as possible about Africa's relation to the Bible. The attention to Hagar's African heritage also conforms to recent efforts of black biblical scholars to ferret out the African references in scripture that Western biblical scholarship has heretofore ignored and thus made invisible.

From this rereading of Hagar's story comes the second step involved in providing god-talk mindful of black women's experience. Heuristics and issues emerge that are used in subsequent chapters in *Sisters in the Wilderness* to explore the nature of African-American women's experience in both the black and white American worlds. Though most of the issues in the Hagar story could be used to lay fully open the many dimensions of black women's experience, space limitations allowed only a few to be used. Therefore, I selected from Hagar's story those issues that had, simultaneously, personal, social and religious significance for black women and for the African-American community: the predicament of motherhood; the character of surrogacy; the problem of ethnicity; and the meaning and significance of wilderness experience for women and for the community. Hence Chapter 2 in this book, "Tensions in Motherhood: From Slavery to Freedom," explores what appears to be evolving tensions in African-American understandings of the function of black motherhood. Chapter 3, entitled "Social-Role Surrogacy: Naming Black Women's Oppression," explores the nature of black women's experience with surrogacy in both antebellum and postbellum America.

Chapter 4 approaches the subject of ethnicity from the perspective of skin color, "the badge of African-American ethnicity" in North America. Rather than probe the character of racism with regard to black women's experience, this chapter shows how skin-color consciousness and the value put upon color have birthed a pathological pattern in American culture that continues to this day. This pattern is named "white racial narcissism." However, the aim of the chapter is not to be accusatory. Rather, its aim is to show a method by which the devaluation and abuse of black people, both female and male, through the centuries has been gradually cemented into America's national consciousness.[12]

Chapter 5, "Sisters in the Wilderness and Community Meanings," draws brief analogies between Hagar's experience in the wilderness and African-American women's understanding of their wilderness experience. Then the chapter shows how black women's experience and the black community's experience come together in a symbolic sense attached to the African-American notion of wilderness. A discussion of the intellectual, social and political significance of this black wilderness symbolism ends the chapter.

Part II of *Sisters in the Wilderness*, "Womanist God-Talk," begins with Chapter 6, "Womanist God-Talk and Black Liberation Theology." This chapter discusses certain classical texts in black liberation theology: James Cone, *A Black Theology of Liberation*, second edition; James Cone, *God of the Oppressed*; James Deotis Roberts, *Liberation and Reconciliation: A Black Theology*; and Cecil Wayne Cone, *The Identity Crisis in Black Theology*. Based on insights from the explorations in the earlier chapters, the womanist god-talk in Chapter 6 dialogues with black liberation theology in the areas of theological methodology, doctrine and ethics. The dialogue is focused in each area by specific issues. In the area of method in liberation theology, the focus is upon the use of the Bible, the understanding and function of experience and the notion of the theological task. In the area of doctrine the womanist god-talk attempts more to enlighten than to dialogue; that is, it reveals the questions about the doctrine of atonement that arise when African-American women's surrogacy experience is reflected upon. The womanist god-talk on this subject invites black liberation theologians into conversation with women about atonement, since black liberation theology has not, to date, given consideration to the meaning of atonement in its enterprise. In the area of ethics the womanist discussion in this chapter uncovers an ethical task black theologians, female and male, exercise in their work.

Chapter 7, "Womanist-Feminist Dialogue: Differences and Commonalities," enters into dialogue with a variety of feminist voices: African, Asian, white-American, Hispanic and other womanist. The first part of this chapter focuses on the theological differences between some feminist/womanist texts and the content of *Sisters in the Wilderness* on such issues as the meaning and use of such terms as *virginity* (as in the Virgin Mary), the understanding in different cultures of what is acceptably female and other issues. The last part of the chapter indicates some of the common ground upon which womanists and feminists stand theologically. Some feminist theological positions very much relevant for the womanist god-talk in *Sisters in the Wilderness* are not included. This is because these positions need more conversation with my position than this present book can provide. For instance, theologian Carter Heyward's position on "mutual relation" and "righting relationships" has affinity with my position. At some point we and other feminists who hold this position need to discuss the differences we each espouse on these issues. But we need a full text to do this. Obviously Beverly Harrison's work and other work in women's reproduction rights and in reproduction technology have a lot to say to my womanist suggestion that black women's history be understood as reproduction history; that is, reproduction history that uses labor as a hermeneutic to interpret black women's biological and social experience of reproducing and nurturing the species and labor as an interpretative tool for analyzing and assessing black women's creative productions as well as their relation to power structures in both the black and white worlds. Certainly I need to give this more thought. This observation about black women's history as reproduction history, like some of the other ideas in the book, is suggestive. Though relevant to the content of *Sisters in the Wilderness*, some of these suggestive ideas will be developed more fully in another context. They are mentioned in this text because I think we womanist theologians must get as many ideas "out there" as possible when we have the chance—that is, ideas relevant to whatever subject we are treating at the time. Most of us know racism and sexism in the publishing business and in theological education lets only a few black people (female and male) into positions that allow us to have a public voice and to publish. Therefore we must share as much with each other as we can so that many, many ideas relevant to our people can get abroad, even if the ideas are developed later by someone other than the original contributor.

The last chapter in *Sisters in the Wilderness* is entitled "Wornanist Reflections on 'The Black Church,' the African-American Denominational Churches and the Universal Hagar's Spiritual Church." This chapter begins with my faith statement celebrating the idea of "The Black Church." I make a distinction between "The Black Church" and the African-American denominational churches. Then I catalog some sins against black women practiced in some of the African-American denominational churches. I also introduce the Universal Hagar's Spiritual Churches, which bear the name of Hagar in the Bible. Most of my knowledge of the Hagar churches has come from personal visits, conversations and from the work of Hans Baer, who has produced the only extended study of the Universal Hagar's Spiritual Churches that I could find. No scholar has focused extensively upon women in the Hagar's churches. Chapter 8 is called reflections rather than something more academic because it presents the awful side of the African-American denominational churches that has not to date been documented and has never been included in the scholarly treatments of these churches. The awful side is black women's experience of sexist oppression at the major leadership and other levels of church life. The word reflection in the title allows me to reference the accusations and evaluations of the African-American churches made to me in conversation with other black women struggling, amid this sexist oppression, to honor their ministerial call from God.

One last word must be said about womanist god-talk in general. As black women retrieving our experience from "invisibility," each of us retrieves from the underside of the underside partial facts about ourselves and partial visions of missing parts of our experience. So, in theology, our womanist work together is to connect these pieces of fact and vision. Like a mosaic, these "colored pieces" will eventually make many designs of black women's experience. These designs, as well as the pieces that compose them, will be available to serve as "pieces" for future generations of black women seeking to understand and describe black women's experience anew in light of the relation between the past and changing times.

Hence the method in womanist theological books often attempts first to provide pieces of fact and pieces of vision subjected to the critical reflection of the particular theologian. The second step is the constructive one. *Sisters in the Wilderness* is representative of that first step. Another book will have to contain my second, constructive step.

Many womanists perhaps agree with Mary Daly that an over concern for method in theology has got something to do with patriarchal authority, with people who want to control and with the sin of what Daly calls "methodolatry." But I think we womanist theologians want to be ever conscious of the way we are doing things in theology so that we do not lose our intention for black women's experience to provide the lens through which we view sources, to provide the issues that form the content of our theology and to help us formulate the questions we ask about God's relation to black American life and to the world in general.

# Part I

# Sisters in the Wilderness

# Chapter 1

# HAGAR'S STORY:
# A ROUTE TO BLACK WOMEN'S ISSUES

In accord with biblical scholars Phyllis Trible and Elsa Tamez, this study regards Genesis 16:1–16 and Genesis 21:9–21 as related episodes in Hagar's
life. The two accounts come from different sources written down at different
times. They may have circulated as variants of the same story in the oral tradition of Hebrew folks.[1]

When reread with the slave woman Hagar as center of attention, Genesis 16:1-6 illustrates what the history of many African-American women
taught them long ago; that is, the slave woman's story is and unavoidably has
been shaped by the problems and desires of her owners. In these texts Hagar
is introduced as the solution to a problem confronting a wealthy Hebrew
slave-holding.family composed of Sarai (Hagar's owner) and Abram, Sarai's
husband.[2] Sarai is barren and has borne Abram no children. But "she had an
Egyptian slave-girl called Hagar. So Sarai said to Abram, 'Listen, now! Since
Yahweh has kept me from having children, go to my slave-girl. Perhaps I shall
get children through her.' And Abram took Sarai's advice" (Genesis 16:1–2).

### Motherhood: A Forced Condition

Early in the text motherhood is an important issue. Obviously Sarai believes
it is Yahweh who controls pro-creation in the family, but it is she who controls Hagar. So, for Hagar, motherhood will be a coerced experience involving
the violation of her body over which she, as a slave, has no control. The texts
report that after Abram lived in the land of Canaan for ten years. Sarai "took
Hagar her Egyptian slave-girl and gave her to Abram, as his wife. He went to
Hagar and she conceived" (Genesis 16:2–4a). From Sarai's position motherhood is a privilege that will grant her status, for in her world of the ancient
Near East a barren woman lost status. "There was no greater sorrow for an
Israelite or Oriental woman than childlessness."[3] While Hagar had no choices

in matters of forced motherhood, the law provided options for wealthy free women like Sarai who were barren. Gerhard von Rad reports:

> The wife could bring to the marriage her own personal maid, who was not available to her husband as a concubine in the same way his own female slaves were. If she gave her personal maid to her husband, in the event of her own childlessness, then the child born of the maid was considered the wife's child. The child was born "on the knees of the wife herself" (Cf. ch. 30:3, 9)! From the legal and moral standpoint, therefore, Sarah's proposal was completely according to custom.[4]

Other legal options were also available to these wealthy slave holders. Nuzi law, which the ancient Hebrews were believed to have often followed, stipulated that the husband of a barren wife could adopt a male slave from his household who would then become heir to the family fortune and see to the master's welfare in his old age.[5] That Abram had considered this option is suggested in Genesis 15:2–3. But regardless of the choice exercised, as far as Hagar is concerned the law guarantees that these slave holders will have complete authority over her body and its reproductive capacities.

It is Sarai's option for motherhood (via Hagar) that allows us to see the nature of aspects of the social process affecting the welfare of slave and slave owner alike. Through the lens of motherhood we see the struggle between power and powerlessness in human relationships disrupt peace in a family unit, breed enmity between women and send a poverty-stricken female slave (Hagar) scurrying into the wilderness. "And once she knew she conceived, her mistress counted for nothing in her eyes. Then Sarai said to Abram. 'This outrage done to me is your fault! It was I who put my slave-girl into your arms but now she knows that she has conceived, I count for nothing in her eyes. Yahweh judge between me and you'" (Genesis 16:4b–6a).

Exegetes have traditionally interpreted this passage so that attention was focused upon the conflict between Hagar and Sarai. And it is usually suggested that this conflict arose because Hagar began to feel that she should take Sarai's place because she was producing the offspring for Abram.[6] Such an interpretation implies that Hagar did not know that the law prescribed stringent punishment for slave surrogates who tried to put themselves on an equal basis with the barren wife. Of course there is nothing in the text to let us know what Hagar knew about the laws governing this situation.

From Hagar's perspective there might be some other realities to consider. For instance, before Sarai gave Hagar to Abram, she had complete control over Hagar because Hagar was her property and handmaid. The job of a handmaid, according to Elsa Tamez was "to look after her mistress, [do] domestic work, and [serve] as wet nurse" if the mistress had children.[7] No one else in the household, not even Abram, could make Hagar do anything without Sarai's permission. Hagar's well-being was determined by Sarai. And there is nothing in the text to suggest that Hagar and Sarai were at odds with each other before the issue of motherhood became a major concern for Sarai—and for Abram because of Yahweh's promise to him in Genesis 15 of many descendants. The word used in Genesis 16 to describe Hagar is šipḥâ, meaning "a virgin, dependent maid who serves the mistress of the house."[8] This means that Hagar was a virgin when she was made to lie down with Abram. Female slaves, especially those owned by slave masters, were often rented out as concubines by their masters. Obviously, Sarai had not allowed such a fate to befall Hagar.

Could it be that Hagar, because of her Egyptian heritage and her protection against rape by Sarai, had status among other female slaves? Did she lose pride and status because of Sarai's betrayal of her virginity? Could it be that Hagar's argument with Sarai had nothing to do with her wanting to take over Sarai's position with Abram, but that Hagar's resentment was because Sarai's betrayal of her would become obvious when her pregnancy by Abram became obvious? Could it be that both women were concerned about loss of status but for different reasons? Could it be that in the consciousness of foreign slaves like Hagar there was no particular value assigned to female slaves on the basis of their reproducing babies who became the property of the slave owners?

Obviously these questions cannot be answered until we know more about female slaves during the time of Abram and Sarai. But it is apparent that exegetes have interpreted Hagar's anger toward Sarai in Genesis 16:45 with regard for a patriarchal value system operative in the world of these slave holders—a system that put final authority in the hands of men like Abram. It is also apparent that the redactors who finally connected the many stories making up the book of Genesis were not attempting to preserve the stories of women's relation to each other. Therefore important details may be missing. The redactors' aim was to preserve the story of Yahweh's election and covenant with Abram and therefore with Israel.[9] Since these stories were first transmitted orally and were only written down centuries later, we cannot know the precise form and content in which they originally circulated.[10]

However, if Genesis 16:5 is taken seriously from the perspective of the slave woman Hagar, it can be interpreted as an instance clearly illustrating the right of ownership and domination patriarchal law provided for one class of females (such as Sarai, the slave holder) over another class of females (such as Hagar, the slave). Yet it seems that Sarai's authority is limited here. Her placing of the blame upon Abram seems to be an appeal for him to exercise the law which prohibited (and prescribed punishment for) slave women who sought to be empowered. Also, from Hagar's perspective, one can ask whether Sarai thought Abram, in his relations with Hagar, had encouraged her to feel empowered and to manifest this feeling? Why, for instance, does Sarai phrase her accusation to Abram in language that suggests intimacy rather than legal relation between Hagar and the slave master ("I . . . put my slave-girl into your arms")? And does her ultimate appeal to the divine patriarch Yahweh suggest that she doubts that Abram will, himself, take action against Hagar? Von Rad interprets Genesis 16:5–6 as instances in which both Sarai and Abram respond to Hagar's belligerence by relating to each other and to Hagar on the basis of what the law allowed. Von Rad claims that

> the maintenance of justice in the house was the man's affair in any case (the cry *ḥᵃ māsī ʿalekā* cannot be translated, "My wrong be upon you," but rather, "My wrong is your responsibility," i.e., you are competent and responsible to restore my right. The cry was the customary legal formula with which one appealed for legal protection). Sarah goes the limit with her counterstroke: she appeals to the highest judge, who sees every secret thing.[11]

Phyllis Trible interprets Abram's response as indicating his choice "not to exercise power and thus remain passive."[12] Technically, however, Hagar no longer belongs to Sarai. She has given Hagar to Abram as second wife. But he returns Hagar to Sarai: "'Very well,' Abram said to Sarai, 'your slave-girl is at your disposal. Treat her as you think fit'" (Genesis 16:6). Sarai is thus in control again, but with Abram's permission. She can determine the punishment for Hagar, who according to modern exegetes broke the law forbidding "a serving maid who has a child by her master . . . to put herself on a par with her mistress."[13] So "Sarai accordingly treated her so badly that she ran away from her" (Genesis 16:6b). Rather than being passive, Abram has actively taken charge by allowing Sarai to avenge herself. He has acted according to the law.

Hagar becomes the first female in the Bible to liberate herself from oppressive power structures. Though the law prescribes harsh punishment for run-away slaves, she takes the risk rather than endure more brutal treatment by Sarai. The harshness of the force Sarai exerts upon Hagar is indicated in the passage by the verb (*'nh*), which is also used in Exodus to indicate the suffering experience of all the Hebrews when they were slaves in Egypt.[14]

But powerlessness defies power and thus affects the welfare of the family and the slave. Hagar, the surrogate mother, runs away into the wilderness. Her leaving means that Sarai cannot become a mother as she had planned. There will be no son to carry on Abram's posterity and inherit the family fortune. This could signal the extinction of the family line, a very serious matter for Abram and Sarai. As John Marshall Holt points out, "The patriarchs knew no other society than the family. . . . Once the Hebrews departed from the Mesopotamian homeland they lived in Palestine without participating to any great extent in the larger society of a state or a national group." Holt goes on to say, "In the absence of any strong demand for loyalty in other directions, the Hebrews of the patriarchal age devote their whole effort toward the family and its work."[15] Just as the welfare of Abram's family is insecure at this point, so is Hagar insecure. She has run off into the wilderness as a lone woman without family support or protection. Courageous though her liberation action may be, Hagar is without the support and physical sustenance a pregnant woman needs.

### Survival, Quality of Life and God

Nevertheless Hagar, by way of her own speech and religious experience, comes through to the reader as a person momentarily in control of her destiny. In the wilderness to which she has escaped, the issues of survival and quality of life come to the surface in her story. And the divinity is at work in the process. The text reports that "the angel of Yahweh found her by a spring in the desert, the spring on the road to Shur" (Genesis 16:7). With reference to the identity of the divinity here, *The New Jerusalem Bible* states that in most ancient texts the angel of Yahweh "is not a created being distinct from God . . . but God himself in visible form."[16] Most biblical scholarship agrees that in the patriarchal narratives "there is no clear distinction between the angel of the Lord and Yahweh himself."[17] Thus the divinity is with Hagar in the midst of her personal suffering and destitution. And Hagar herself is obviously on the way to Egypt, for Shur is thought to have been located on the Northeast border of Egypt.[18]

But Yahweh has other plans for Hagar, which will determine her survival and the quality of life she must form and endure for several years. First, God invites her to speak, asking, "Hagar, slave-girl of Sarai, where have you come from, and where are you going?" (Genesis 16:8). The angel of Yahweh still identifies Hagar as Sarai's property, but seeks from Hagar her own words about her past and her sense of destination. Hagar speaks about neither her past nor her future. Rather, she tells only the present: "I am running away from my mistress Sarai" (Genesis 16:8b). Hagar's response here suggests that Hagar still sees herself as property. Then, in what appears to be God's support of slavery, the angel of Yahweh says to Hagar, "Go back to your mistress and submit to her" (Genesis 16:9). If Hagar obeys, she can be sure that her autonomy will be severely restricted.

We cannot help but question this response given to Hagar by the angel of Yahweh. Did God not know about Sarai's brutal treatment of Hagar? Elsa Tamez connects this response with Yahweh's concern for the survival and future quality of life for Hagar and Ishmael. She says:

> What God wants is that she and the child should he saved, and at the moment, the only way to accomplish that is not in the desert, but by returning to the house of Abraham. Ishmael hasn't been born. . . . Hagar simply must wait a little longer, because Ishmael must be born in the house of Abraham to prove that he is the first-born (Deut. 21:15–17) and to enter into the household through the rite of circumcision (chap. 17). This will guarantee him participation in the history of salvation and will give him rights of inheritance in the house of Abraham.[19]

While Tamez's observation has merit, her initial attempt to put this aspect of Hagar's experience with God into a liberation mode stretches the text beyond what it declares. The angel of Yahweh is, in this passage, no liberator God. However, given what we now know about high infant mortality rates in the ancient Near East and about promise and covenant as major themes in the Hebrew testament, we can agree with Tamez's claim about survival. (In the book of Genesis covenant and promise are associated with survival, election and blessing.) We can also speak of quality of life with regard to God's concern for Hagar at this point. God apparently wants Hagar to secure her and her child's well-being by using the resources Abram has to offer. But in this passage, God is not concerned with nor involved in liberation.

Nevertheless, the angel of Yahweh makes a promise to Hagar similar to the promise Yahweh makes to Abram in Genesis 15:2–6. "The angel of Yahweh further said to her [Hagar], 'I shall make your descendants too numerous to be counted'"(Genesis 16:10). This means that Hagar, a foreign female slave whose future would ordinarily not advance past slavery,[20] is given hope not only for the survival of her generation but also hope for the possibility of future freedom for her seed. God forecasts the "methods" Hagar's son, in adult life, will possibly use to secure his well-being:

> Now, you have conceived and will bear a son,
>     and you shall name him Ishmael,
>     for Yahweh has heard your cries of distress.
> A wild donkey of a man he will be,
>     his hand against every man, and every man's hand against him,
>     living his life in defiance of all his kinsmen
>
> *(Genesis 16:11–12)*

Using a birth announcement formula like those appearing in several other places in the Bible, the narrator suggests that Ishmael's adult life will be far from peaceful.[21]

From our modern perspective, this announcement may resemble a curse more than a blessing. But the birth announcement and the promise ("I shall make your descendants too numerous to be counted") are connected. The promise assures survival, and the birth announcement forecasts the strategy that will be necessary for survival and for obtaining a quality of life.[22] This is a blessing, suggesting that Ishmael will be free and a warrior. He will be able to help create and protect the quality of life he and his mother, Hagar, will later develop in the desert.

### Surrogacy Roles and Wilderness Experience

The last few verses in the Genesis 16 episode in the story remind the reader of the various surrogate roles Hagar assumes or is made to assume in the narrative. She is forced to substitute for Sarai in the reproduction of a male heir for Abram. In her job as handmaid to mistress Sarai, she will also function as wet-nurse for any children who are born, thereby substituting for the mistress in the nurturing role. The human role in the "Yahweh promise modality" has (before Hagar) been filled by a male, the patriarch. Hagar steps into the usual male role of receiving a promise of numerous posterity. Naming of shrines, wells and other places was done by men, but Hagar's authority substitutes for male authority. The text claims, "Hagar gave a name to

Yahweh who had spoken to her. 'You are El Roi,' by which she meant, 'Did I not go on seeing here, after him who sees me?' This is why the well is called the well of Lahai Roi; it is between Kadesh and Bered" (Genesis 16:13–14). While the text does not actually identify Hagar as the person who named the well, it does suggest that Hagar's experience with God at the well was so significant that the well thereafter bore a name issuing from Hagar's experience of naming. Therefore, Hagar is responsible for the name and is in that sense its author.

As Phyllis Trible points out, Hagar is the only person in the Bible to whom is attributed the power of naming God, who has ministered to her and empowered her in these surrogate roles:

> The expression [Genesis 16:13a] is striking because it connotes naming rather than invocation. In other words, Hagar does not call upon the name of the deity (*qr'bšm yhwh*; cf. Gen 12:8; 13:4). Instead she calls the name (*qr'šm-yhwy*), a power attributed to no one else in the Bible. . . . The maid . . . after receiving a divine announcement of the forthcoming birth, sees (*r'h*) God with new vision. . . . Her naming unites the divine and human encounter.[23]

Equally significant here is the nature of the name Hagar assigns to God, that is, "El Roi." Helmer Ringgren, in his discussion of the names found in the patriarchal narratives, indicates the uniqueness of the name Hagar chose:

> El is . . . familiar as the highest god of the Canaanites (as of most of the Semitic peoples). . . . These names [i.e., those compounded with El] are never associated with the patriarchs, either as individuals or as tribes; instead, with the exception of El Shaddai, they are always linked to specific cultic sites. . . . El olam, "the Everlasting God," appears in Genesis 21:33 in connection with Beer-sheba. El ro'i, "God of seeing," appears in Genesis 16:13 at another sanctuary in southern Palestine. Beyond this we have no information about these two divinities.[24]

While Hagar's God may be, as Ringgren suggests, a localized form of "a single great divinity,"[25] it is interesting that this deity is not associated with Hagar's oppressors, the patriarchal family.

Viewed within the context of Hagar's Egyptian heritage, this act of naming the deity takes on added significance. Though El may also be, as Roland de Vaux contends, an altered form of "Baal" in the text "under the influence of Yahwism,"[26] the name of Hagar's God (pointing to sight and therefore eyes of the deity) recalls certain Egyptian myths associated with the God Ra, his eye and the creation of humans. As Egyptian myth has it:

> Man, far from being the crowning achievement of creation . . . comes into being only incidentally, from the tears shed by Ra. After Shu and Tefnut [other deities] had been created, they had been left in the happy care of Nun, the Primordial Waters, possibly until they should mature. But Ra's eye (the sun itself) left his head to follow and look after them. Naturally Ra had to make another one to take its place. When the original Eye of the Universal Lord finally returned and saw that it had been replaced, it reproached its master angrily, and Ra wept. From these tears men came into being.[27]

Earthlings being who they are, Egyptian myth provides further insight about Ra's eye and human conduct:

> And it came to pass when Ra . . . had established his kingship over men and gods together . . . mankind planned evil thoughts against Ra. . . . His majesty discerned the thoughts that were planned against him by mankind. And His Majesty . . . said to the gods who were among his following: "Come, fetch me my Eye, and also Shu, Tafnnt, and Geb [other gods], together with the Fathers and Mothers who were with me when I was as yet in Nun. . . . Thou shall come to the Great palace, that they may give me their counsel." Then Ra said to Nun: "O thou Eldest God, . . . behold mankind, who came into being from my Eye! They have planned evil thoughts against me. Tell me what you would do about it!" And . . . the Majesty of Nun said, "O my son Ra, . . . great is the fear of thee when thine Eye is against those who have planned against thee!" . . . And they all [the gods] said to His majesty: "Let thine Eye go forth to smite for thee those who plan evil. However, the Eye has not sufficient power within itself to smite them for thee. Let it go forth as Hathor [the mother goddess capable of both good and destruction]!"[28]

The point here is that Hagar's naming of God gathers additional meaning when we look at her action in relation to Egyptian traditions as well as Hebrew traditions. In the context of Egyptian myth the deity's eye (sight) has been involved in the creation of humanity only incidentally and not through planned choice. The parallels here between Hagar's experience with God in the wilderness and the work of Ra's Eye are considerable. The God in the wilderness has been involved in the creation of Ishmael in the sense that

God gives Ishmael his identity, that is, name and temperament. Hagar's God (like Ra) has incidentally become involved in the creation of man (Ishmael). There is no prior connection between Hagar and the God, while there is a connection between Abram and his God prior to the Hagar-Sarai incident and prior to the birth of Isaac. The appearance of Hagar's God (and God's involvement in Ishmael's creation) is not "an invocation" but a spontaneous happening. Also, the connection of motherhood (the goddess Hathor) and Ra's Eye in the Egyptian myth is an interesting parallel with the connection of God's sight and Hagar's motherhood in the Hebrew testament. Finally, in both the Egyptian context and the biblical context, the issue of women's surrogate roles comes to the surface. When Ra's Eye is transformed into Hathor, she becomes a surrogate for Ra. Hagar is obviously the surrogate for Sarai.

The fact that Hagar does not call upon the God of the slave holders Sarai and Abram and the fact that she does not name her God in accord with their (Sarai and Abram's) patriarchal traditions lifts up another bit of Egyptian tradition. This tradition helps us connect the image of the belligerent Hagar in the household of Sarai and Abram with the image of Hagar in the wilderness, who may not have lost any of her belligerence. Egyptologist Adolph Erman provides this insight:

> According to Egyptian faith, one could do nothing better for anyone than by inscriptions and representations to "cause his name to live," and nothing worse than to allow it to perish. The Egyptians zealously endeavoured to root out and destroy the names and figures of people they hated; this act of revenge was common at all periods, and was practiced by kings as well as by private individuals.[29]

In light of Hagar's Egyptian heritage, in light of her brutal treatment by Sarai and Abram's complicity in this brutality, a question can be raised. Is Hagar's naming action a strike against patriarchal power at its highest level, since the ultimate head of this ancient Hebrew family was its patriarchal God? Was Hagar's naming of God an act of defiance and resistance as well as an expression of awe?

This act of naming is Hagar's last word in the Genesis 16 account. Verses 7 through 14 show Hagar, the surrogate mother, involved in wilderness experience. This experience holds in solution a woman's self-initiated liberation event, woman's alienation and isolation, economic deprivation, pregnancy and a radical encounter with God, which empowers the female slave of African descent to hope and to act. It is this first wilderness experience that brings to the surface the many surrogate roles Hagar has and will assume. The final two verses in the Genesis account (verses 15, 16) narrate the results of Hagar's return to the household of the slave owners Sarai and Abram. "Hagar bore Abram a son, and Abram gave his son borne by Hagar the name of Ishmael." Thus Hagar's power of naming has been surrendered to the patriarch Abram. Verse 16 (from P) informs the reader that Abram is what we would call an old man. But the fact that Hagar returned to the household of her slave-owner after her self-initiated liberation demonstrates her faith and her radical obedience to her God.

A provocative string of stories bridges the gap between the first episode of Hagar's story and the second episode, which appears in Genesis 21:9–21. Most of the stories contain some motif in human sexuality essential for understanding either the relation of God to the patriarch's history, or God's response to sexual abuse, or the origin of certain tribes' kin to the patriarch or the patriarch's attempt to offer his wife's body to ensure his own survival.

In chapter 17 God seals his covenant with Abraham by commanding a sign demonstrated by snipping skin on the human penis, that is, circumcision. Chapter 18 reveals God's concern for the reproductive capacities of Abraham's wife Sarah and for the sin of Sodom. Chapter 19 tells of God's destruction of Sodom because of its alarmingly inhospitable manner and sexual excess. Also recorded in this chapter is the incest by which the Moabite and Bene-Ammon tribes came into being. In chapter 20 Abraham is once again offering Sarah up as his sister (to mate with a king) because he "thought there would be no fear of God here and I would be killed for the sake of my wife" (Genesis 20:11–12).

Chapter 21 begins with another motif in human sexuality, birth, and tells of the fulfillment of the promise of a child to Abraham and Sarah. Isaac is born. Once the child is weaned, Hagar and Ishmael come back into the Genesis narrative in 21:9–21. Obviously relations between Sarah and Hagar, and Hagar's young son, Ishmael, have not improved. The text claims, "Now Sarah watched the son that Hagar the Egyptian had borne to Abraham, playing with her son Isaac. 'Drive away that slave-girl and her son,' she said to Abram, 'this slave-girl's son is not to share the inheritance with my son Isaac'" (Genesis 21:9–10). The Elohist, like the Yahwist in chapter 16, emphasizes Hagar's ethnicity and lowly station. Both women are identified as mothers. But we do not know whether Sarah actually took Ishmael as her own as she stated in Genesis 16. The reference to "this slave-girl's son" leads us to conclude that Sarah did not consider Ishmael her son. However, there is ambiguity here.

Sarah's concern about Ishmael inheriting suggests that Ishmael is not a slave, because among the early Hebrews (and in early Mesopotamian law) the slave sons of the master's concubines could not inherit "unless their father had given them equal rank with the sons of free-born wives, by legal adoption."[30] Legal adoption by the father did not automatically indicate acceptance by the wife (for example, Sarah). But neither custom nor law gave Sarah power to affect the adoption. Her ability to affect decision-making depended upon the degree to which the patriarch, who had all power, would allow himself to be influenced—apparently in Sarah's case, here, this was not a lot.[31]

Economic realities, specifically inheritance, are the central issues here. Hagar is poor; and apparently Sarah does not want Hagar's station elevated, as it no doubt would be if Ishmael received the inheritance from his father that the firstborn son was supposed to receive. According to early Hebrew custom, and Assyrian and Nuzi law, the eldest son received a double portion of his father's wealth. Law forbade the father from showing special privilege to the son of the wife he preferred and thereby protected the firstborn son's inheritance rights.[32]

Hiding beneath these economic realities centered in inheritance are power and property dynamics that could seriously affect the lives of Hagar and Sarah in the future. Among these ancient Hebrews, wives could not inherit their husband's wealth. Therefore, neither Sarah nor Hagar would inherit anything from Abraham should they outlive him. The responsibility for Sarah's sustenance and care would ordinarily fall upon the firstborn son as chief inheritor of his father's wealth. But if this firstborn son, Ishmael, also becomes head of the family and/or tribe, Sarah may have considerably less power and status than she has as a wife of Abraham and as she would have as mother of the son who inherited the larger share of the wealth and therefore power. Needless to say, Isaac would have considerably less wealth, power and status as brother of the firstborn son. Sarah faces another possible threat. If Hagar is allowed to remain in the household, Abraham may stipulate that a gift be given her at the time of his death. Slave women who had children by the master could receive such awards. This concern of Sarah's about inheritance seems to reinforce the idea that she had not accepted Ishmael and thus could not expect the care from him that adopted children were supposed to render their parents in their old age. Sarah's hostility here might also have been aggravated by what she perhaps knew about contemporary women in the surrounding cultures. Roland de Vaux reports:

The social and legal position of an Israelite wife was . . . inferior to the position a wife occupied in the great countries round about. In Egypt the wife was often the head of the family, with all the rights such a position entailed. In Babylon she could acquire property, take legal action, be a party to contracts, and she even had a certain share in her husband's inheritance.[33]

If Ishmael could claim his right of primogeniture, Hagar's power and status could only increase. Most of what is presented in the text suggests that Ishmael was the son of Abraham and Hagar was regarded as mother, since Sarah appears not to have taken him. However, Hagar is not to realize an elevation in status among these Hebrews. Sarah's demand for the expulsion of mother and child was heard by Abraham:

> This greatly distressed Abraham, because the slave-girl's child too was his son, but God said to him, "Do not distress yourself on account of the boy and your slave-girl. Do whatever Sarah says; for Isaac is the one through whom your name will be carried on. But the slave-girl's son I shall also make into a great nation, for he too is your child" (Genesis 21:11–13).

Whereas God's voice entered the Genesis 16 episode in conversation with Hagar and not her oppressors, in this episode (Genesis 21) God first communicates with Hagar's oppressor Abraham. In both episodes God sides with Sarah. Here God reaffirms the covenant made with Abraham and qualifies the promise made to Hagar. In Genesis 16 God does not tell Hagar that the promise made to her is in any way connected with Abraham. Rather, God "has heard her cries of distress" (verse 11). Therefore, the gift of numerous progeny will be given her. Now, in Genesis 21, God authenticates the promise to Hagar on the basis of her connection with Abraham. It is God who ultimately destroys Ishmael's right to claim primogeniture and receive the appropriate inheritance. Abraham heeded the advice of God.

So, "early next morning, Abraham took some bread and a skin of water and giving them to Hagar, put the child on her shoulder and sent her away" (verse 14).

### Homelessness and Economic Realities

At this point in the narrative, the issue of economic realities connects with the issue of homelessness. Abraham has given Hagar and his son no economic resources to sustain them in their life away from his family. Hagar

and Ishmael seem consigned to a future of poverty and homelessness. While
the Elohist indicates that Ishmael is young enough to be carried away in
his mother's arms, modern scholarly opinion places Ishmael's age at about
seventeen at the time he and Hagar were expelled from Abraham's house.[34]
Regardless of Ishmael's (or Hagar's) age, bread and a skin of water would not
sustain them on their journey, which apparently had no destination. The
text claims, "She wandered off into the desert of Beersheba. When the skin
of water was finished she abandoned the child under a bush. Then she went
and sat down at a distance, about a bowshot away, thinking 'I cannot bear to
see the child die.' Sitting at a distance, she began to sob" (Genesis 21:15–16).

To recognize Hagar's and Ishmael's frightening and insecure predicament at this point, we must understand something about the composition
and function of the family among these ancient people. According to de
Vaux, "The family consists of those who are united by common blood and
common dwelling place. The 'family' is a 'house'; to found a family is 'to
build a house' (Ne 7:4)." De Vaux goes on to say, "Noah's family included
his wife, sons and their wives. . . . Jacob's family comprises three generations.
. . . The family included the servants . . . who live under the protection of
the head of the family."[35] Even for the slave, "to be without family is to be
without protection."[36]

So Hagar and Ishmael, expelled from the family, or "house," of Abraham and Sarah, were not only without economic resources; they were without protection in a nomadic culture where men ruled the families, tribes and
clans. As mother and child wander off into the desert of Beersheba, we cannot
help but wonder how their survival will be secured. Though this desert or
wilderness is the site of many important events in Hebrew and ancient Israelite history,[37] it is hardly a place where a lone woman and child ought to be
wandering without sustenance, shelter or protection.

There were some rules peculiar to nomadic life that might finally have
alleviated the poverty and homelessness of Hagar and Ishmael. These rules
had to do with hospitality and asylum. Roland de Vaux says:

> Nomad life . . . gives rise . . . to a law of asylum. In this type of society
> it is impossible and inconceivable that an individual could live isolated,
> unattached to any tribe. Hence, if a man is expelled from his tribe . . .
> for any reason . . . or he leaves it . . . he has to seek the protection of an-
> other tribe. There he becomes what modern Arabs call a dahil, "he who
> has come in," and what their forefathers call a jar. The tribe undertakes
> to protect him, to defend him against his enemies and to avenge his

blood, if necessary. These customs are reflected in two Old Testament institutions, that of the ger (which is the same word as the Arabic jar) and that of cities of refuge.[38]

About hospitality, de Vaux says it "is a necessity of life in the desert, but among the nomads this necessity became a virtue, and a most highly esteemed one. The guest is sacred."[39]

In Hagar's case there might have been a problem since she was an expelled slave and a woman. That is, her inferior status as ex-slave was compounded by her sex. But if Ishmael was free because of adoption by his father, Abraham, their chances of joining another tribe could have been better. Whether Hagar's slave status would change in new family and tribal connections is not known. Probably much would depend upon Ishmael's age at the time of expulsion. If he was in fact seventeen, perhaps he could negotiate for a home for himself and his mother.

Information in the biblical texts, however, suggests that Hagar and Ishmael might not have become attached to another family or tribe. One is led to believe that with the aid of God, Ishmael and Hagar maintained an autonomous existence. The Genesis 21 narrative reveals that when their resources for survival (water and bread) had run out, Ishmael was near death and Hagar was a short distance away crying, unable to bear seeing her son perish. "God heard the boy crying, and the angel of God called to Hagar from heaven. 'What is wrong Hagar?' he asked. 'Do not be afraid, for God has heard the boy's cry in his plight'" (Genesis 21:17).

Unlike the Yahwist narrative (Genesis 16), the Elohist narrative (Genesis 21) does not present an image of an immanent deity. Rather, in Genesis 21 God is transcendent, calling down to Hagar from heaven. Neither is Ishmael mentioned by name as he is in Genesis 16, though the words "God has heard" (Genesis 21:17) reflect the meaning of Ishmael's name.[40] Again, as in Genesis 16, God asks Hagar a question. This time, however, Hagar is not given a chance to speak. God gives her a command that, if obeyed, will end the separation between mother and child (Ishmael is under a bush and Hagar is some distance away crying). Tender loving care is in order. So God bids her to "'Go pick the boy up and hold him safe, for I shall make him into a great nation.' Then God opened Hagar's eyes and she saw a well, so she went and filled the skin with water and gave the boy a drink" (Genesis 21:18–19). Hagar is assured that, contrary to the child's near-death appearance, he will be great. God renews the promise made to Hagar in Genesis 16 and to Abraham in Genesis 21:13. Ishmael will survive. We assume Hagar obeyed, for God gave her new vision to see survival resources where she saw none before.

The last two verses in the Genesis 21 narrative reflect the real autonomy of Hagar and Ishmael, an autonomy facilitated by the reality that "God was with the boy" (verse 20a). The issue of homelessness is resolved in the statement, "He grew up and made his home in the desert, and he became an archer. He made his home in the desert of Paran" (verses 20–21a). The fact that he lived in the desert and was an archer could suggest the idea of raiding, which was a practice among the early nomadic tribes. Unlike war, raiding had as its object not killing, but carrying off plunder and escaping unharmed.[41] Ishmael's home (and we would suppose at this point Hagar's home also) is a place where the Israelites, after the Exodus from Egypt, wandered for thirty-eight years.[42] Perhaps raiding was a way Ishmael increased his wealth and was possibly able finally to head the tribe originally bearing his name.

Hagar's autonomy is manifested in the last act she performs in the Genesis 21 narrative. Assuming a role ordinarily prescribed for males in most ancient Near Eastern households, Hagar gets a wife for Ishmael from Egypt (verse 21b). This last action of Hagar suggests several possibilities about the kind of "house" she may want to establish. Apparently she does not want to perpetuate the culture of Abraham and Sarah. Perhaps she wants to reinforce the influence of Egyptian culture, since she chooses Ishmael's wife from among her own people. Or it could be that Hagar, in the choice of Ishmael's wife, is attempting to strengthen or establish Egyptian ties that might prove useful for the kind of nomadic existence she and Ishmael will live in the desert. Egypt was a great center of sophisticated culture and power. Or it could be that Hagar wanted to perpetuate the inheritance customs of Egypt, which were reckoned by the mother and not the father.[43] Whatever her reasons for choosing an Egyptian wife for Ishmael, Hagar may have dealt with the problem of homelessness and poverty by founding her own "house" or tribe. The Hagarites may be more related to Hagar than we have been led to believe. Lee A. Starr, writing in the early twentieth century, has this to say:

> Dwelling in the eastern part of Palestine, over whom the tribe .of Reuben achieved victory . . . the Hagarites were a strong and wealthy tribe . . . evident from the Bible account of the victory gained by the Reubenites (I Chrn. v:18–22). The spoils taken from the nomads on the occasion of this battle were fifty thousand camels, two hundred and fifty thousand sheep, two thousand asses and an hundred thousand captives. "And they took away their Cattle" and "there fell many slain."[44]

Addressing the problem of the tendency among scholars to dissociate Hagar from the Hagarites and Hagarenes, Starr says:

> No one questions the claim that Dan was the ancestor of the Danites; Reuben of the Reubenites; Ephraim of the Ephraimites; Edom of the Edomites; Moab of the Moabites; Ammon of the Ammonites; Midian of the Midianites, etc. Why should we deviate from the common rule when we come to the Hagarites and Hagarenes?[45]

(Could it be that the battle between Reuben and the Hagarites is an ancient Hebrew rendering of a victory of patriarchy over matriarchy?) We can only provide a speculative response to this question. However, the Genesis 21 narrative suggests that Hagar and Ishmael fared well, because God was with the child as he grew. Both the Genesis 16 and 21 narratives reveal the faith, hope and struggle with which an African slave woman worked through issues of survival, surrogacy, motherhood, rape, homelessness and economic and sexual oppression.

The African-American community has taken Hagar's story unto itself. Hagar has "spoken" to generation after generation of black women because her story has been validated as true by suffering black people. She and Ishmael together, as family, model many black American families in which a lone woman/mother struggles to hold the family together in spite of the poverty to which ruling class economics consign it. Hagar, like many black women, goes into the wide world to make a living for herself and her child, with only God by her side.

## Chapter 2

## TENSIONS IN MOTHERHOOD: FROM SLAVERY TO FREEDOM

Like Hagar's story, African-American women's story has been closely associated with motherhood. Sociologists LaFrances Rogers Rose and Joyce Ladner claim that the social and economic significance of motherhood in Africa did not lose its importance when African women were brought to America and enslaved. The close bond between black women and children that existed in Africa was reinforced in the slavocracy. Many slave women were left alone to nurture their offspring because the fathers lived on other plantations or were used as "studs" to father a host of other children—or the father was the slave holder, who did not claim his black children. Slave mothers worked in the fields and were often hired out in other capacities if they were city slaves. Yet they often simultaneously nursed and nurtured their children. In parts of Africa mothers were market women, earning their own living and simultaneously nurturing their children. Thus many African women and African-American female slaves had a long heritage of public and private functions associated with motherhood. All of this African-derived female knowledge was useful in the slavocracy. Slave women could nurse and nurture their own children and also "mammy" the slave master's children.

One should not assume, however, that African-American women's history is an immediate and unaltered link with an African traditional past. From the beginning of her history in North America, the black woman was controlled by a host of alien social and political forces. Anglo-American social and family demands controlled her life during slavery. African-American social, political and family needs shaped her life after slavery into the present. Hence, in the course of her long history in America, the black woman has often found herself trapped in a mesh of cultural redefinitions, role exploitation and black male-female crises that have seriously affected her well-being.[1] Whatever her role as mother and nurturer in Africa, the new world of American slavery adjusted it to meet American institutional needs at the time.

Yet there is no denying that black women's roles as mothers and nurturers have been important for the development of institutional life in both the Anglo and the African-American communities. Attempts to understand social life in the African-American community must take seriously the history of the black woman's motherhood roles, which were institutionalized in the slavocracy as "mammy"[2] and were later redeemed from negative connotations and reinstitutionalized in some African-American denominational churches as "mothers of the church." Mammies had considerable authority in the context of white family life in the antebellum South. Mothers of the church were not only powerful figures in the church. They were also greatly respected and had considerable power in the communities in which they lived.[3]

From antebellum time in North America until the present, African-American literary history has revealed the importance of black mothers for the development of community life. It has also shown how black mothers used religion to support themselves emotionally, psychologically and spiritually when they were exploited first by the white world and later by some members of the black community. After the Civil War, some African-American literary history began to suggest that certain religious customs practiced by black mothers and nurturers during slavery caused problems for the kind of social change necessary in the African-American community following emancipation.

But in the lyrics of some African-American spiritual songs—created during slavery—women's roles are associated with birthing and nurturing functions in a positive way. One encounters lines celebrating "Mary had a baby," and that "Mary and Martha feed my lambs, feed my lambs." Of the one hundred and thirty spiritual songs in the Ballanta Taylor collection published in 1925, twenty-three songs contain positive references to mother. Five contain references to Mary "who had a baby" and to Mary and Martha. On the whole, then, spiritual songs project a positive image of women as helpful and caring mothers and nurturers. In these documents of slave culture there is no suggestion of conflict in the community about how black women's mothering and nurturing roles ought to function.

Like the spiritual songs, many slave narratives describe black mothers and nurturers burdened by a system of bondage. Unlike the spiritual songs, the narratives tell how the relation between slave owners and slave women was exploitative and affected the well-being of slave mothers. Linda Brent's slave narrative describes her Aunt Nancy, a slave woman, caught in the conflict between white and black demands upon her mothering and nurturing roles.

The relation between the slave-owner's Wife and the slave woman is, like Sarah's and Hagar's relation, built upon the exploitation of the slave woman's body and labor. Brent reports that her Aunt Nancy

> had always slept on the floor in the entry near Mrs. Flint's chamber door that she might be within call. When she married she was told she might have the use of a small room in an outhouse. . . . Mrs. Flint . . . was expecting to be a mother, and if she should want a drink of water in the night, what could she do without her slave to bring it? So my aunt was compelled to lie at the door, until one midnight she was forced to leave, to give premature birth to a child. In a fortnight she was required to resume her place on the entry floor because Mrs. Flint's baby needed her attentions. She kept her station there through the summer and winter, until she had given premature birth to six children, all of whom died.[4]

In another narrative an old slave woman tells of her aunt's exploitation as a "breeder woman" for a white slave owner. This breeder woman was forced to birth children for the slavocracy every twelve months.[5]

Yet slave mothers were dedicated to the care of their young ones. Even the labor practices of the slavocracy did not interfere with the mothering and nurturing functions of some antebellum black women. Charles Ball, a slave writing in 1836, tells us of slave mothers nursing their babies as they worked in the fields. One slave woman fastened her child to her body in a crude knapsack as she worked in the fields, and "in this way carried [her baby] all day and performed her task at the hoe with the other people."[6]

Apparently great strength was required of the slave mother. This strength was manifested not only by her ability to perform the difficult tasks associated with her mothering and nurturing roles. Strength was also manifested in her ability to endure and to gain victory over the suffering and pain often accompanying these tasks. That this endurance and victory were directly related to the mother's dependence upon God and religious faith is revealed in both spiritual songs and slave narratives. There are these lines from a spiritual that declare

> O yonder's my old mudder been a-waggin at de hill so long, It's about time she cross over, Get home bime-by, Keep prayin' I do believe.[7]

> My mother died with a staff in her hand, She had so much Trouble in this land, But she held onto God's hand.[8]

I wonder were my mudder deh, See my mudder on de rock
Gwine home on de rock gwine home in Jesus' name.[9]

Linda Brent's narrative shows how the slave mother's religion shaped her relationships with her children and other people in the slavocracy. Brent tells of her grandmother's untiring efforts to purchase the freedom of her children and of the grandmother's belief that God supported her efforts.[10] She tells of her grandmother's ordeal of witnessing the death of her last surviving daughter and of the supportive role played by her religion and faith:

> My grandmother was summoned to the bedside of this, her last remaining daughter. She was very ill, and they said she would die. Grandmother had not entered Dr. Flint's [the daughter's owner's] house for several years. They had treated her cruelly. . . . At last Uncle Philip came into the house. I heard someone inquire, "How is she?" and he answered, "She is dead." . . . He whispered, "Linda, she died happy . . . don't add to my poor mother's trouble." . . . Ah, yes, that blessed old grandmother. . . . She . . . had borne the pelting storms of a slave mother's life. . . . She has always been strong to bear, and now, as ever, religious faith supported her. . . . That poor back was fitted to its burden. It bent under it, but it did not break.[11]

Another slave describes a mother's use of religious ritual as she tries to rear him. He says that he and his mother were close. She taught him to pray and how to survive because she feared that he would be sold or that she would be sold. She spent much time in prayer and she always asked God to take care of him.[12]

One of the most moving personal testimonies came from Sojourner Truth. At a women's rights convention in 1851, in Ohio, she told of her reliance upon Jesus to support her as she bore the pain connected with being a slave mother:

> Dat man ober dar [a white clergyman on the rostrum] say dat womin needs to be helped into carriages and lifted ober ditches, and to have de best place everywhar. Nobody ever helps me into carriages or ober mud puddles, or give me any best place! And ain't I a woman? Look at my arms! I have ploughed, and planted and gathered into barns, and no man could head me! And ain't I a woman? . . . I have borne thirteen children, and seen 'em mos' all sold off to slavery and when I cried out with my mother's grief, none but Jesus heard me! And ain't I a woman?[13]

Apparently the roles of slave mothers and nurturers were determined more by the institutions of slavery than by the internal demands of the slave community. Their roles were fixed. They were primarily to labor, reproduce and nurture. But mothering and nurturing tasks could range from birthing children to breastfeeding white children, to caring for the family needs of the master and his household, to tending to children as she worked in the fields, to protecting the lives of hundreds of slaves she helped escape from slavery to freedom (as did Harriet Tubman).

The American slavocracy was an all-compassing legal, political and economic system that affected every relationship in the slave community. Therefore the social process in the antebellum slave community turned black motherhood into something totally different from what was thought to be the model of motherhood in white society. The mothering and nurturing function of the African-American slave woman extended beyond the mere limits of female role activity into areas of control that should have belonged to the black man (according to American standards of male role functioning).

It was the black mother who often protected the children and family as far as they could be protected during slavery.[14] It was a black female nurturer, called Moses by her people, who led regiments and scouted for the Union Army during the American Civil War.[15] Sometimes it was the slave mother who was given permission by the slave master to operate her own business and thereby provide economic security for her children. An ex-slave woman tells the story of her mother, whom her slave master allowed to go into business to support herself and her children. The slave mother had to give her slave master one half of what she earned working in the garrison of Fort Washington, Maryland. There, she "carried on a little business of selling pies, hot coffee, etc., to the marines and exchanging the same for rations." Within three years she was able to buy a horse and wagon to carry her goods to the fort. Her business continued to prosper until the poor white people "became jealous in a body and waited on the major and gave vent to their feelings."[16]

Incorporated, then, within the mothering and nurturing functions of slave women were often the tasks of protecting, providing for, resisting oppression and liberating. All of these tasks suggest strength. But it must be emphasized that strength is not necessarily synonymous with power, nor does it here imply an idea of black matriarchy. Gerda Lerner correctly declares: "The question of black matriarchy is commonly misunderstood. The very term is deceptive, for 'matriarchy' implies the exercise of power by women."[17] The antebellum black mother had no real power. The power above her and her family was the white antebellum slave master and his family. But it is perhaps not too farfetched to suggest that in their struggle to survive and nurture their own, many antebellum black mothers often had as their helpmate not the black man but black religion. The black male was the lowest in authority in the slave system.[18] Hence black mothers and nurturers depended upon their religion for psychological and emotional support. And black Christian religion became, after the Civil War, greatly dependent upon these black women for its form and sustenance.[19]

In his article "Slave Songs and Slave Consciousness," Lawrence Levine hypothesizes that slave religion extended slave consciousness so that "life is lived on a twofold plane; it takes its course as human existence and, at the same time shares in a transhuman life, that of the cosmos of the gods."[20] Levine suggests that the slave's response to any situation reflected a spiritual interpretation of reality "un-dichotomized" by separation of the sacred from the secular. And it is probably true, as Bert Loewenberg and Ruth Bogin claim, that slaves used their religion as a fixed psychic point to counter the uncontrollable flux in their social world.[21] This was perhaps true for all slaves.

But in terms of some slave mothers and religion, it also seems that an additional internalization process operated. God and religion fulfilled some very basic needs that could not be fulfilled by the slave community or the black man. Thus the slave narratives often portray black mothers exhibiting a vigorous spiritual self-confidence even though their sexuality has been completely brutalized and exploited by white men of every social class. Though they were continuously raped, used as breeder women and made accessible to the sexual appetite of all white males, many slave mothers endured with strength and dignity. They endured because, as one slave mother taught her daughter, they believed there was "nobody in the wide world to look to but God."[22]

### *Tensions in the Community over Motherhood*

In some African-American literary history following the antebellum period, black writers infer that this kind of God-consciousness and God-dependence supporting black mothers is problematic. They suggest that for some black mothers, this consciousness and dependence created needs that could only be fulfilled within the limits of the black mother's religion. James Baldwin, an avid student of African-American religion, demonstrated this in a scene in his novel *If Beale Street Could Talk*. Here, a black Christian woman can only make love to her husband by psychologically substituting God for the husband. Thus the woman's pillow talk is also her god-talk, from which the husband is excluded.

Postbellum black writers were trying to present the black woman's mothering and nurturing roles in relation to the transformative social processes occurring in the black community after the Civil War. Especially important was the process of strengthening the black male's role as father and giving him uncontested authority over black family life. During slavery this control had been exercised first by the slave master and his family and next by the slave woman.

In the newly freed African-American community, this business of transferring authority to the black male represented a process of translating power in the ex-slave community into a more stable patriarchal model. There are indications that even before the Civil War the institutionalization of black religion into various forms like African Methodist Episcopal carried with it the subordination and oppression of women. The following testimonies of black mothering and nurturing figures Jarena Lee, Maria Stewart and Old Elizabeth show how sexism accompanied the practice and understanding of institutional religion in the black community during and directly after the antebellum period in North America:

> JARENA LEE: I went to see the preacher in charge of the African society . . . the Rev. Richard Allen . . . to tell him that I felt it my duty to preach the gospel. . . . He then replied, that a Mrs. Cook, a Methodist lady, had also some time before requested the same privilege. . . . But as to preaching, he said that our Discipline knew nothing at all about it—that it did not call for women preachers. . . .
>
> On second day morning, I took a stage and rode seven miles to Woodstown, and there I spoke to a respectable congregation of white and colored, in a school house. I was desired to speak in the colored meeting house, but the minister could not reconcile his mind to a woman preacher—he could not unite in fellowship with me even to shaking hands as Christians ought.[23]

> MARIA STEWART: What if I am a woman; is not the God of ancient times the God of these modern days? Did he not raise up Deborah, to be a mother and a judge in Israel? Did not queen Esther save the lives of the Jews? . . . I say if such women as are here described have once existed, be no longer astonished, then brethren . . . that God at this eventful period

should rise up your own females to strive by their example both in public and private to assist those who are endeavoring to stop the strong current of prejudice that flows so profusely against us [women] at present.[24]

ELIZABETH: Our meeting gave great offense, and we were forbid holding any more assemblies. Even the elders of our meeting joined with the wicked people, and said such meetings must be stopped, and that women quieted. . . . The persecution against me increased, and a complaint was carried forward . . . and the elders came out with indignation for my holding meetings contrary to discipline—being a woman.[25]

In the development of African-American musical and literary history, it is in blues art that the process of power transferal from female to male begins to show itself. Some blues artists, consciously or unconsciously, diminish the reflection of the black woman's God-consciousness and God-dependence in relation to her role as mother and nurturer. She is often pictured as completely dependent upon the quality of male-female relationships for the emotional and spiritual support she needs. Neither her religion nor her God is mentioned in a substantial way. And her mothering and nurturing function reflected in blues art had less to do with children and more to do with the care and love for black men.

### *"Mamma-Baby" in Blues Literature*

Emerging shortly after the Civil War during the reconstruction period, the lyrics to many blues songs often present black women in conflicting roles as mamma and baby simultaneously. Reflecting an ambivalence about mothering roles, the blues lyrics diminish the independent strength of mothers and portray weakened female figures. Consider the following blues songs:

SONG #1

> Hey, Hey, Mamma, Baby, what's the matter now?
> Hey, Mamma, Baby, what's the matter now?

SONG #2

> Lord, I'm going away now,
> I'm going away to stay,
> Lord, I'm going away now,
> I'm going away now,
> I'm going away to stay!

Be all right, pretty Mamma
Might need my help some day . . .
Baby, bring me a cold towel
For my head, my aching head.[26]

SONG #3

. . . and the sun going down, . . .
dark gone catch me here.
Uumh, oh dark gone catch me here.
I haven't got no loving sweet woman,
that love will be near . . .
Lord, that I'm standing at the crossroads,
Babe, I believe I'm sinking down.[27]

There are many more lines in blues songs that portray this ambiguous ad-mixture of the roles of mamma-woman-baby in relation to the black woman: "Black woman, black woman, baby, you know you paid your dues"; "Blues in the bottle . . . I've got the stopper in my hand sweet mamma"; "I got holes in my pockets baby, I got patches in my pants, I'm behind with the house-rent, mamma, Lord."[28] All lines portray a weakened "mamma."

Some of the blues poetry of Langston Hughes provides a very clear view of the blues artist reshaping the image of the black woman's mothering and nurturing roles. In his *Selected Poems*, the section entitled "Shadow of the Blues" has a poem, "Sylvester's Dying Bed," which demonstrates this reshap-ing process:

(stanza 1)    I woke up this mornin'
                'Bout half-past three.
                All the womens in town
                Was gathered 'round me.

(stanza 2)    Sweet gals was a-moanin'
                "Sylvester's gonna die!"
                And a hundred pretty mammas
                Bowed their heads to cry.

                . . .

(stanza 4)    Black gals was a-beggin,
                "You can't leave us here!"
                Brown-skins crying, "Daddy!
                Honey, Baby! Don't go, dear!"

(stanza 5)     But I felt ma time's a-comin',
                And I know'd I's dyin' fast.
                I seed the River Jerden
                A-creepin' muddy past—
                But I's still Sweet Papa 'Vester,
                Yes, Sir! Long as life do last!
(stanza 6)     So I hollers, "com'ere, babies,
                Fo' to love you daddy right!"
                And I reaches up to hug 'em—
                When the lawd put out the light.[29]

Throughout the poem there is a conflict in the male/female imagery that is finally resolved in the assertion of masculine dominance and female dependency. Initially the females are referred to as "womens," an adult female designation. But in stanza two the "womens" become "sweet gals" —thereby infusing the adult image with an element of adolescence. In line three of stanza two, however, the black females become the stronger, more basic figures of "pretty mammas" —suggesting reproduction and nurturing. Then, in stanza six all images of the females in the poem collapse into the final image of "babies" —implying utter dependence. But the development of the male imagery in the poem involves only two steps: from the contradictions expressed in stanza four (that is, "Daddy" and "baby") to the single authority of "Papa 'Vester" in stanza five and "daddy" in stanza six.

Whereas the black woman in some blues art is still "mamma," she is no longer "mamma" like the Rock of Gibraltar. She is "mamma" with a certain dependency, like a baby. Though her suffering prevails, the black woman in blues art has not the uncanny spiritual and emotional endurance of her literary progenitor, the antebellum slave mother. The blues woman is only human, supported by neither God nor man. She merely "hangs her head and cries" in the face of trouble while her man may "take a train and ride" to escape it. The fact that most blues art does not associate the black woman's mothering and nurturing role with religion (as do some of the lyrics of the spiritual songs and many of the slave narratives) diminishes her characteristic strength, which she believed came from God through her religious faith. When blues artists de-emphasized religion, they not only lessened the importance of the mothering and nurturing function of the black woman, but they also directed attention away from the exploitation of these roles by forces inside and beyond the postbellum black community.[30]

The works of some postbellum black protest novelists and dramatists advance the blues artists' trend of casting aspersions on the effect of the black mother's religion upon the performance of her mothering and nurturing tasks. But contrary to the blues artists, some of the postbellum protest writers show black mothers depending very much upon the African-American denominational churches, the black preacher and black religion to support their mothering and nurturing roles. However, the protest writers criticize this relation. They question the compatibility of the black mother's religion with the demands a complex urban world makes upon her. Unlike the blues artists, writers James Baldwin and Richard Wright stage their protest about the relation of the black mother to religious phenomena on a much more sophisticated sociological level. Both men agree that the black mother's church religion (mediated by the black preacher) has made her oblivious to the real needs of black people and to the destructive nature of the social, political and legal forces governing black life in white America.

### Black Mamma, Black Preacher, Black Protest

In his play *Amen Corner*, James Baldwin creates a black mother character who consciously rejects her black husband as she selects black religion to help her perform her mothering and nurturing tasks.[31] The results are, of course, disastrous for the family. The father dies destitute and unhappy, having been deprived of his place in the family because of the mother's call to preach. The son goes out into the world as a musician to find his black manhood, which his mother had tried to smother in the obligation of a forced religious commitment. Baldwin believes black mothers hold fast to religion for psychological, emotional and physical security black men cannot or will not provide.[32] According to Baldwin, the instability of her family and socioeconomic condition, the corrupt elements in her black urban community and white oppression cause the black mother to develop an "unnatural" dependency upon religion. This dependency renders her extremely vulnerable before the religious authority in the black church or exalts her to a position of religious authority through which she exploits other people.

An important point to recognize about some protest writers' portrayal of the black mother in relation to religious phenomena is that Christian religion does not often play a supportive, productive role. In his novel *The Long Dream*, Richard Wright reveals the great degree to which a black preacher and his theology are indifferent to the suffering of black mothers. First

Wright presents a black mother questioning God following the lynching of her son Chris and the mutilation of his body by the white lynchers:

> "Chris, baby, this ain't you! Now, naw, God! This can't be." Mrs. Sims cried, clinging hysterically to the dead body. "Gawd didn't do this to me! He couldn't! And you got to do something to stop this from happening to black women's children. . . . Gawd, take your sun out of the sky! Take your stars away! I don't want Your trees, Your flowers no more! I don't want Your wind to blow on me when my son can die like this. . . . I'm standing 'fore Your throne asking You to tell me: What did I ever do wrong? Where's my sin? . . . Gawd, talk to me. As long's I live, I'll be asking You to tell me why my son died like this."[33]

Then Wright presents the black preachers' response to the incident:

> In Fishbelly's [the protagonist] Black-Belt living the echoes of Chris's death died slowly away. From pulpits, sweating black preachers thundered cryptic sermons describing all death as the work of God's mysterious Hand meting out divine justice to the earth's sinful inhabitants.[34]

In some of his fiction Richard Wright suggests the Christian religion has failed to meet the black mother's needs because it has confounded her understanding of black suffering and has caused her to accept untenable explanations for it. She, in turn, tries to pass these ineffective explanations to her children as tools for dealing with white oppression.

Richard Wright's major protest, then, is against the black mother's dependence upon Christian religion for support in her mothering and nurturing roles. He suggests that this religion exploits her intellect by stunting the growth of her critical faculties, thereby limiting the action she can choose to alter her family's oppression. The black preacher's contribution to all of this is that his theology bears a relationship with the social forces that oppress the black woman and the black community. This is clearly revealed in that section of Richard Wright's novel *Native Son* where the black preacher visits the main character, Bigger Thomas, who is in jail accused of murdering a young, rich, white woman. In order to communicate the degree to which this religion (via the black preacher) has subjugated the black mother, Wright establishes the following sequence in one passage. First, Bigger, seeing the black minister before him in his jail cell, makes a mental association:

> He was . . . Reverend Hammond, the pastor of his mother's church. He feared that the preacher would make him feel remorseful. He wanted

him to go; but so closely associated in his mind was the man with his mother and what she stood for that he could not speak.[35]

Bigger attempted to direct his hearing away from the preacher's exhortations, for Bigger "knew without listening what they meant; it was the old voice of his mother telling of suffering, of hope, of love beyond this world."[36] And the preacher's words reinforce Bigger's premonitions: "Fergit ever' thing but yo' soul son. Take yo' mind off ever' thing but eternal life. . . . Fergit yuh's black. Gawd looks past yo' skin 'n inter yo' soul, son."[37] The preacher begins a long sermon about the creation not knowing that Bigger, in his mind, has already "killed" the creation story. Richard Wright tells the reader that those who wanted to kill Bigger thought that he was not human, that he was not "included in the picture of creation; and that was why he [Bigger] had killed it." Wright says that in order for Bigger to live he had to create a new world for himself, and for that he was to die.[38] Bigger's mother can endure struggling and suffering because the preacher had defined these as prerequisites for Christian salvation. The preacher says to Bigger:

> Look son Ah'm holdin' in mah hands a wooden cross taken from a tree. A tree is the worl' son. 'N nailed t' this tree is a sufferin' man. Th's whut life is, son. Sufferin. How kin yuh keep from b'lievin' the word of Gawd when Ah'm holdin' befo' yo' eyes the only thing tha' gives a meanin' t' yo' life?[39]

These "Christian philosophies" make possible the action of Bigger's mother in his jail cell—an action that disgusts Bigger and causes him to loathe himself and her. She crawls around on her knees in his cell, going from "white racist to white racist" begging them to spare the life of her son. Her religion does not allow her to see that her son has decided that if he must die, he will die like a man. This is the point of Richard Wright's stringent critique of the black-mother-black-preacher-Christian religion relationship. This religion, with the help of the black preacher, has blinded the black mother to such an extent that she can neither value nor recognize the tensions inherent in the expression of black manhood. Apparently Baldwin and Wright are in partial agreement here, though Baldwin pays more attention to the fanatical aspect of black religion and how it oppresses both women and men.

Wright and Baldwin, in part, build their images of the black mother upon the foundations laid by both antebellum and postbellum blues writers. The antebellum image of black motherhood yielded the "strong black mamma," capable of uncanny endurance and dignity because of her faith in the effectiveness of her religion. The postbellum blues artist presented an image of the black woman (without religious faith or involvement) that emphasized the dependency and weakness of the black mother vulnerable before a host of emotional, economic, domestic and social crises. Baldwin and Wright, on the other hand, merge the two images (antebellum and blues) into one—but with an important difference. Though their female characters are absorbed in their mothering and nurturing roles, though they are dependent upon religion, they are exploited by this religion and by some black preachers. This experience makes these women inept in dealing with oppression. Richard Wright, more than Baldwin, raises serious theological questions about the Christian religion in relation to black mothers' and black people's experience of racial oppression in America. Wright raises the theodicy question of why a good God lets innocent people suffer along with the guilty.

### Black Women Authors Differ

Some postbellum women writers provide images of black motherhood that are radically different from what their male counterparts (that is, Wright and Baldwin) have projected. Two examples are Margaret Walker and Alice Walker. Margaret Walker's novel *Jubilee* reinforces the image of the slave mother, but more detail is added. Alice Walker in her novel *The Color Purple* recasts the image of black motherhood, emphasizing the importance of the development of "SELFconsciousness" and a new spirituality on the part of black mothers. Neither of these two female writers criticizes the function of Christian religion in relation to black mothering and nurturing roles. However, other black women writers like Zora Hurston and Nella Larson (both part of the Harlem Renaissance movement in the 1920s) find fault with the effect some black preachers have upon the lives and roles of black mothers.

In *Jubilee*—set in the antebellum South —Margaret Walker emphasizes the positive role religion plays in the development of what every African-American slave mother needed, that is, survival intelligence. The endurance of the protagonist Vyry is assured by the shrewd survival intelligence she developed under the tutelage of Mammy Sukey and Aunt Sally, both mothers and both religious women. One part of this survival intelligence had to do with plantation politics of learning how to be visible and accessible while simultaneously keeping out of the way of Big Missy, the slave-master's cruel wife. A second part had to do with learning how to survive physically on the basis of the correct knowledge of the effects of roots and herbs. The third part of survival intelligence had to do with developing a deep spirituality that provided psychological and emotional support in the time of trouble. The parts were held together by Vyry's God-consciousness and absolute dependence upon God, which allowed her at an early age to understand her life processes in a positive light even though she was a slave. Thus in *Jubilee* Margaret Walker emphasizes an important point about African-American mothers not considered by male blues and protest writers. The concern of many African-American mothers has been for the survival of their children, the family and the race. The economic, spiritual and physical assault upon black life in America by white people and white-controlled institutions has caused the African-American mother to try to develop survival strategies her family can use. She has not always been successful, but she has depended upon her religion to help her develop these strategies and to muster the courage to survive when survival gave no promise.

Often these survival strategies took the form of spiritual values. Black literary critic Mary Burgher describes this reality well when she says that spiritually, black mothers are usually the strongest in the community. They maintain and transmit values and ideas that support and enrich the black community "as a viable unit." Burgher describes these transmitted values as belief in a promised land beyond bondage and oppression; belief that black people have the natural "resourcefulness to find strength in . . . weakness, joy in sorrow and hope in what seems to be despair."[40] Burgher goes on to say that these "values suggest that the black mother . . . sees herself not as a breeder nor as a matriarch but as a builder and nurturer of a race, a nation."[41] In the work of Margaret Walker and many other black women, the image of black motherhood is

> a strong, hard-working woman who does what is necessary . . . to ensure the survival of her children. . . . Although frantic with the defeats that have occurred through the years, the Black mother . . . never quits on you.[42]

✳ Few black male writers have taken seriously the intensity of the black mother's commitment to the survival of her children and her willingness to do what is necessary (including being a mammy, a domestic or stealing food from the white folks) to maintain the life of her offspring. Therefore, some black male writers, such as Richard Wright, portray the black mother as an impediment to the black male's struggle for manhood in America.[43]

Margaret Walker's depiction of Vyry as the "strong black mamma" supported by her religious faith reiterates what slave women's narratives and what some other postbellum black female writers declare about the black mother: "She was the great Black bridge I crossed over on."[44] In accord with this kind of statement, Walker offers an eloquent description of the black mother Vyry, to whom Innis Brown (Vyry's husband) pays tribute:

> She [Vyry] . . . a woman who stood much outrage . . . had a wisdom and a touching humility It was more than her practical intelligence, or her moral fortitude; more than the fundamental decency and innate dignity. . . . She was touched with a spiritual wholeness. . . . Peasant and slave, unlettered and untutored, she was nevertheless the best true example of the motherhood of her race, an ever present assurance that nothing could destroy a people whose sons had come from her loins.[45]

Yet, prior to Margaret Walker's time, some black female writers interpreted as problematic some black mothers' relation to black Christian preachers. Zora Hurston and Nella Larson criticized the emotional exploitation of black women by black preachers who hid their exploitative tactics in the submissive theology advocated in their sermons. While Hurston's book *Jonah's Gourd Vine* portrays an intelligent black mother emotionally bedazzled by her philandering preacher husband, Nella Larson in *Quicksand* portrays an octoroon woman rejected by (and rejecting) the values of white upper-class culture. Larson's character turns to the religious values of the black community modeled in the black preacher she ultimately marries. Zora Hurston's mother-character Lucy dies leaving a word of advice all black women would do well to heed: "Don't love nobody bettern' yo' self, do you'll be dying before your time is out." Lucy has loved her preacher husband best of all. Nella Larson's mother character, smothered by religion in the black community, dies burdened and oppressed by excessive childbearing.

Alice Walker represents one of the most able voices of a cadre of modern black women writers who are trying to recast the image of the black mother for the black community.[46] Walker's novel *The Color Purple* does what black feminist literary critic Barbara Christian understands as finding a female voice for mothers so they can tell their own stories realistically.[47] Walker uses feminist issues to shape the situations in which her mother characters find themselves. Their stories are about domestic violence, rape, racial oppression, the white male exploitation of nature, black sexism, consciousness-raising, sexuality, work, survival and liberation. Because she employs a feminist framework to present the image of African-American mothers, Alice Walker radically recasts both the image of black mothers and the nature of the religious perspectives black mothers' need for self-realization. It is this radical recasting of images in a feminist mode that distinguishes Walker's work from that of the other writers considered in this study.

Alice Walker begins *The Color Purple* not by introducing a strong black mamma. Rather she introduces the reader to a vulnerable woman-child plagued by domestic violence in the home of her parents and later in the home of her husband. Fourteen-year-old Celie has been raped by her stepfather. Because she knows very little about how her body functions, she is surprised when she gives birth to children by him. After giving her children away, Celie's stepfather forces her to marry Mr. Albert, who beats her constantly because he believes "Wives is like children. You have to let 'em know who got the upper hand. Nothing can do better than a good sound beating."[48]

Like the blues artists, Alice Walker does not emphasize women's roles as mothers and nurturers of children. Though every major female character in the book is a mother, none has the responsibility of rearing her biological offspring. Unlike blues artists, Alice Walker wants us to recognize that the inordinate demands men make upon the nurturing capacities of black mothers are destructive for women (for example, Mr. Albert's demands upon Celie, and Harpo's demands upon Sophia). Walker's work suggests that the exertion of male power to make sure women meet these demands constitutes sexism in the black community.

From the beginning of the novel this sexism is in place. The exploitation of black women's sexuality occurs throughout the book. The bodies of the mothers become targets for the gratification of male lust. Nettie's rape by her stepfather is prevented because Celie offers her own body instead. Mr. Albert, Celie's husband, expels Nettie from their house because she refuses his advances. Men have been so brutally intent upon their own gratification in their sexual relations with Celie that she does not discover her body's erotic zones until another woman points them out to her. The white prison warden rationalizes his abuse of the body of (the black woman) Mary Agnes on the grounds that he has indulged in a bit of fornication that "everybody is guilty of."[49]

Freeing the black mothers from debilitating impotence, Alice Walker presents an image of women emerging into self-awareness, power and autonomy. Consciousness-raising; new notions about female sexuality, about God, man and church; new notions about female bonding and women's economic independence are the "tools" Walker uses to move Celie (the main mother-character) from impotence to empowerment. Celie's progress toward empowerment begins when she and the bisexual woman Shug bond in true friendship. Shug is the catalyst causing the changes in Celie's consciousness. She nurtures Celie through the transformations in thinking and action necessary for Celie to become an autonomous woman, taking full responsibility for her own life. Shug guides Celie through her struggle with self-hate and shame to the final realization of her independence as a self-confident lesbian woman.

Shug helps Celie to reexamine certain religious values Celie has held all her life—religious values supporting her bondage rather than her empowerment as a new, liberated woman. This reexamination centers on notions of God, man and church. This reflection shows Celie her image of God as man has limited her perception of the connectedness of all reality. Shug convinces Celie that church is not a place to find God. Rather, church is a place where people come to share God because "Any God I ever felt in Church I brought in with me . . . the other folk did too."[50]

Celie's change of consciousness about "God-as-man" frees her psychologically from the fear of her husband, who was as stern as any God she had imagined. After years of silently suffering, Celie "enters into creation."[51] Her revaluing and her departure from her husband's house with Shug liberate her for self-discovery. Shug helps her achieve economic independence. So when Celie returns to Georgia where her husband and his children reside, she is a new woman with a new morality, a new sense of herself and a new financial independence. She has moved from impotence to full autonomy, from self-abasement to self-confidence, from passivity to active responsibility.

Alice Walker's use of feminist issues to structure *The Color Purple* brings a "new word" to talk about black motherhood in African-American literature. Speaking to the community, Walker communicates an inclusive understanding of who is to provide the nurturing for children. Walker portrays mothers (Celie, Shug, Sophia, Mary Agnes) who are separated from their children. But these children are lovingly nurtured by family members and others beyond the family. Jack, Odessa, Harpo and Mary Agnes love and nurture Sophia's children as Sophia serves out her lengthy incarceration. Sophia and Harpo nurture Mary Agnes's child while she seeks a singing career. In the "redistribution" of children, Walker suggests that the nurturing of children is the task of the entire black community—male and female.

Walker also presents an image of black mothers nurturing one another in order to help each other develop self-love and self-esteem. Shug nurtures

Celie into a fully responsible moral agent who can take control of her own life and destiny. In her recasting of the image of motherhood, Walker shows the redemptive character of lesbian relationships for some women's lives. Walker also depicts the heterosexual relation between Samuel and Nettie as loving and as productive for both people. Thus Walker suggests that there are loving and nurturing possibilities in both homosexual and heterosexual relationships.

Finally, Walker transforms the character of the religious perceptions the black mothers use to help them in their progress toward self-consciousness and freedom. At the beginning of *The Color Purple*, when Nettie tells Celie "I hate to leave you here with these rotten children [Mr. Albert's children]," Celie answers, "Never mine, never mine, long as I can spell G-O-D I got somebody along."[52] Thus Celie continues her long painful correspondence with God whom she imagines to be old, white and a man. Celie maintains this image of God as long as she nurtures Mr. Albert and his children and works in his fields—as long as she denies herself and possesses a consciousness primarily occupied with self-sacrifice and with surviving the brutality men inflict upon her. As long as she lives in transcendent relation to her own experience, she is content to image God as male, old and white.[53] But when Shug helps Celie begin her process of self-discovery, Celie starts to understand that her notion of God must change, because "you have to git man off your eyeball before you can see anything a'tall."[54] Thus Celie's God becomes an internal experience rather than a physical manifestation to be worshiped like the man Jesus. Her new understanding of God is similar to that expressed by one of the women in a play by black feminist playwriter Ntozake Shange—the woman who testified "I found god in myself and I love her/fiercely."[55]

That Alice Walker intends to challenge black people to examine their concept of God in relation to liberation is demonstrated by a letter Nettie sends to Celie. After serving almost thirty years as a missionary to the Olinka people in Africa, Nettie says that for her and her husband God is different. God is more spirit and more internal. Most people think God "has to look like something or someone—a roofleaf [the Olinka perception of God] or Christ—but we don't." Nettie claims that "not being tied to what God looks like, frees us."[56]

Walker has tried, in her portrait of black mothers and their transformed religion, to reshape some traditional black understandings of mothering and nurturing roles.[57] Unlike the antebellum black artists, Walker does not present an image of the "strong black mamma" made invulnerable by her faith in

God. Rather, she shows black mothers and nurturers vulnerable before a host of destructive domestic and social forces. But unlike blues writers, who also present vulnerable women, Walker does not suggest that women should deal with these destructive forces by hanging on tighter to men. She suggests that mothers get victory over oppressive social forces by bonding with one another and opposing their oppression rather than "praying 'cause praying was all I know to do."[58]

Unlike the protest writers Richard Wright and James Baldwin, Alice Walker portrays religion as a positive force supporting black mothers in their transformative processes. But she shows that the black mother's religion must move beyond male-female imagery in order to accommodate the black mother's realization of self-esteem, autonomy and liberation. The idea of the divine spirit working within humans is more efficacious for women's development of self-worth than notions of God in male or female form. Like Margaret Walker, Alice Walker does not project an image of a black male preacher exploiting the nurturing capacities of black women. Alice Walker merely gives us Shug's words and Celie's acceptance of them: "You have to git man off your eyeball before you can see anything a'tall."[59] This statement includes male gods and human men. This is a radical departure from the image of God supporting some of the mothers in the other novels. In the antebellum literature, Wright, Baldwin, Margaret Walker, Nella Larson and Zora Hurston either project or assume images of a traditional male God. But Shug's and Celie's God lives in a feminist faith that abides in the spirit rather than in creeds or in the orthodoxy of institutional religion.

However, Alice Walker, Margaret Walker, Richard Wright, James Baldwin, Zora Hurston and Nella Larson would perhaps agree on at least one point—that black women have been devout in their mothering and nurturing tasks. They have believed God supported them in their struggle. Perhaps these writers would also agree that, more often than not, the rank-and-file black woman believes as Celie believed: "Long as I can spell G-O-D I got somebody along."[60]

### Motherhood in a Context of Resistance

Through black mothering and nurturing depicted in the deposits of African-American culture we see social process in the black community (in both the antebellum and postbellum periods) affected by the God-consciousness and God-dependence of African-American women. Whether positively or negatively assessed by the various artists used in this study, the African-American mother's God-consciousness and absolute dependence upon God provided hope in personal and community relationships where hope seemed absurd. Therefore, systems of bondage like racism and sexism did not bring permanent lethargy to the community.

Black mothers often defied laws and custom in order to nurture black people with care and compassion. Sometimes they suffered severe consequences for this defiance. Historian Benjamin Brawley reports that "in the South any free Negro who entertained a runaway might himself become a slave. Thus in South Carolina in 1827 a free woman with her three children suffered this penalty." Her crime was that "she gave succor to two homeless and fugitive children six and nine years old."[61] For the slave mother, caring for slave children also meant telling the child who her father was even though there were laws against this. The octoroon slave Louisa Picquet shares an incident in which her mother received a penalty for this offense. Owned by John Randolph, this slave mother was fifteen years old when Louisa was born. John Randolph's wife had a child only two weeks older than the slave mother's child Louisa. Randolph was the father of both children. Louisa's mother told Louisa her father was her slavemaster, John Randolph. For this "offense" of telling the child about her parentage, the slave mother was sold away from her child.[62] Harriet Tubman defied the law in order physically and spiritually to nurture hundreds of black people from bondage in the South to freedom in the North.

Some scholars also make reference to a practice among free black communities during the antebellum period where "free colored men owned their women and children in order that the latter might escape the invidious law against Negroes recently emancipated." The same report tells of the practice among the free people of Northfold, Virginia, where "several women owned their husbands."[63] Slave women did what they could to enhance relationships in the family and community, even if they had to assume what was customarily thought of as "male roles."

During the antebellum period, every person was affected by the laws, customs and economics of the slavocracy. The well-being of black mothers and nurturers was constantly threatened. But these women often built networks of female support and resistance to aid themselves in whatever tasks they were involved in. Jarena Lee and Old Elizabeth—in their nurturing tasks as preachers—tell of the women who readily opened their houses for women to preach when black male authorities in the churches denied them ordination or use of church buildings. Lee tells of the women who walked with her for ten or even twenty miles to her preaching engagements and to visit the sick. Historian Deborah Gray White, in her treatment of slave women's reality, also speaks of the female slave networks. She claims that "adult female cooperation and interdependence was a fact of female slave life." Further, "The self-reliance and self-sufficiency of slave women, therefore, must not only be viewed in the context of what the individual slave woman did for herself, but what slave women as a group were able to do for one another."[64]

Apparently this kind of networking extended to parenting in the black community during the antebellum era. Jarena Lee and Zilpha Elaw left their children with other women in the community for extended periods while they traveled through the country preaching the gospel. The children survived and thrived. In the postbellum period this female networking extended into the African-American denominational churches and possibly into later developments like the club movement among black women.

What all this suggests is that the modern phenomenon of black mothers like Rosa Parks acting as catalysts for social change stems from a long tradition of black mothers and nurturers who were catalysts for social change in and beyond the African-American community—even though some social processes in the community restricted black women's opportunities while expanding black men's opportunities. A case in point is the sexism that confronted black women in their effort to become ordained ministers and the lack of restrictions based on sex for black men seeking the same opportunity. This sexism exists today in both the African-American denominational churches and also exists in most of the male theology that issued from the churches after slavery and before the 1980s.

Other structures of domination have had an impact upon the lives of African-American mothers and nurturers. Surrogacy is one such structure. Hagar and African-American women have a common bond in this surrogacy theme threading through their stories. The following chapter focuses upon the area of African-American women's history where this structure of domination reveals itself.

# Chapter 3

## Social-Role Surrogacy: Naming Black Women's Oppression

Because she was a slave, Hagar had no control over her body or her labor. Her body, like her labor, could be exploited in any way her owners desired. Her reproduction capacities belonged to her slave holders, Abraham and Sarah. Thus surrogacy became a major theme in Hagar's story of exploitation. Surrogacy has also been a major theme in African-American women's history. But whereas Hagar's experience with surrogacy was primarily biological, African-American women's experience with surrogacy has been primarily associated with social-role exploitation.

Two kinds of social-role surrogacy have negatively affected the lives of African-American women and mothers: coerced surrogacy and voluntary surrogacy. Coerced surrogacy, belonging to the antebellum period, was a condition in which people and systems more powerful than black people forced black women to function in roles that ordinarily would have been filled by someone else. For example, black female slaves were forced to substitute for the slave-owner's wife in nurturing roles involving white children. Black women were forced to take the place of men in work roles that, according to the larger society's understanding of male and female roles, belonged to men. Frederick Law Olmsted, a northern architect writing in the nineteenth century, said he "stood for a long time watching slave women repair a road on a South Carolina plantation."[1] Sometimes black women were even forced to substitute for the slave owner and his wife in governing roles connected directly with the slave-owner's household. Historian Deborah Gray White tells of a white North Carolina planter who put a slave woman (and not his wife) in charge of all domestic duties in his household.[2] This slave woman was not a mammy. Rather, she was the lover of the slave owner. During the antebellum period in America, this coerced surrogacy was legally supported in the ownership rights by which slave masters and their wives controlled their property, for example, black women. Slave women could not exercise the choice of refusing surrogacy roles.

After emancipation, the coercion associated with antebellum surrogacy was replaced by social pressures that influenced many black women to continue to fill some surrogacy roles. But there was an important difference between antebellum surrogacy and postbellum surrogacy. The difference was that black women, after emancipation, could exercise the choice of refusing the surrogate role, but social pressures often influenced the choices black women made as they adjusted to life in a free world. Thus postbellum surrogacy can be referred to as voluntary (though pressured) surrogacy.

Poverty among African Americans often pressured some black women into certain surrogacy roles. For poor black women voluntary surrogacy could mean that, as domestics employed by white families, these women could still perform nurturing tasks for white children.[3] In the black community black women could be pressured by social circumstances to step into the role of head of household in lieu of absent male energy and presence.

Today the growing surrogacy industry in North America and the escalating poverty among black people can pressure poor black women to become heavily involved in this industry at the level of reproduction. Though legislation has been passed that makes surrogacy contracts non-binding for surrogate mothers, poverty can influence black women to honor such contracts.[4] However, the point here is that since emancipation, black women have been able to exercise choice with regard to surrogacy roles, even though economics and other social forces exert undue influence upon the choices black women make.[5]

A closer look at these two modes of social-role surrogacy in the two different periods (antebellum and postbellum) reveals the difference between the modes and describes an aspect of black experience heretofore invisible in the scholarship about black history, religion and culture.

### Coerced Surrogacy Roles and Antebellum Realities

In the antebellum South coerced surrogacy roles involving black women were in the areas of nurturance, field labor and sexuality. Some of the traditions associated with these three areas have helped develop stereotypical images of black women that have survived from antebellum times to the present.

One such tradition was that of the southern black mammy. Standing in the place of the slave-owner's wife, mammy nurtured the entire white family. A long and respected tradition among southern whites, mammy was an empowered (but not autonomous) house slave who was given considerable authority by her owners. According to the existing scattered reports of mammies and how the tradition operated, we know many southerners thought "mammy . . . could do anything, and do it better than anyone else. Because of her expertise in all domestic matters, she was the premier house servant and all others were her subordinates."[6] Eliza Riply, a southern white woman who received nurture from a mammy, remembers her as

> a "supernumerary" who, after the children grew up . . . managed the whole big and mixed household. In her [Eliza Riply's] father's house, everyone was made to understand that . . . all applications were to go through Mammy Charlotte. Nobody thought to go to the judge or his wife for anything.[7]

Susan Epps's recollection of mammy attests to the fact that it was often the mammy who taught and instilled values in white children—a teaching role that southern ideology usually assigned to white Christian mothers. Mammies acted as protectors of their young white charges. Epps recalls that "it was Mammy who stood between her 'honey child' and the cold, cold world."[8] On many occasions, mammies advised slave owners about business matters.

Testimony by ex-slaves themselves also attests to the value and power of mammies in southern households. Drucella Martin remembered "that her mother was in full charge of the house and all 'marse children.'" Katherine Epps of Alabama said that her mother "worked in the Big House, 'aspinnin and 'asussin de white chillun." Epps also claimed that the mistress was so fond of her mother "that when she learned . . . the overseer had whipped the woman whom everyone called 'Mammy,' she dismissed him and gave him until sundown to remove himself and his family from the plantation." An ex-slave woman in Louisiana recalled the unusual respect given to some mammies. She said that "all the niggers have to stoop to Aunt Rachael just like they curtsy to Missy."[9] Deborah Gray White therefore concludes that mammy was primarily devoted to white families and their children. A house servant, mammy had complete control of the management of the white household. "She served as friend and advisor. She was, in short, surrogate mistress and mother."[10]

However, historian Eugene Genovese makes the point that while mammies were devout in their care of white children and families, they were also just as dedicated to their own families and to the well-being of black people. They often interceded to prevent slaves from receiving floggings and abuse, and they performed other services beneficial to the slave community. Therefore, Genovese claims, mammy's tragedy was not that she abandoned her own people. The tragedy was that she was powerless to offer her gifts to black people "on terms they could accept without, themselves, sliding farther into a system of paternalistic dependence."[11] Though tenable, Genovese's observation forgets some black women who, beyond the plantation, bore the title of mammy but who were subtly engaged in liberation efforts. One such woman was Mammy Pleasant, whose given name was Mary Ellen.

Early in life Mammy Pleasant was a slave in Georgia, but her intelligence was recognized by a planter who sent her to Boston for training. Here, according to W. E. B. Du Bois's account of her life, she was made a household drudge and eventually married.[12] She inherited fifty thousand dollars from her husband's estate. With this money she migrated to California and made a fortune. Describing the liberation activity of Mammy Pleasant, Du Bois reports that she wanted her epitaph to read: "She was a friend of John Brown."[13] It was rumored that she financed John Brown's raid. In accord with the mammy tradition of advising wealthy white men about business, Mammy Pleasant in California "was the trusted confidante of many of the [white] California pioneers like Ralston, Mills and Booth."[14]

Much mythology surrounded the figure of the black mammy. White pro-slavery arguments picture mammy as a contented and well-taken-care-of house servant whose activities in the house of her owners were "in keeping with . . . Victorian ideals of womanhood prevalent in nineteenth century America." In addition to being maternal, the ideal Victorian woman was virtuous, asexual, pious, tender and understanding.[15] Mammy exhibited some of these characteristics. Therefore, it could be argued that slavery was a tool for converting some "heathen" black women into "civilized" models of womanhood. Mammy was living proof that the conversion could be accomplished.

Mythology about mammy's well-being in her old age was apt to be just as exaggerated as notions of her "fit" into Victorian notions of womanhood. Mammy's old age was often full of suffering. Deborah Gray White reports that many of these mammies, when old, were not treated well by their owners. They were often abandoned. White cites the case of Frederick Douglass's grandmother, who suffered this fate. As a devoted nurse to white children and as housekeeper, this grandmother nevertheless lived to see her own children, grandchildren and great-grandchildren sold away from her. When she got too old to work, the slave owners whom she had so devoutly served built her a little hut in the woods and left her there to care for herself, even though she was very frail. "As Frederick Douglass put it, they turned her out to die." White describes other forms of abuse some mammies suffered. One mammy named Aunt Betty nursed her master from infancy to adulthood. Then she experienced a fatal destiny when "during one of his drunken rampages, he took his shotgun and killed her."[16] Nevertheless, the mammy role was probably the most powerful and authoritative one slave women could fill. And although slave women—in their coerced roles as mammies—were often abused, they were also empowered.[17]

This was not the case, however, with slave women laboring beyond the Big House, that is, the slave-owner's dwelling. In the area of field labor, black women were forced into work usually associated with male roles.[18] In the fields slave women and slave men performed the same tasks. Black feminist scholar Bell Hooks claims that on large plantations "women plowed, planted . . . harvested crops. On some plantations black women worked longer hours in the fields than black men."[19] What this amounted to, in terms of coerced surrogacy, was black female energy substituting for black male energy. This resulted in what Hooks refers to as the masculinization of the black female.[20] Unlike the mammy role of the female house slave, the masculinized roles of the female field slave did not empower black women in the slave structure to the extent that mammies were empowered. In the fields the greatest amount of power a slave could hold was a position of slave driver or overseer. Usually, only males could ascend to these roles. Thus the driver was a male slave. Though a few black males served as overseers, this role was usually filled by white men of a lower social class than the slave owner.

In their autobiographies many female slaves described the masculine work roles black women were forced to fill. Ex-slave Bethany Veney tells of helping her cruel slave owner haul logs, drive out hogs and set posts into the ground for fences.[21] Louisa Picquet, a slave, told her story in 1861 and mentioned that slave women drove ox wagons, tended mills and plowed just like men.[22] Another slave, Mary Prince, told of a female slave simultaneously performing tasks associated with both male and female roles:

> A French Black called Hetty, whom my master took in privateering from another vessel and made his slave . . . was the most active woman I ever saw, and she was taxed to her utmost. . . . She came in from milking the cows, and put the sweet-potatoes on for supper. She then

fetched home the sheep, and penned them in the fold; drove home the cattle, and staked them about the pond side; fed and rubbed down my master's horse, and gave the . . . hogs and cows their suppers; prepared the beds, and undressed the children, and laid them to sleep. I liked to look at her and watch all her doings, for hers was the only friendly face I had as yet seen, and I felt glad that she was there. She gave me my supper of potatoes and milk, and a blanket to sleep upon, which she spread for me in the passage before the door of Mrs. I____'s [the slave-owner's wife] chamber.[23]

Like some of the mammies, the slave woman coerced to perform the masculine tasks sometime met death at the hands of their owners. Prince describes Hetty's end:

Her death was hastened (at least the slaves all believed and said so) by the dreadful chastisement she received from her master during her pregnancy. It . . . was as follows. One of the cows had dragged the rope away from the stake to which Hetty had fastened it, and got loose. My master flew into a rage and ordered the poor creature [Hetty] to be stripped quite naked, notwithstanding her pregnancy, and to be tied to a tree in the yard. He then flogged her as hard as he could lick, both with the whip and cow-skin, till she was all over streaming with blood. He rested, and then beat her again and again. . . . Poor Hetty . . . was delivered after severe labor of a dead child. She appeared to recover after her confinement . . . but . . . ere long her body and limbs swelled to a great size; and she lay on a mat in the kitchen, till the water burst out of her body and she died.[24]

Apparently, in the consciousness of many slaves, the masculinization of the roles of female slaves erased gender boundaries in relation to work. It may well be that this forced substitution of female energy for male energy, which field tasks would ordinarily be thought to require, was a root contributor to some male slaves' lack of gender distinction in their use of pronouns. Union Army officer Higginson said he asked a slave the meaning of a certain female custom and received an answer "framed with their usual indifference to the genders of pronouns." The slave's response was "he [meaning she] in de lonesome valley, sa."[25] (Today, in both the larger American society and in the African-American community, the tendency to signify only masculinity with the use of the words "the blacks" may derive, in part, from this early American, practice of masculinizing black females through their work.)

This focus upon coerced surrogacy roles of female slaves in the areas of nurturance and field labor reveals that women who filled the masculinized roles beyond the Big House were less respected than mammies, were given no recognition for their service, seldom realized the endearment of the white folks as did some mammies, got worse food and clothing and often received more brutal punishment. These masculinized female field slaves were thought to be of a lower social class than the female house slaves who usually did "women's work," consisting of cleaning, spinning, cooking, sewing and tending children.

All slave women no doubt knew that to refuse any role assigned them in the slavocracy meant severe punishment or even death. The slave woman Harriet Tubman was a notable exception. She refused all roles assigned to her by slave owners and lived with a price upon her head. In her autobiography she tells of the time she was preparing to go South and liberate more slaves. She was watched for everywhere. Slave holders had held a meeting in a courthouse in Maryland and increased the reward for her capture. They discussed the various cruel ways by which she should be tortured and put to death.[26] Nevertheless, Tubman continued in her role as liberator of slaves—a role usually thought to be filled by males.[27]

More than in the areas of nurturance and field labor, coerced surrogacy in the area of sexuality was threatening to slave women's self-esteem and sense of self-worth. This is the area in which slave women were forced to stand in place of white women and provide sexual pleasure for white male slave owners. The Victorian ideal of true womanhood (for Anglo-American women) supported a consciousness which, in the area of sexual relations, imagined sex between free white men and their wives to be for the purpose of procreation rather than for pleasure. Many white males turned to slave women for sexual pleasure and forced these women to fulfill needs that, according to racist ideology during the time, should have been fulfilled by white women.

In her narrative *Incidents in the Life of a Slave Girl*, Linda Brent presents a vivid description of her slave owner, Dr. Flint, who tried to force her into one of these illicit relations in which she would have provided him sexual pleasure. Brent escaped his advances by fleeing from his house and hiding for seven years in a crawl space in the roof of her grandmother's home. Octoroon slave woman Louisa Picquet was not as fortunate as Linda Brent. Picquet was purchased by a Mr. Williams when she was about fourteen and a half years old. She told an interviewer about the nature of her relation with this slave owner:

Answer [by Louisa]:

> . . . I was sold to Mr. Williams. I went right to New Orleans then.

Question [by interviewer]:

> . . . Well how was it with you after Mr. Williams bought you?

A. Well, he took me right away to New Orleans.

Q. How did you go?

A. In a boat. . . . Mr. Williams told me what he bought me for, soon as we started for New Orleans. He said he was getting old, and when he saw me he thought he'd buy me, and end his days with me. He said if I behave myself he'd treat me well; but if not, he'd whip me almost to death.

Q. How old was he?

A. . . . I guess pretty near fifty. . . . That's the reason he was always so jealous. He never let me go out anywhere.

Q. Had you any children in New Orleans?

A. Yes; I had four.

Q. Who was their father?

A. Mr. Williams.

Q. Was it known that he was living with you?

A. Everybody knew I was housekeeper, but he never let on that he was the father of my children. I did all the work in his house—nobody there but me and the children.

    . . .

Q. Were your children Mulattoes?

A. No, Sir! They were all white. They look just like him. The neighbors all see that. . . . I told him one day, I wished he would sell me . . . because I had no peace at all. I rather die than live in that way. Then he got awful mad, and said notin' but death should separate us; and, if I run off, he'd blow my brains out. Then I thought, if that be the way, all I could do was just pray for him to die.[28]

Louisa also relates details of the sexual liaison between a white slave owner and the female relatives of another slave woman named Lucy, who had white skin, "light hair and blue eyes." The slave holder purchased Lucy's sister Elcy and lived with her until she died. Then he purchased Elcy's and Lucy's sister Judy. He lived with her. Louisa thought the slave master's sexual liaison with Elcy was beneficial to Elcy, because he taught her to read and write and he taught her music. Apparently this slave master and Lucy's brothers and sisters were instrumental in buying Lucy and setting her free.

In his slave narrative William Wells Brown tells of a female slave Cynthia purchased by a slave trader who told her she would either accompany him home to St. Louis and become his "housekeeper" or he would send her as a field worker to one of the worst plantations on the Mississippi River. Cynthia accepted the first offer and became the slave-trader's mistress and housekeeper.[29]

There was in the antebellum South a kind of institutionalizing, of female-slave/slave master sexual liaisons that was maintained through something called the "fancy trade." This was a special kind of slave trading involving the sale of beautiful black women for the exclusive purpose of becoming the mistresses of wealthy slave owners. Though New Orleans seems to have been the center of this trade, it also flourished in Charleston, South Carolina; St. Louis; Lexington; Richmond, Virginia; and Columbia, South Carolina.[30] The famous octoroon balls that occurred in New Orleans allowed rich white men to meet and purchase these black women, who became their mistresses and often bore their children. Beyond this special kind of arrangement, slave owners also frequented the slave quarters and established sexual connections with any female slave they chose. The woman in either kind of arrangement had no power to refuse this coerced surrogacy. Sometimes she hoped for (and was promised) her freedom through these sexual liaisons with the slave master. But more often than not, her expectations were futile, and she was "sold off to plantations where . . . [she] shared the misery of all slaves."[31]

All three antebellum forms of coerced surrogacy have contributed to the formation of negative images of black women that prevail in America to this day. From the mammy tradition has emerged the image of black women as perpetual mother figures—religious, fat, a-sexual, loving children better than themselves, self-sacrificing, giving up self-concern for group advancement. Delcy in William Faulkner's *Requiem for a Nun* is such a figure. Sophia in *The Color Purple* protests against this image in her conversation with her white charge, Miss Eleanor Jane, who believes that all black women love children, including white ones. Sophia's response to her is "I love children. . . . But all the colored women that say they love yours is lying."[32]

The antebellum tradition of masculinizing black women by means of their work has given rise to the idea that black women are not feminine and do not desire to be so. This phenomenon of masculinization of the female slave in the South was also supported by the general attitude among slave holders that blacks could stand any kind of labor, could not be overworked and were "comparatively insensitive to sufferings that would be unbearable to whites."[33] This meant, then, that black women were considered to have far more physical strength and more capacity for pain than white women. The image of black women as superwomen has emerged from these kinds of ideas and practices. In our time, Michele Wallace has written *Black Macho and the Myth of Superwoman*, which attempts to shatter this image of black women and instead present them as vulnerable, angry, hurt, frightened and not very successful in their struggle to rid their lives of sexist oppression.

One of the most prevalent images of black women today has its roots in the antebellum slave-woman/slave-master sexual liaison. Black women as "loose, over-sexed, erotic, readily responsive to the sexual advances of men, especially white men" derives from the antebellum southern way of putting the responsibility for this sexual liaison upon "immoral" slave women—black females whose "passionate" nature was supposed to have stemmed from their African heritage. Deborah Gray White discusses the making of this image under the rubric of "Jezebel." According to White, this "Jezebel" was not pious and hence did not "lead men and children to God." Neither was she prudent nor domestic. "Domesticity paled in importance before matters of the flesh."[34]

Bell Hooks contends that this kind of white, antebellum image-making about black women's sexuality has contributed greatly to the process of devaluing black womanhood that continues to this day. According to Hooks, the rape of slave women led to the devaluation of black womanhood in the American psyche. And television keeps this notion of black womanhood alive today. Hooks says American television continues to project images of the black woman "as 'fallen' woman, the whore, the slut, the prostitute."[35]

All forms of coerced surrogacy evidence the exploitation of the slave woman by the slavocracy. Like the slave system among the ancient Hebrews (Abraham and Sarah), slavery in the United States demanded that slave women surrender their bodies to their owners against their wills. Thus African-American slave women (like the Egyptian Hagar) were bound to a system that had no respect for their bodies, their dignities or their motherhood, except as it was put to the service of securing the well-being of ruling class families. In North America fierce and violent struggle had to afflict the entire nation before southern slave women could experience a measure of relief from coerced surrogacy roles.

## Voluntary Surrogacy and Postbellum Realities

When the American Civil War ended and the master-slave relation was officially terminated in the South, black people tried to determine for whom or what black women would not stand in place. They were especially anxious to relieve black women from those coerced surrogacy roles related to field work and to black women's sexuality involving black-female/white-male sexual liaisons. Ex-slave women themselves are reported to have said that "they never mean to do any outdoor work, that white men support their wives and they [black women] mean that their husbands shall support them."[36] Black men were just as anxious for black women to quit the fields. According to historians Carter G. Woodson and Lorenzo Greene, "The Negro male when he worked for wages ... tended to imitate the whites by keeping his wife and daughters at home."[37] Both black men and black women were obviously trying to pattern black family life after the patriarchal model of family sanctioned in mainline America. This would, of course, necessitate "feminizing" black female field workers by relieving them of those roles where female power and energy matched and often surpassed that of black males. The black field women would have to become proficient solely in those tasks the larger American society associated with women's work. If this practice of consigning black women to the home had been able to be consistently adopted after emancipation, the black family would have developed into a more rigid patriarchal structure.

Of even greater concern to black males and females were their efforts to terminate the forced sexual relations between black women and white men that existed during slavery. Inasmuch as marriage between African-American women and men became legal after freedom and droves of black women and men came to official locations to be married,[38] sexual liaisons between black women and white men could be curtailed, although white men (without regard for black marriage) still took advantage of some black women. Hooks points out that after black Reconstruction (1867-77) "black women were often ... [pressured] into sexual liaisons with white employers who would threaten to fire them unless they capitulated to sexual demands."[39]

Nevertheless, there was not nearly as much sexual activity between black women and white men after slavery because black women could refuse to substitute for white women in providing sexual pleasure for white males. Nancy White, a contemporary black female domestic worker, testified about refusing this role of playmate to white male employers:

I've had to ask some [white male employer's] hands off me and I've had to just give up some jobs if they got too hot behind me.... I have lost some money that way, but that's all right. When you lose control of your body, you have just about lost all you have in the world.[40]

Nancy White makes it clear that some white female employers approved of black women standing in their places to provide sexual favors for their husbands. White says,

One day that woman [her white female employer] told me that she wouldn't be mad if I let her husband treat me the same way he treated her. I told her I would be mad ... if he tried to treat me like I was as married to him as she was.[41]

She goes on to describe her method of declining this surrogate role her female and male employers wanted to assign her. Says White, "I had to threaten that devil with a pot of hot grease to get him to keep his hands to hisself."[42]

While black women and men did realize a small measure of success in determining surrogate roles black women would not fill after emancipation, certain social realities limited black women's power to choose full emancipation from all surrogacy roles. Poverty and the nature of work available, especially to southern black families, caused many black women to participate in some of the most strenuous areas of the work force. Black people were also involved in what historian Joel Williamson describes as an acculturation process that began in slavery and continued in freedom. These realities pressured black women to choose to continue in two surrogate roles: that of substituting female power and energy for male power and energy, and that of mammy. However, the nature of the mammy role changed somewhat when it served black people instead of white families.

Black women were pressured to choose to substitute their energy and power for male energy and power in the area of farm labor in postbellum America. Greene and Woodson tell of urban Negro male laborers in 1901 who saved money and invested in farms. "It was not uncommon ... to see Negro mechanics owning well-kept farms, which were cared for chiefly by wives and families."[43] Wives of poor black sharecroppers in the South worked everyday in the fields beside their husbands.[44] The United States Census of 1910 reported that 967,837 black women were farm laborers and 79,309 were farmers.[45] In 1910 Addie W. Hunton reported that black women were still engaged in agriculture "from its roughest and rudest form to its highest and most attractive." Of the two million black workers involved in farming, more than half were black women. She said that the fifteen million and more "acres owned and cultivated by Negroes represent not only the hardihood and perseverance of the Negro man but also the power of physical and mental endurance of the woman working by his side." Black men who owned farms often left the management of the farm to the women in the family while the men had employment elsewhere.[46] Hunton speaks of knowing "a number of women who were successful farmers and supported their children in a boarding school by their earnings."[47]

There were other areas in which some black women stepped in and filled roles that might be thought to require male power and strength. When many black people migrated from the South to the North to fill factory jobs during World War I, black women worked in all kinds of difficult positions. Paula Giddings describes their work in the metal industries where they "drilled, polished, punch-pressed, soldered." Black women did the heavy work in laundries, and in the garment industry they were hired in factories to labor in any position that had to be filled.[48]

### The Black Mammy Memorial Association

It was the surrogate role of mammy that some blacks and whites consciously tried to perpetuate beyond slavery and reconstruction. In Athens, Georgia, in the early twentieth century, Samuel Harris, the black principal of Athens Colored High School, dreamed up the idea of starting the Black Mammy Memorial Institute in that city. With the help of prominent white citizens, this institute was founded. Nine white educators and businessmen filed a petition with the county clerk for a charter on September 19, 1910, and the institute was authorized to operate for twenty years. According to a brochure published by the Black Mammy Memorial Association, the institute was to be

> a memorial where men and women learn ... how to work and to love their work; where the mantle of the "Old Black Mammy" may fall on those who go forth to serve; where the story of these women will be told to the generations that come and go; where better mothers for homes will be trained; a building from which those who go forth in life may speak louder in their works than their words.... The Monumental Industrial Institute to the Old Black Mammy of the South will be devoted to the industrial and moral training of young Negro men and women. The work that is to receive special emphasis is the training of young women in Domestic Arts.[49]

Obviously the prominent white citizens wanted to perpetuate mammy roles so that the comfort of the white family could be assured by a type of black female servant who (after slavery) was properly trained in the skills of nurturing, supporting and caring for the well-being of white children. During slavery the Big House itself had been the "school" where the training of house slaves took place. Here, mammy modeled her role for generations of young black female house slaves and thus the mammy skills could be passed on and the mammy tradition could be maintained. With the passing of the coercion associated with slavery, with the absence after emancipation of black female children from the work force in the Big House, and with free black women's reluctance to spend nights in their white employers' houses, black females could not be thoroughly trained in the antebellum style of mammying. Therefore, a school dedicated to training black women in these skills could substitute for the Big House and be an adequate training place.

Not so obvious, but possible, is the suggestion that black educator Mr. Harris was seeking the financial means from white people to provide education to the black masses, many of whom had been field slaves or were the direct descendants of field hands. The assumption could be made that by training black women in the skills of mammying, they would also choose to use these skills to foster the well-being of the black family and the black community. By learning how to be mammies, black women (especially those with field-work heritages) would learn to be the kind of mothers and nurturers who could organize and manage black households as white households were organized and managed.

A variety of skills went into the performance of this managerial task. Mammy had to be skillful at exerting authority in the household while being careful not to offend or usurp the power of the main authority figures, the slave master and his wife. She was skilled in about every form of what was thought to be women's work, that is, sewing, spinning, cooking, tending to children, cleaning. This meant that she could supervise other members of the household work force. With regard to human relations in the family, she knew how to be a diplomat, a peacemaker who often healed relationships that had gone awry. Mammy had lived in close proximity to "quality" white people and therefore understood upper-class white values. Her life had been shaped by them, and she knew how to use them to shape the lives of others, especially the children.

All of these skills that mammy had were needed after emancipation if the black community was to continue a process of acculturation in which black people became what historian Joel Williamson describes as "more white," that is, more mainline American. To illustrate his point, Williamson makes reference to free black people who, during slavery, educated their children with white values. He also illustrates his point by describing some of the activity of ex-slaves after emancipation. According to Williamson, in the Reconstruction period, black people attempted to reject everything that had the appearance of servility and to embrace white cultural ideals.[50]

Testimony of some ex-slaves seems to corroborate Williamson's claim about rejecting servility. Lee Guidon's description of the renaming that ex-slaves engaged in after the Civil War is a case in point:

> After freedom a heap of people say they was going to name theirselves over.... They changed up so it was hard to tell who or where anybody was.... Some of the names was Abraham, and some called theirselves Lincum. Any big name 'cepting their master's name.[51]

But there is evidence demonstrating that some ex-slaves kept the names they had because, in freedom, they wanted to indicate that they had been "raised" by quality white folk during slavery. Therefore Guidon's father said, "Fine folks raise us and we gonna hold to our own names."[52] This suggests that even though slaves wanted in freedom to reject all appearances of servility, some of them also wanted to hold on to and perpetuate the values of the quality white folks they had been in contact with during slavery. There was belief among some slaves that some quality white folks lived by higher ethical standards than poor whites and poor blacks. A Georgia ex-slave man, Tines Kendricks, describes his mother's father as an overseer who was not a Kendricks (the slave-holding family's name) because the Kendricks "wasn't ... mixed up in nothing like that [i.e., raping slave women]. They didn't believe in that kind of business."[53] Nicey Kinney, an ex-slave woman also living in Georgia, was grateful for the values her master and mistress taught her. She believed these values sustained her through a bad marriage to a poor black man. Kinney said she thanked her former owners "for the pains they took with the little nigger gal that growed up to be me, trying to show her the right road to travel.... I'se still trying to follow the road that leads to where they are."[54] (Her former owners were dead and she believed them to be in heaven.) Cato, an ex-slave living in Alabama, tells of his days as a slave when he was taken by "Missy Angela" to live in the Big House. He was a very young child. His slave owners built a special room for him onto the Big House because Cato was "one of their blood." They never hit him, and they promised that they would never sell him away from them. Thus Cato concludes that his slave owners were "the best-quality white folks."[55] In the understanding of some ex-slaves, the adherence to white cultural ideals and quality white folks' values was important for cleanliness in the black home. An ex-slave woman, accounting for the difference between "the Davis and the Bethea Negroes" during slavery, says

> My God, child, you could go through there [the slave quarter] and spot Sara Davis niggers from the Bethea niggers time you see them.... We [she was a Davis Negro] was raised decent ... and that how come me and my children is that way to this very day. There that child in the house now, she does put fresh sheet on all us bed every week just like they was white people's bed.[56]

It was in the area of conditioning ex-slaves to continue to perpetuate and/or to be trained in quality white folks' cultural ideals and values that mammy's skills were so important for the black family. One of the key ideals and values was the sanctity of patriarchalism in the family. The fact that mammy knew how to exert authority in household management while not usurping the power invested in the patriarchal male head of the household meant that if other ex-slave women could be taught this, the patriarchal acculturation of the black family could continue. The model of female authority that ex-slave field women saw and experienced in the work force was that of women who were captains of industry in the fields. Often their authority extended to both female and male field hands. Williamson makes reference to an ex-slave, "Captain Margaret," who was a captain of industry in the fields of one plantation.[57]

Apparently the freedmen did not want to perpetuate a model of authority subordinating black men to black women. Williamson's description of black male authority after slavery suggests that the development of patriarchal values in the black family was reinforced by social, legal and economic customs of black men:

> In Reconstruction, Negro males, like white males, asserted themselves by insisting that wives spend more time in home management and less in field work, by demanding that mothers care for their children, and by exhibiting such common masculine exclusiveness as leaving the wives at home while they themselves attended fraternal and political gatherings. In legal and economic matters, black men assumed the power to speak for their wives and children.[58]

Williamson cites two cases showing patriarchal patterning in the training of young black males:

> In January 1866 on one Carolina cotton plantation, Ned affixed the mark of his wife, Victoria, to a contract with the landowner, and their son, Zack, made his mark "with Ned's consent." On the same contract, another laborer named Frank Tom made his own mark and those of Giles and Neil, his wife and his son.[59]

There can be little dispute that mammies had the desired skills needed to support male dominance, to nurture children, to accomplish the tasks associated with good household management and to know how to get along with "quality" white people tasks necessary after slavery to support a black patriarchal model of family life and to "induct" former slaves into "white ways of life." So, as the mammies began to die out during the postbellum period, it became desirable to some black people (as it was to some white people) to find a way to pass on the skills belonging to the mammy profession. Thus the Black Mammy Memorial Institute would serve black as well as white needs.

However, after emancipation the mammy reality (as far as black life was concerned) underwent changes that began to terminate the kind of mammy tradition that existed during slavery. One transformation had to do with the name mammy. Apparently during the antebellum period, a common practice among many slaves was to call their own mothers Mammy.[60] At some point the mammy nomenclature was lost, and black people began to refer to their maternal figures as Mother or some other appellation more in accord with the names prevalent in mainline American culture. But black people apparently retained their respect for the kind of dedication to the family (especially to children) that mammies demonstrated. The institution of mothers of the church that developed in some black churches after emancipation perhaps has some kinship with the antebellum mammy tradition. Like the slave mammy, the mother of the church exerts considerable authority in the church family. But more often than not she uses her power in a way that does not challenge the power and authority of the patriarchal head of the church, usually a male preacher. She is often called upon to be a healer of relationships within the congregation. She is well versed in and knows how to pass along the highest values for living the Christian life. Her power and influence often extend beyond the church into her community, because she has been empowered by one of the central authority agents of the community—the African-American church—to provide care and nurture for the children of God.

Another area in which the mammy role experienced transformation, albeit a limited one, was that of protecting children. Inasmuch as a conscientious effort was afoot to invest the primary power and authority in black males and fathers (that is, to bring notions of black manhood in agreement with the manhood notion of mainline American culture), it was necessary for the black community to begin to see not a woman but the black man or the black father as protector—as the one who stood between black children and the cold, cold world. Some forces in white society exerted much energy aborting these manhood and fatherhood efforts to protect the black family. The Ku Klux Klan came to life shortly after the emancipation of slaves. One of its aims was, through the use of violence, to stamp out any manifestation of black male power, the very power necessary for the protection of the family. Then, in the twentieth century, certain governmental welfare policies have had the effect of hindering the building of the black father's financial strength, important for protecting the family economically. Today, black working fathers cannot reside with their destitute families if the mother is to receive welfare payments for the children.

Both of these realities (Ku Klux Klan and welfare as it is presently structured) have helped contribute to the continuous devaluation of black fatherhood in North American society. This means that the mammy chore of protector—as the one standing between children and the cold, cold world—has remained the responsibility of many black women. But there are differences between the mammy role as protector in the white context and the mammy role as protector in the black context. These differences cast a shadow of ambivalence upon the black mother's role of protector. The differences are of two sorts. First, this mammy role in the black context lacked the financial and institutional resources that supported the mammy role in which black mammies stood between *white* children and the cold, cold world. Second, black people have, since emancipation, come to expect the protector role in the family to be filled by the black man, as the protector role in the white family is expected to be filled by the white male. Thus "mammy roles" of any variety are looked upon with disdain by most black people as the black community focuses its attention upon strengthening models of black masculinity. The black woman in the protector role in the black community is not respected and is often critically labeled matriarch.

This assessment of the mammy reality in postbellum America is not meant to suggest that all black women chose to appropriate the mammy style of female authority figure in the home and community exclusive of all other styles. Possibly the way of being mother or female authority figure in many black homes and communities, in the early days after slavery, was a mixed bag; that is, insights and characteristics of the former field hands and captains of industry in the fields merged with insights and characteristics of former mammies in the Big House. How this could have happened, one can only speculate. Perhaps the African-American denominational churches were arenas where field women's ethos and mammy's knowledge of what was thought to be upper-class values merged in the work of sustaining the life of the church. The suggestion of this kind of blend of field and house could, in part, account for certain philosophies and action on the part of black women that are obvious to this day. The following testimony of an ordinary contemporary black woman points to this mix: "I do not need a man to feed myself," she says. "I scrubbed and cooked and busted suds at home and then went out there and did the same for white women." She continues: "I had two children and kept them just like they should have been kept. . . . I believe in knowing some of everything out there [in the public arena beyond the home]."[61] This woman's testimony shows a mixture of what could be considered a fieldwoman's posture (working hard inside and outside the home), mammy's concern for proper values (keeping children "as they should have been kept") and the task of knowing the way of the world of both mammy and field woman.

Whatever may be the case with regard to the style of power and authority black women exert in their homes and beyond, one thing is certain. Surrogacy has been a negative force in African-American women's lives. It has been used by both men and women of the ruling class, as well as by some black men, to keep black women in the service of other people's needs and goals. By appropriating the biblical Hagar stories, African-American people have kept the issue of surrogacy alive in the community's memory. Thus generations of African Americans can understand the struggle black women wage against the devaluation of their womanhood that social-role surrogacy supports.

### Old Oppression, New Threat

Even today, the newly developing "breeder women" industries (commercial surrogacy institutes) pose a threat to poor women of color in North America. If black women take seriously the wish of the director of one of these commercial surrogacy institutes, they have cause to be alarmed. Ethicist Elizabeth Bettenhausen reports that one of the early operators of an agency arranging these pregnancies looked forward to the day when embryo transplants would eliminate the need to use the surrogate's egg (thus reducing her claim to the child) and when the surrogates would be recruited in foreign countries [or in poor African-American communities?] where poverty would drive women to accept less pay for functioning as the surrogate uterus.[62]

What many black women know is that some of the language associated with commercial surrogacy today is a throw-back to American slavery, when certain slave women were set apart to function as "breeder women." Women participating in today's surrogacy industry are sometimes referred to as "breeders." During slavery, breeder women were mated with any male the slave holder chose so that the women could birth children every twelve months. These children would become the property of the slave holder. If the white slave holder could not find a male he deemed adequate for mating with the "breeder woman," he would mate with her himself. Slave women were mated with a "stud," just as race horses are today and for the same reason profit.

In Hagar's time Mesopotamian law legitimated surrogacy, which was evidently adopted by many Semitic people. The question for black women today is whether forced surrogacy can happen again in their history. Can black women again be used by groups more powerful than they to produce children for the profit of other more powerful groups? Will the law legitimate surrogacy to the point that black women's ovaries are targeted for use by groups more powerful than poor black women? Will surrogacy become such a common practice in wealthy women's experience that laws are established to regulate it—laws that work to the advantage of the wealthy and the disadvantage of the poor? Given the declining birth rate among middle-class white women, will poverty pressure poor black women to rent their bodies out as incubators for wealthier women unable to birth children? Will it become the custom for some middle-and upperclass women to choose to remain in their careers and not become pregnant but pay poor black women to carry and birth their children? Reproduction technology has perfected the process whereby one woman can be implanted with the reproduction material of another woman and man. Then the host woman births a child having the physical characteristics of the woman and man who furnished the reproduction material. Thus a black woman can carry and birth a white child. Is Elizabeth Bettenhausen correct when she labels this surrogacy phase of women's reproduction history "Hagar Revisited"? Are American women stepping into an age of reproduction control so rigid that women will be set against each other like Hagar and Sarah? Will the operation of certain reproduction technologies, acting in white women's favor, put even more strain upon the already strained relation between black and white women?

# Chapter 4

## COLOR STRUCK: A STATE OF MIND

One day, a white child shouted in my ear "nigger" as if he were saying "cur," and I was startled. I had never heard the word before, and I went home and asked what it meant, and my parents looked apprehensively at each other as if to say, "it's come...." I went to church and I wondered why God let this thing continue.... Then I began to daydream: it will not always be this way. Someday, just as chattel slavery ended, this injustice will also end; this internal suffering will cease; this ache inside for understanding will exist no longer.... But always I was seeking for the real answer, not the daydream. Always I wanted to know. I lay awake at night pondering in my heart, why? Why? Why?

—Margaret Walker
*How I Wrote Jubilee and Other Essays on Life and Literature*

Here, an African-American woman reminisces about an emotionally wounding experience she suffered as a child. And like many African-American people, the child wants to know why the racial oppression of black people exists and continues. At this point Hagar's story and African-American women's history diverge a bit. Hagar's story in the Bible does not provide enough information for us to respond to the "why" of her enslavement. The Bible does not tell how or why the Egyptian woman Hagar came to be the slave of a Hebrew woman—given Egypt's overwhelming power and leadership in antiquity and the Hebrew people's relative obscurity and powerlessness. Nor does the text indicate whether Hagar's skin color had anything to do with the nature of her bondage among the Hebrews and her miserable treatment by Sarah. But in America skin color makes a difference. Thus African-American women's skin color has had a lot to do with their enslavement and with the continuation of their oppression. Hagar's ethnicity was based on national identity, while African-American women's ethnicity is indicated by their skin color or the drop of "black blood" that flows through their veins.

Africa, a source of black American heritage, has been and often still is depicted in many American sources as a wilderness continent inhabited by "subhuman savages," not civilized according to European (white) standards. Blackness is looked upon with disdain. In North America popular culture, religion, science and politics have worked together to assign permanent negative value to the color black. This has led to the formation of an American national consciousness that considers black frightening, dangerous and/or repulsive—especially when this is the color of human bodies.

In subtle and not so subtle ways, this repulsion and devaluing of the color black is communicated in the everyday life of American culture; white, on the other hand, receives highest valuation. While this black/white symbolism has gone on for centuries in Western culture, as some of the following examples show, more recent incidents illustrate that Americans still tend to assign black to evil and white to good without hesitation or reflection about the message this conveys.

- Angel food cake is white, and devil's food cake is dark.
- *Blackmail* is illegal.
- The American economic crash of 1873 was referred to as Black September. The Great Depression began with a stock market crash on Black Friday. When the stock market fell in 1987 the day was referred to throughout the media as Black Monday.
- When the motion picture "Ghost" showed in American movie houses a few years ago, it continued the association of whiteness with heaven and blackness with hell. The hero in the movie died and ultimately walked into a bright, white light apparently leading to heaven. When the villains in the movie died, jet-black figures escorted them, apparently into hell.
- An April 12, 1992, episode of the television series "Murder, She Wrote" reenacted the practice of blackballing, associating black with guilt and white with innocence. On the show a group of wealthy men were voting on the ethical behavior of a member of their group. Each man was given a black and a white marble. If he believed his colleague to be innocent, he was asked to cast in the white marble. If he believed his colleague to be guilty, he was asked to cast in the black marble.
- No doubt, many Protestant church choirs and congregations continue to sing on many occasions "wash me whiter than snow, Lord, whiter

than snow," which associates the color white with purity and perfection.

- In the early days of the industrial revolution in America, when the factory system was emerging, management circulated "black lists." These lists named workers whom management designated as troublemakers or undesirable for one reason or another. Being blacklisted (blackballed) still means being excluded by others from a job, an organization or a social group perceived as desirable.
- Blackening a person's reputation means to soil or stain it, to defame the person. Yet association with white can lessen an acknowledged evil; for example, a "white lie" isn't considered a real lie, a real evil, at all.

This conditioning about the negative value of the color black has not just been confined to the white world. Many black Americans have internalized this negative disposition toward black. When I was growing up in a black community in the South, I heard this jingle regularly: "If you white, you're all right. If you yellow, you're mellow. If you brown, you can stick around. But if you black, get way back." Truly enough, this jingle taught us children the realities regarding skin color in the dominating white culture. But, unfortunately, we were not taught an opposing ideology that contradicted this jingle. Neither were we shown the evil effects that resulted from belief in what the jingle claimed—evil effects destroying unity in the African-American community, especially unity among women. Many black female writers have alluded in their works to the discrimination against black-skinned women in the black community, for example, Gwendolyn Brooks's *Maud Martha*, Toni Morrison's *The Bluest Eye*, Zora Hurston's *Their Eyes Were Watching God*, Nella Larson's *Passing* and Alice Walker's definition of a womanist contained in her book *In Search of Our Mothers' Gardens: Womanist Prose*.

There is, then, at least one response that can be given to the black female's "why" question posed at the beginning of this chapter. For generations, Americans have been conditioned to hate and fear black, to regard it as evil and illegal and to consider black skin indicative of intellectual and moral inferiority. The American national conscience is thoroughly saturated with the idea of bad black and good white, of inferior black and superior white.

However, this is not response enough to the questions posed at the beginning of this chapter. In the "why" of Margaret Walker's question is also the "how." How did this negative attitude toward the color black (and therefore black skin) become so entrenched in the American psyche? To respond to the question, this chapter will show that the national and religious arrogance of early English settlers was foundational for their prejudice against black people, females and males. Upon this foundation the settlers built the rationales supporting their devaluation of black people. Once this degraded image was firmly implanted in the American conscience, black people could be made chattel slaves for life, could be homeless and poor throughout their history, could be brutalized by law enforcement agents without white Americans realizing that these conditions compromised the basic notions of freedom championed in America.

Beyond the colonial period into the nineteenth century this prejudice against the color black manifested itself—with the aid of science—in the century's discourse about race. All of this has generated a negative, oppressive and pathological force that persists in American national consciousness. The term *white racial narcissism* is used in this chapter to name this force that degrades black and elevates white. This pathological narcissism expresses itself in an "exaggerated concern with [white] power and control, the result of which is interpersonal exploitation [of black people]" and deficient social consciousness with regard to darker races.[1] White, racial, narcissistic groups disregard and "flout conventional rules of shared living" with [dark] racial groups, "viewing these rules as naive or inapplicable" to the racially narcissistic group. This group is indifferent to the rights of darkly colored others.[2] Racial narcissism, then, indicates overvaluation of one group's skin color to the pathological point of using the group's power and authority to persecute others who are not of that skin color. Whether or not a particular kind of color narcissism manifests itself in the culture depends upon the amount of power and authority wielded by the racial group.

White racial narcissism is apparent in these kinds of remarks from white people: "I don't know what I would do sometimes if I didn't have my whiteness to support me." (This statement was made by a white woman in a black studies course at a school where I taught.) "I might be poor, but I ain't no black nigger." (This statement was made by the wife of an unemployed West Virginia coal miner to a white minister.) This kind of thinking is widespread in America, indicating that many people's sense of self-worth comes from an unnatural regard for their whiteness. White racial narcissism indicates a malfunction in the American national psyche that can ultimately lead the culture to self-destruct or can lead the powerful racially narcissistic group to genocide members of a less powerful racial group. One way of dealing with white racial narcissism in the culture is for the victimized group to stand against the powerful, racially narcissistic group in a permanent posture of self-defense.

This pathology in the American psyche started in colonial America but had its roots in Europe and England before these people came to American shores.[3] Its roots among the English were, in part, planted in arrogance.

### National/Religious Arrogance and Racial Narcissism

Cotton Mather reflected a bit of national arrogance when he spoke before a Massachusetts legislative body in 1700.[4] He said, "It is no Little Blessing of God, that we are a part of the English Nation."[5] Mather's statement reflects a general attitude prevailing among Englishmen.

> It was of the utmost importance to know that they were Englishmen, which was to say that they were educated (to a degree suitable to their station), Christian (of appropriate Protestant variety), civilized, and (again to an appropriate degree) free men.[6]

Within the context of this kind of thinking, the steps to white racial narcissism involved a logic first degrading the Native Americans and then the imported Africans. Anyone who was not English, who was not educated to a suitable degree, and who—above all else—was not Christian and was not from a Christian nation was deficient and was called heathen by Christian Englishmen. Non-English, non-European, non-Christian people, so-called heathens, could not be free in the sense that Englishmen were free—capable of directing destiny in the way the God of the biblical scriptures intended. Thus the Native Americans in the new world—being neither educated, Christian nor "civilized"—were not of the same ilk as Englishmen. The Native Americans were thought to be "separate from" and "inferior to" free, civilized, Christian Englishmen. Subduing them fed the Englishmen's sense of national superiority, since they perceived Native Americans as grouped in "nations" occupying and controlling specific land masses in America. To take their land and diminish their numbers illustrated to Christian men from the nation of England that they were superior to what *they* viewed as savage nations in the American wilderness. Furthermore, in subduing the Native American nations they saw a challenge to subdue nature, which the Bible reported that God gave man—that is, Christian man—dominion over. Thus, as Winthrop Jordan points out, "Conquering the Indian symbolized and personified the conquest of the American difficulties, the surmounting of the wilderness." For, "To push back the Indian was to prove the worth of one's own mission, to make in the desert a highway for civilization," which was the Christian duty of civilized men who, of course, Englishmen thought themselves to be.[7] Untamed, unruled nature and "heathen" Native Americans were thought to be as distant and different from Christian Englishmen as cotton from corn.

### The Impact of Aesthetic Values

While the colonists' evaluation of Native Americans as different and inferior had (before the coming of Negroes) to do with English national and religious biases, the same evaluation applied to Negro slaves had to do with English values regarding color, especially blackness. A century before the nineteenth, when England and the American colonists were heavily involved in the slave trade, the Oxford English Dictionary defined black as "deeply stained with dirt; soiled, dirty, foul.... Having dark or deadly purposes, malignant; pertaining to or involving death, deadly, baneful, disastrous, sinister.... Foul, iniquitous, atrocious, horrible, wicked.... Indicating disgrace, censure, liability to punishment."[8] To the English mind, then, "black was an emotionally partisan color, the handmaid and symbol of baseness and evil, a sign of danger and repulsion."[9]

Because of these attitudes toward black, the physical characteristics of black-skinned people (such as nose and lip size, bust and hip size of the women) were deemed ugly by the Englishmen. Hence in the literature of Elizabethan England the opposite of blackness, fair skin (and rose cheeks), was depicted as the ideal standard of beauty, especially women's beauty.[10] Nothing could be truer than Winthrop Jordan's observation that for Englishmen, ideas about blackness also suggested ideas about its opposite: whiteness. Thus white and black "connoted purity and filthiness, virginity and sin, virtue and baseness, beauty and beneficence and evil, God and the devil."[11]

What was beginning to be structured here with these aesthetic values was the ideological foundation for white racial narcissistic attitudes that would, with regard to the Negro, ultimately ground inferiority in nature. No eighteenth-century English-speaking philosopher was more dedicated to this kind of grounding than David Hume, who said:

> I am apt to suspect the Negroes, and in general all the other species of men (for there are four or five different kinds) to be naturally inferior to the whites. There never was a civilized nation of any other complexion than white.... No ingenious manufactures amongst them, no arts, no sciences. On the other hand, the most rude and barbarious of the whites, such as the ancient Germans, and the present Tartars, have still

something eminent about them, in their valour, form of government or some other particular. Such a uniform and constant difference could not happen, in so many countries and ages, if nature had not made an original distinction betwixt these breeds of men.... In Jamaica... they talk of one Negro as a man of parts and learning; but 'tis likely he is admired for very slender accomplishments like a parrot, who speaks a few words plainly.[12]

Thus it is no wonder that color prejudice against blacks flourished early among the English-speaking American colonies.[13] By the beginning of the eighteenth century the thought of blackness as depraved and evil was so "entangled with the basest status in American society...that...it was almost indecipherably coded into American language and literature."[14] Skin color or blackness had, by the eighteenth century, become "an independent rationale for enslavement."[15] In *White Over Black* Jordan makes reference to Samuel Sewell, who in 1709 wrote in his diary that a "Spaniard [a black one] had petitioned the Massachussets [sic] Council for freedom but that 'Capt. Teat alledg'd that all of that color were slaves.' "[16]

### *The Impact of Religion*

The debasement of the color black, and therefore of the Negro, did not derive only from aesthetic values informed by dictionary meanings. The Bible and white interpretations of biblical stories also fed into this debasement of blackness and black people. Leslie Howard Owens makes the point that the distinction between blackness (as inferior and evil) and whiteness (as superior and good), which became deeply embedded in American consciousness, also finds support in the Hebrew testament. Owens cites Amos 9:7 as an illustration. God, angry at the Israelites, tells them "you are no more to me than these Cushites," who were dark-skinned Ethiopians. Owens indicates that some of the colonial ministers, such as Jonathan Edwards, Thomas Hooker and George Whitefield, "sermonized at length on his [the devil's] habits, sprinkling their jeremiads with the color of sin—black." So, concludes Owens, "Church-going colonists, like American society in general, were thus amply indoctrinated with physical descriptions of the color of evil [black]."[17]

However, seventeenth- and eighteenth-century Englishmen and American colonists were not the first Christians to express antipathy toward blackness. Consider this portrait of the devil appearing in *The Epistle of Barnabas* in the first century:

The way of the Black One is crooked and full of cursing, for it is the way of death eternal with punishment, and in it are the things that destroy their soul: idolatry, forwardness, arrogance of power, hypocrisy, double-heartedness, adultery, murder, robbery, pride, transgression, fraud, malice, self-sufficiency, enchantments, magic, covetousness.[18]

There was also the prevailing interpretations of the Noah-Ham story in Genesis 9:20–27, in which Ham, or perhaps Canaan, looked upon his father's nakedness. Noah then cursed Canaan, decreeing that Canaan shall be "a slave of slaves...[unto] his brothers." Somehow colonists interpreted this story so that blackness and slavery were equated, although blackness is not mentioned in the biblical story. The perpetual enslavement of black people was interpreted to be ordained by this curse. Therefore, in some colonial reasoning, the enslavement of black people was intended by God and "recorded" in scripture.[19]

### Economic Impact

Aesthetic values, interpretations of biblical texts or stories and the analogies Englishmen made between the African natives and the animals on the continent of Africa helped them arrive at the conclusion that the Negro was less than human and was more akin to animals—like the apes inhabiting Africa. Thus chattel slavery could happen and continue in the American colonies because "black people were viewed as beast, as cattle, as 'articles' for sale."[20] All of these ways of thinking about the Negro supported the major economic reality in the American colonies in the mid- and late-eighteenth century. Charles Nichols describes this economic reality, claiming that slavery was "the very basis of colonial industry and commerce in the eighteenth century." Thus the slave trade was the primary source of wealth during the colonial period.[21] Throughout the antebellum period, slave trading "offered an opportunity for real economic advancement."[22] Doctors, lawyers and just plain (and often illiterate) men made money from the slave trade. Doctors examined the slaves being sold and testified to the state of their health. One of their tasks was to determine the fitness of slave women being sold to bear children. Lawyers prepared the legal documents accompanying the sale of slaves. And ordinary men often got wealthy buying and reselling slaves.[23]

In the seventeenth century colonial powers in the United States did not allow their acquisition of wealth to interfere with the distinctions they made between economic realities facing poor black women and those facing poor white women. These differences, of course, exacerbated the tensions between poor black and white women. This distinction began to show itself in Virginia with the "tithe" or tax law. In 1629 the law identified taxable persons as "those that worke in the ground of what qualitie or condition soever." In 1643 a new tax law was passed declaring that "all adult men were tithable and, in addition, Negro women." Maryland followed this policy in 1654. On the other hand, servant women (or poor white women) were taken out of the fields and put in domestic jobs. This meant they were exempt from the tax. However, free women of color were not exempt. Maryland law stated:

> Whereas some doubts have arisen whether negro women set free were still to be accompted tithable according to the former act, it is declared by this grand assembly that negro women, though permitted to enjoy their freedom yet ought not in all respects to be admitted to a full fruition of the exemptions and impunities of the English, and are still lyable to payment of taxes.[24]

Jordan makes an enlightening point: "This official discrimination between Negro and other women was made by [white] men who were accustomed to thinking of field work as being ordinarily the work of men rather than women."[25] In his tract written in 1565, John Hammond of Maryland provides a clue that shows how the low opinion some white males had of black women figured into the distinction they made between black women's and poor white women's employment realities. Hammond confirmed that servant women (poor, white women) "were not put to work in the fields but in domestic employments." Then he adds: "Some wenches that are nasty, and beastly and not fit to be so employed are put into the ground [put into the fields to work]."[26] Black women were thus distinguished from white women and suffered economic injustices from the state that other women would not. Because of their black skin color Negro women would, in the larger society's definitions, lose the gender distinction society made between men and women. Regarded as "nasty and beastly," they would be required to do any kind of work the slavocracy demanded.

### Enter Statistics, Politics and Science

This discussion of national and religious biases and of aesthetic values about color indicate that as the American national consciousness developed, one of its strongest currents would be a kind of white racial narcissism, which perpetuated its life by feeding on ideas about "bad" blackness and about the Negroes' intellectual and moral inferiority. This racial narcissism came clearly to the surface in the nineteenth century as national statistics, politics and science joined together to "prove" the intellectual and moral inferiority of black people.

Supporting the longevity of the slave system, the statistics had to do with the 1840 census, or the sixth annual American census. The problems in this census were uncovered by Dr. Edward Jarvis, a white doctor living in Massachusetts. He discovered the census report was full of lies about the Negro. It tried to suggest that freedom in the North had led to widespread insanity and idiocy among northern Negroes.[27] Jarvis's investigation discovered that the census had reported insane Negroes in some northern territories where no Negroes lived. Some northern cities were reported to have as many colored lunatics as people living in the city. But the instances of Negro insanity decreased as the census moved deeper and deeper into southern slave territory. Thus the census gave the impression that slavery was more conducive to mental health than freedom. Jarvis published his findings in the *American Journal of Medical Science*. John Quincy Adams became aware of Jarvis's findings and tried repeatedly to get the United States Congress to denounce the census of 1840. Congress never did. It is no wonder that twelve years later a young white man reading the 1840 census remarked, "Who would believe . . . without the fact in black and white before his eyes, that every fourteenth colored person in the state of Maine is an idiot or lunatic?"[28]

When Adams confronted John Calhoun personally about the errors in the 1840 census, Calhoun said, "There were so many errors they balanced one another and led to the same conclusion as if they were all correct."[29]

At this point nineteenth-century politics entered in as John Calhoun became secretary of state and advanced pro-slavery arguments regarding the admittance of Texas to the Union. Calhoun favored admitting Texas as a slave state. England opposed this action. To convince England and to prohibit the consolidation of European opinion on the matter, Calhoun had to make a convincing case in favor of slavery. So he marched out the census of 1840 to prove that Negroes did not fare well in freedom. But he needed still more reinforcement for his argument, so he turned to science. Some of the proponents of the newly developing science of physical anthropology quickly came to his aid, providing "scientific" data to support his claims. Some of the leaders in this field were Dr. Samuel Morton, Dr. Josiah Nott and Morton's disciple George R. Gliddon. Much of their work and most of their negative claims about Negro intellect were supported by noted Harvard University zoologist Louis Agassiz. Morton's work in this discipline claimed that human skull size determined the character of a person's intelligence and moral fiber. The larger the skull, the larger the brain and the more intelligent and moral the person. Morton and other physical anthropologists claimed white people's skulls were larger than all others, and black people's skulls were smaller than all others. Therefore white people were naturally intellectually and morally superior, while black people were naturally intellectually and morally inferior.[30] Further, Morton and Gliddon claimed to provide documented proof that even in ancient Egypt Negroes had been slaves. According to these physical anthropologists, during all of their existence on earth Negroes had been servants/slaves to the "more intelligent" races, that Negroes had always served Caucasians even in the most distant past. Calhoun, armed with this "scientific" knowledge, sent word to the American minister in Paris "that to abolish slavery in areas where Negroes were few would not raise the inferior race to the condition of freeman, but deprive the Negro of the guardian care of his owner." Further, "to abolish slavery in the areas where Negroes were many would result in a deadly strife . . . war of the races all over the western hemisphere."[31]

Several magazines and journals popularized these "scientific" views of black inferiority. One of the most widely read was DeBow's Review. By the time of the Civil War, the American public was convinced of the intellectual inferiority of black people. The abolition of slavery in the United States did not purge the American psyche of its white racial narcissism, which could only respect the white image, white intellect and white morality.

After the war the southern planter class depended upon the brawn and manual skill of ex-slaves to regain what it had lost economically. As the planters tried to create a new labor force in order to rebuild the war-torn South, they had to deal with this white racial narcissistic way of thinking, especially among poor whites.

### Terror and Poverty for Ex-Slaves

As Negroes organized and began to find jobs after the Civil War, they were thrown into fierce competition with poor white people. The black labor force was a source of bitterness for these whites because white employers had a low opinion of poor white workers and often expressed their preference for black workers.[32] White employers referred to poor white workers as lazy and shiftless.

This preference on the part of the planters had nothing to do with respect for black people or with thinking Negroes were equal to whites. Rather, several economic and social realities were the determining factors. First, poor whites would not work for the same amount of money as ex-slaves. Second, there were some jobs whites would not take because they thought these jobs were "Negro jobs." Often white employers tried to hire the former slaves because many of the freedpersons were still submissive to whites. As one employer put it, "They [ex-slaves] often acquiesced to social relations, which would have been regarded as insulting to the [white] free-born American."[33] Finally, poor whites believed their common whiteness created a social bond between them and their white employer. Distinguishing themselves from the freedpersons by referring to themselves as "free-born Americans," white workers expected better food at lunch than blacks received, separate eating and work space and more egalitarian treatment than blacks got from white employers. In fact, one old white planter told his son to hire a Negro carpenter instead of a white one in order to avoid "the trouble of entertaining him in your house."[34]

These economic realities created severe tension between poor black freedmen and poor whites. But historian Gerald Jaynes is right to emphasize that economics were not the sole cause of these tensions. Pointing to the significance of whiteness for poor whites, he writes:

> While two and a half centuries of unsuccessful competition with slave labor must have been a festering catalyst to the development of a population of Negrophobes, it is untenable to argue that racial antagonism was solely a product of capitalism and black slavery. Much recent scholarship on the origins and growth of racism and racial ideology has confirmed the judgment of nineteenth-century historian George Bancroft that to white colonists "the negro race was from the first regarded with disgust, and its union with the whites was forbidden under ignominious penalties. With racism so deeply imbedded in society, the mass of laborers, white and black, were, in 1865 [after the war], probably incapable of taking a stance toward one another other than one of conflict."[35]

It seems, then, that since poor southern whites in the period immediately following the Civil War were looked down upon and could not derive feelings of self-worth from their work,[36] their feelings of self-worth had to come from another area in which the society had already invested great value. White skin and membership in the white race had superior intrinsic value, while blackness was supposed to indicate intrinsic inferiority. Obviously poor whites had internalized this value and expected to receive preferential treatment because of it. In the reconstruction of the South after the war this principle of white superiority/black inferiority had to be reinforced in order to prevent insurrection by poor whites. As one historian put it, reconstructing the South meant that employers had to come up with a plan that "could utilize black and white labor in a reasonably efficient manner and preserve white supremacy, especially for the disadvantaged white."[37]

To facilitate this process and also to secure themselves economically, many poor southern whites organized into groups that used violent tactics against blacks—or anyone who tried to help blacks advance toward equality with whites in any area. Two of these groups, the Regulators and the Ku Klux Klan, demonstrate how this pathological fascination with whiteness (white racial narcissism) manifested itself in the actions of white people and contributed to the homelessness, poverty and death of many black people. In southern Kentucky in 1867 an organized group of Regulators terrorized the freed black people, notifying them that they must leave their homes on or before February 20. "White men were notified that all tenements rented to freedmen would be burned." Jaynes reports that "there resulted an exodus of freedpeople into the cities,"[38] and these freewomen and men were without homes in the city. Ex-slaves themselves have left vivid descriptions of how the Ku Klux Klan terrorized their lives and often left them homeless. One ex-slave claimed,

> After us colored folks was 'sidered free and turned loose, the Ku Klux Klan broke out. Some colored people started to farming . . . and gathered the old stock. If they got so they made good money and had a good farm, the Ku klux would come and murder 'em. The government builded schoolhouses, and the Ku klux went to work and burned 'em down. They'd go to the jails and take the colored men out and knock their brains out and break their necks and throw 'em in the river.[39]

White hate for black people was so strong that one klansman, who was being hanged for murdering his wife, said "he didn't mind being hung, but he didn't want a damn nigger to see him die."[40] These violent and unpunished acts on the part of white people caused many ex-slaves to conclude that "it was the poor white man who was freed by the war, not the Negroes."[41]

Like the southern white, the white northerner was infected with this same white racial narcissism, though it did not always express itself in massive violence—except for occasional race riots. In 1863 a race riot occurred when northern white dock workers, angry because of the war draft and because black workers were being imported from the South to break their strikes, turned on the Negroes and drove them from the docks and from their homes.[42]

Regardless of any egalitarian rhetoric northerners might have spouted immediately after the Civil War, their real feelings about black inferiority and white superiority were just below the surface of their speech and were not different from those expressed by the poor southern white. Historian August Meier sums up the matter:

> The majority of Northerners had never had any exalted notions of racial equality, and once memories of war had begun to fade, and the political and economic exigencies of keeping a solid Republican South (on the basis of an enfranchised Negro population) had passed, reconciliation and nationalism quite naturally became the order of the day. Reconciliation between the sections was correlated with a rising anti-Negro prejudice, and was accomplished largely at the expense of the Negroes, as the North acquiesced in discriminatory treatment by the South and even came to justify it. By the end of the century public opinion in the North had come to feel that Negroes were an inferior race, unfitted for the franchise, and that white domination was justified.[43]

What this meant was that the entire "freedom-loving" nation turned blind eyes to the Regulators' and the Klan's violence against black women and men. Thus white supremacy could begin to reign again in the redeveloping South as it already reigned in the victorious North. In fact, in 1865 only six northern states were allowing Negroes to vote on the same basis as whites. By the time the fifteenth amendment was passed extending equal voting rights to all male Americans, only ten northern states were permitting Negroes to vote on the same basis as whites."[44] With regard to the Negro male, the South disregarded the fifteenth amendment completely, was not forced to honor the amendment and could therefore still honor the pre–Civil War decision in the Dred Scott case, proclaiming "the Negro has no rights a white person is bound to respect." The administrators of both orders of state (southern and northern) obviously had taken to heart the "scientific findings" of those nineteenth-century American scientists who claimed the Negro was intellectually and morally inferior to whites.[45] Word had filtered down to the white lower classes.

The twentieth century brought no relief from the manifestation of white racial narcissistic attitudes. When Franklin Roosevelt became president, poor unemployed whites and blacks in cities as well as the sharecroppers got some help through work-relief programs financed by the federal government. But there was a tendency to decrease work subsidies to Negroes because some white welfare administrators and fact-finders had a low opinion of the Negroes' intellect and high regard for white people's whiteness. Some of the literature about the Great Depression of the 1930s is sprinkled with references showing vestiges of the century-old ideology degrading blackness. White racial narcissism was indeed in place and guiding the thoughts and actions of white America.

The idea that the Negro was more akin to animals than to other "races of men" was echoed in Lorena Hickok's 1934 letter to Harry L. Hopkins, head of the Federal Emergency Relief Administration under President Franklin D. Roosevelt. Writing from Augusta, Georgia, Hickok, a white woman fact-finder for the government, claimed that "some of the Negroes down here are rather terrifying . . . in appearance. They seem so much bigger and blacker than the Negroes up North, and many of them look more like apes than like men."[46] Writing to Mr. Hopkins about Negroes in Savannah, Georgia, Hickok said:

> I imagine the whites in places like Savannah must be a little afraid of the Negroes. More than half the population of the city is Negro—and such Negroes! Even their lips are black, and the whites of their eyes! They're almost as inarticulate as animals. They are animals. Many of them look and talk and act like creatures barely removed from the Ape. Some of them I talked with yesterday seemed to me hardly more intelligent than my police dog. Only a little more articulate, that's all. At that, I could barely understand them.[47]

Inevitably this white love of white and hate of black expressed itself in skewed notions about black people's economic rights. Hickok continues:

> For these people [i.e., Negroes] to be getting $12 a week—at least twice as much as common labor has ever been paid down there before—is an awfully bitter pill for Savannah people to swallow, even the most kindly disposed and tolerant of them. I don't say the "most enlightened of them" because—Northerner that I am, raised in the sentimental tradition that all men are created equal—I'm not so sure these Southerners aren't right. What makes it tougher for the Savannians, as they call

themselves, is that while these illiterate creatures, whom they regard as animals, are getting more than they ever had in their lives before, hundreds of white workingmen are unable to get CWA jobs, and their families are hungry.[48]

The "scientific notion"—provided by Harvard scientist Louis Agassiz—that the Negro brain was comparable to the brain of a child seven months in its mother's womb is akin to the idea expressed to Hickok by a white social worker who said: "I believe these huge Negro case loads may be due largely to the Negro psychology. . . . They are children, really."[49]

It was Hickok herself who summed up the South's philosophy of preferential employment for whites, suggesting that Negroes should always be poor with or without an economic depression in America. This kind of thinking was and is a product of the white racial narcissistic consciousness. Hickok illustrated it well when she said:

> I've heard something . . . from white people themselves down here. The attitude, quite naturally, I suppose, is that if two men are hungry, a white man and a black man, and one of them must go on being hungry, it must be the black man, of course. And if the black man has a job, and the white man hasn't any, the black man must give it up to the white man, of course, if he wants it. Sometimes I think the white people in the South would be perfectly happy if we'd take over the job of feeding all the Negroes just enough to keep them from starving in droves and cluttering up the streets and alleys with their dead bodies![50]

Black people complained to Hickok that white men were taking their truck jobs, white women were taking their waitress jobs and white people were threatening employers if they did not fire Negroes and hire whites. Even the unions used these tactics.

Regardless of any sophisticated analysis one might give of the causes and effects of the great, worldwide economic depression in the 1930s,[51] it is clear that economic destitution did not inspire white Americans to relinquish notions of the inherent inferiority of Negroes and their own inherent superiority. In this belief, the white North and the white South came together. The fact was, and still is, that the "sustenance" that kept white racial narcissism alive (such as theories of Negro intellectual and moral inferiority) also sustained every social system affecting black and white life—the educational system, the Christian religious systems, the political system, the economic system, the welfare systems, the legal systems.

### *For Instance: Eugenics*

A significant "scientific" strengthening of the life of white racial narcissism in America came some years before the Great Depression in the popularizing of the science of heredity called eugenics, which was begun and named by the British scientist Francis Galton (a cousin of Charles Darwin). Galton intended the name "to denote the 'science' of improving human stock by giving the more suitable races or strains of blood a better chance of prevailing speedily over the less suitable races."[52] Eugenics sought to apply Darwin's theory of evolution to society. Its advocates believed "that biological decline is occurring or is likely to occur [in] modern nations." Among its major claims, as reported in some of the American scientific texts of the time, were these: (1) over time, a master race can be produced by mating males and females with superior intelligence and health from the superior race (assumed to be Caucasian); (2) a mixing of members of the superior race (Caucasian) with members of an inferior race (African and Asiatic) produces a weakened race; (3) inferior races are primitive and have little or no capacity for building, developing or adapting fully to civilization; members of the inferior races are often feebleminded or childlike in their intellectual development; (4) a society must do its best to limit the number of progeny produced by members of the inferior races or the inferior will outnumber the superior and the intellectual and moral standards of the society will be lowered; (5) thus the biologically superior people must reproduce faster than the inferior ones.[53]

No doubt the major tenets of this new science were integrated into the knowledge about black people held by those who administered subsistence programs with which poor Negroes came in contact throughout their history. Historian Daniel J. Kevles reports that in the early part of the twentieth century eugenics made quite a splash in America:

> Thousands of people filled out their "Record of Family Traits" and mailed the forms to Charles B. Davenport's Eugenics Record Office, at…Long Island.…In both countries [England and America], demands for lecturers on eugenics came from ethical, debating, health, and philosophical societies; school and university campuses, women's clubs; medical and nursing associations; and Y.M.C.A.[54]

Articles on eugenics appeared in British and American newspapers; many articles were printed in popular magazines. "Hardly a year went by without a spate of books on eugenics—from scientists…as well as from enthusiastic laymen."[55]

Though World War I slowed down the eugenics craze, it emerged again in 1923 with the publication of journalist Albert Wiggan's best seller, *The New Decalogue of Science*. He brought together the science of eugenics with morality and religion, suggesting that "had Jesus returned in the nineteen-twenties, he would have given the world a new commandment: 'the biological Golden Rule.'" And this rule was "do unto both the born and the unborn as you would have both the born and the unborn do unto you."[56]

Some of the most important men in America supported one or the other of two eugenics societies in the United States—the American Eugenics Society and its sister, the American Genetics Association. John D. Rockefeller, Jr., George Eastman and Irving Fisher (the popular Yale University economist) were members of eugenics societies. To make sure that eugenics principles filtered down to the public, the American Eugenics Society distributed "A Eugenics Catechism" in 1926. It posed questions and gave ideological answers:

Q: Does eugenics contradict the Bible?
A: The Bible has much to say for eugenics. It tells us that men do not gather grapes from thorns and figs from thistles. . . .
Q: Does eugenics mean less sympathy for the unfortunate?
A: It means a much better understanding of them, and a more concerted attempt to alleviate their suffering, by seeing to it that everything possible is done to have fewer hereditary defectives. . . .
Q: What is the most precious thing in the world?
A: The human germ plasm.[57]

As a way of popularizing their ideas, eugenics groups sponsored sermon contests. Preachers, rabbis and their congregations participated in communicating these ideas to their constituencies.

In Kansas City, Missouri, Rabbi Harry H. Mayer chose a special Mother's Day service convoked by the Council of Jewish Women and the Temple Sisterhood to declare, "May we do nothing to permit our blood to be adulterated by infusion of blood of inferior grade."[58]

Many Protestant sermons claimed the Bible was a eugenics book and "Christ was born into a family representing a long process of religious and moral selection."[59]

Even some of the state fairs got in on the action of making the principles of eugenics accessible to the general public. In 1920 the Kansas fair at Topeka sponsored "The Fitter Families" contest. In the breeding sections of the fair, where farmers displayed their fittest purebred livestock, there was a section for human stock. The contest was sponsored by the American Eugenics Society, which distributed a pamphlet to the public claiming "the time has come when the science of human husbandry must be developed." This science must be "based on the principles now followed by scientific agriculture, if the better elements of our civilization are to dominate or even survive."[60] Other state fairs followed the Kansas example and advertised "Fitter Families" contests sponsored by the American Eugenics Society. The Sesquicentennial Exposition in Philadelphia went even farther and appealed to people's sense of tax burden. A board with flashing lights "told" spectators "that every fifteen seconds a hundred dollars of your money went for the care of persons with bad heredity," and that "every forty-eight seconds a mentally deficient person was born in the United States, and that only every seven and one half minutes did the United States enjoy the birth of 'a high grade person' . . . [with] ability to do creative work and be fit for leadership."[61]

The eugenics movement in America in the early part of the twentieth century demonstrated that the country had a new developing "scientific" discipline that could continue perpetuating the idea of the Negro's inherent intellectual and moral inferiority and white people's inherently superior intelligence and moral character. Eugenics principles had been so popularized that by the time of the economic depression of the 1930s, the Anglo-American public was quite accustomed to the idea that the growth of the black population had to be restricted. What better way to diminish a population's growth than by keeping it poor, practically starving and dying at a rate outrageously disproportionate to its numbers? It seems probable that white racial narcissism was manifesting itself in a most destructive form as the country tried to struggle out of a period of extreme national crisis.[62]

This is not to suggest, however, that only southern whites have demonstrated this malady during times of national crises. Neither is this to suggest that—after the eugenics craze waned and economic depression ended—there were no more "scientific" underpinnings for ideas about black intellectual and moral inferiority.

Unfortunately, a new science is emerging in America today that has the potential of holding in place the old theories of inherent black intellectual and moral inferiority and inherent white intellectual and moral superiority. This new science is called sociobiology. It uses evolutionary biology to explain social behavior in animals, including humans. Appropriating Darwin's understanding of natural selection, sociobiology stresses two major principles: the interaction principle and the principle of fitness maximization. The interaction principle maintains that behavior and all other characteristics of animals, including humans, are caused by interaction between genotype and experience. Neither genes nor environment alone cause behavior. Both factors, interacting, are responsible for behavior. The central principle of sociobiology, fitness maximization, maintains that all animals act in a way that maximizes their fitness, that is, their success in sending copies of their genes into succeeding generations. Put simply, sociobiology suggests that social problems like racism and pauperism may also be a matter of genes as well as adaptive stages in the evolutionary process.

Fortunately, some scientists, teachers, writers and ordinary people are taking a strong stand against sociobiology. They are publicly criticizing it for its "deterministic view of human societies and actions." Some critics have likened the work of the sociobiologists to that of the eugenicists "such as Davenport in the early twentieth century."[63] (Davenport and his followers claimed that behavior such as criminality, alcoholism and so forth was genetically derived.) The work of the father of sociobiology, Edward O. Wilson, has been attacked and is charged with being of the ilk of Arthur Jensen's, William Shockley's and other works that claim "a genetic basis of racial difference in intelligence."[64] Some critics have accused Wilson and the other sociobiologists of faulty scientific methodology that erroneously derives theories about human behavior from observations made of lower-animal behavior.[65] The sociobiologists assume a connection rather than prove one. Their theories about the connection between genes and human social behavior come from these assumptions.

Regardless of the dialogue, debate and critique of sociobiology, it is clear that yet another "science" has emerged that can be used to reinforce notions of black inferiority and white superiority. History seems to repeat itself. White racial narcissism in the last years of the twentieth century is getting a "shot in the arm" from science—as it got in the early part of the century from eugenics. Thus white America's present disregard for the life and well-being of black people, female and male, may continue long into the future. White people in control of this country's resources are not apt to be too concerned about the well-being of people whom they believe to be "criminal by nature." They are not apt to be concerned about equality and justice for black people whom white people's "science" has declared to be naturally inferior intellectually and morally. As the pathology of white racist narcissism continues to dominate American national consciousness, the misery of the masses of black people continues. One cannot help but wonder when black people, females and males, will stand tall together and say to America in unequivocal language and deeds: "Enough is enough."

## Chapter 5

# SISTERS IN THE WILDERNESS AND COMMUNITY MEANINGS

Although many themes in African-American women's history correspond with many themes in Hagar's story in the Bible, nothing links the two women together more securely than their religious experiences in the wilderness. Hagar and African-American women (with their children) meet God there in the midst of trouble and what appears to be impending death and destruction. Many African-American slave women have left behind autobiographies telling how they would slip away to the wilderness or to "the haystack where the presence of the Lord overshadowed" them.[1] Some of them governed their lives according to their mothers' counsel that they would have "nobody in the wide world to look to but God"[2]—as Hagar in the final stages of her story had only God to look to. The famous "Ain't I a Woman?" speech of ex-slave Sojourner Truth testifies that she cried out when her children were most all sold off into slavery and "none but Jesus heard me."

For many black Christian women today, "wilderness" or "wilderness-experience" is a symbolic term used to represent a near-destruction situation in which God gives personal direction to the believer and thereby helps her make a way out of what she thought was no way. I recently encountered black women's symbolic sense of wilderness when I lectured at Howard Divinity School in 1992. Arriving earlier than my lecture was scheduled, I went to one of the workshops attended almost exclusively by black female ministers. As the women shared their experiences in ministry, one woman turned to another woman and said, "Tell the group about your wilderness experience." The woman began to tell about her experience in her last parish. A few members of the congregation had all but successfully turned the rest of the congregation against her. Her ministry was about to be destroyed, she said. But she, alone, "took her situation to God as she fasted and prayed." Finally God "came to her," giving her direction. This was a positive turning point and her ministry survived to become one of the most outstanding in the district.

Other women around the table in the workshop began to share what they termed their wilderness experiences in ministry.

In the biblical story Hagar's wilderness experience happened in a desolate and lonely wilderness where she—pregnant, fleeing from the brutality of her slave owner, Sarai, and without protection—had religious experiences that helped her and her child survive when survival seemed doomed. For both Hagar and the African-American women, the wilderness experience meant standing utterly alone, in the midst of serious trouble, with only God's support to rely upon.

As the result of these hard-time experiences and the encounters with God, Hagar and many African-American women manifested a risk-taking faith. Though she obeyed God's mandate for her life, Hagar dared to give a name to the God she met in the wilderness. In a sense, this God is her God, and possibly not the God of her slave holders Abram and Sarai. No other person in the Bible names God. Many African-American women (slave and free) have taken serious risks in the black community's liberation struggle. For example, in the midst of the violence and brutality that accompanied slavery in America, Harriet Tubman, with a price on her head, dared to liberate over three hundred slaves. She served as a spy and a general in the Civil War. She is said to have relied solely upon God for help and strength; she had no one else to look to. Thus we can speak of Hagar and many African-American women as sisters in the wilderness struggling for life, and by the help of their God coming to terms with situations that have destructive potential.

In order to provide a clearer view of the relation between Hagar's experiences in the wilderness and African-American women's experiences in the wilderness, this chapter attempts two tasks. First, it explores the significance of "wilderness" or "wilderness experience" in the African-American cultural context in which black women's, Hagar's and the black community's wilderness experiences are brought together. This consideration is necessary because it takes seriously the womanist theological presupposition that black women's religious experiences are shaped by black women's interaction in a black community composed of both oppressed females and oppressed males. Therefore, to understand black women's experience we need to see how it has been influenced by the faith, thought and life-struggle of the communities of which black women are a part. The second task of this chapter is to suggest the significance of this Hagar-in-the-wilderness symbolism for shedding more light upon certain aspects of the intellectual, social and political life of African-American women and the African-American community. These two tasks, once accomplished, contribute to the challenge posed by the womanist God-talk in the last section of this book.

### *"Wilderness/Wilderness-Experience" in Black and White*

A connection between the wilderness and religious experience has been made by African Americans for hundreds of years. An early appearance of this connection occurs in the spiritual songs, which enable us to speak of "wilderness experience" among slaves as basically religious.[3] This experience made no attempt to be gender exclusive. Women and men were encouraged to participate in it. The following two spiritual songs illustrate the kind of religious activities African-American slaves assigned to this experience:

> Song #1

> *Chorus:* I wait up-on de Lord,
> I wait up-on de Lord,
> I wait up-on de lord, my God,
> who take a-way de sin of de world.
> If you want to find Jesus, go in de wilderness,
> Go in de wilderness, go in de wilderness,
> Mournin' brudder, go in de wilderness....
> You want to be a Christian, go in de wilderness,
> Go in de wilderness, go in de wilderness,
> Mournin' brudder, go in de wilderness....
> You want to get religion, go in de wilderness,
> Go in de wilderness, go in de wilderness...
> If you spec' to be converted, go in de wilderness,
> Go in de wilderness...
> O weepin' Mary, go in de wilderness,
> Go in de wilderness, go in de wilderness...
> 'Flicted sister, go in de wilderness,
> Go in de wilderness, go in de wilderness...
> Say, ain't you a member? Go in de wilderness,
> Go in de wilderness, go in de wilderness...
> Half-done Christian, go in de wilderness,
> Go in de wilderness, go in de wilderness...
> Baptist member, go in de wilderness,
> Go in de wilderness, go in de wilderness...
> O see, brudder Bristol, go in de wilderness,

Go in de wilderness, go in de wilderness...
Jesus a waitin' to meet you in de wilderness, go in de wilderness,
Go in de wilderness, go in de wilderness...[4]

Song #2

How did you feel when you came out de wilderness, came out de
  wilderness, came out de wilderness?
Tell me, brudder, how did you feel when you came out de wilderness,
  came out de wilderness?
Tell me, sister, how did you feel when you came out de wilderness,
  came out de wilderness, came out de wilderness?
How did you feel when you came out de wilderness, came out de
  wilderness?
Did you love your brother when you came out de wilderness, came
  out de wilderness...?
Did you love your sister when you came out de wilderness, came out
  de wilderness...?
Did you love back sliddin' Christians when you came out de wilderness, came out de wilderness...?
Tell me, brudder and sister, did you meet Jesus in de wilderness?[5]

The stanzas of both songs reveal that during the antebellum period in
America, when these songs were created and sung, slaves had a positive concept of wilderness. It was a free and friendly space where one received from
Jesus the strength needed to rise above one's ailments (sadness, sin, affliction,
backsliding, etc.). William Allen described the kind of ritual movement slaves
associated with the wilderness in the nineteenth century:

> One of their customs, often alluded to in the songs... is that of wander-
> ing through the woods and swamps, when under religious excitement,
> like the ancient bacchantes. To get religion is with them to "fin' dat
> ting."[6]

Slave women were often most persistent in their effort to undergo the wilderness experience. Allen, Ware and Garrison tell of a slave named Mosley, who
described her sister's experience searching for religion: "[Mosley's sister] . . .
couldn't fin' dat leetie ting—hunt for 'em—huntin' for 'em all de time—las'
fin 'em."[7] Slaves, female and male, who had found religion in the wilderness
were cautious about letting unconverted slaves into their religious meetings.
Allen reports, "One day, on our way to see a 'shout,' we asked Bristol whether

he was going—'no, ma'am, wouldn't let me in—hain't foun dat ting yet—hain't been on my knees in de swamp.' "8

Evidently slaves thought an environment supporting solitude and reflection was conducive to gaining a true connection with Jesus and to strengthening the kind of God-consciousness needed to support their journeys through life. Getting religion and getting one's consciousness thoroughly saturated with God involved moving one's self bodily into a private space where the God-human encounter could happen undisturbed by competing forces in the environment. Going into the wilderness assured slaves that they would meet Jesus if they persevered.

The wilderness experience, as religious experience, was transforming. Its structure was physical *isolation* (of slave from slave environment); *establishing a relation* (between Jesus and slave); *healing by Jesus* (of whatever malady afflicted the slave); *transformation* (conversion of the slave's more secular bent to a thoroughly religious bent); and *motivation to return* (to the slave community) changed for the better. So, for African-American slaves, female and male, the wilderness did not bear the negative connotations that mainline white pioneer culture had assigned to it. Rather, for the slave, the wilderness was a positive place conducive to uplifting the spirit and to strengthening religious life. Wilderness experience, involving a compatible relation between humans and nature, was to be sought actively. Yet wilderness was a place where the slave underwent intense struggle before gaining a spiritual/religious identity, for example, as a Christian. But the struggle itself was regarded as positive, leading to a greater good than the slave ordinarily realized. To the slave's way of thinking, then, the wilderness-experience was not easy. One tarried and struggled in the wilderness with oneself and finally met Jesus. Of course, the results were emotionally and spiritually invigorating for the slave.

In the dominating white American culture from the seventeenth century to the late nineteenth century two primary attitudes toward the wilderness were in effect. One attitude came from the early pioneers; the other attitude came from the later influence of the European-derived Romantic Movement. In early American culture (pioneer culture) the wilderness was presented as a hostile place unfriendly to humankind. Thus the wilderness was to be conquered rather than lived with in peaceful and reciprocal relation. In his exploration of the meaning and development of wilderness in the (white) American mind, Roderick Nash rightly describes the American pioneer's belief that the wilderness threatened human survival and was thus to be conquered. Hence wilderness "not only frustrated the pioneers physically but also acquired significance as a dark and sinister symbol." According to Nash,

> They [pioneers] shared the long Western tradition of imagining wild country as a moral vacuum, a cursed and chaotic wasteland. As a consequence, frontiersmen actually sensed that they battled wild country not only for personal survival but in the name of nation, race, and God. Civilizing the New World meant enlightening darkness, ordering chaos, and changing evil into good. In the morality play of westward expansion, wilderness was the villain, and the pioneer, as hero, relished its destruction.[9]

Since the aim of the pioneer was to transform the wilderness into civilization, this was "the reward for his sacrifices, the definition of his achievement, and the source of his pride. He applauded his successes in terms suggestive of the high stakes he attached to the conflict."[10]

Of course the wilderness could not be transformed from "savagery" to order without destroying its natural arrangement. Transforming the wilderness not only meant dealing with the natural environment; it also meant civilizing "savage" humans associated with the wilderness, such as the Native Americans identified with the wildernesses of America and the African people allied with the "wilds" of Africa. Slavery was rationalized and argued as the proper "civilizing process" for these "savage" people. And when slavery failed—as it did with Native Americans—destruction of "savage" humans was in order. Genocide of these women and men became, for the Euro-Americans, the proper strategy for subduing wilderness people.

Runaway slaves who escaped into the wilderness and were captured were either taken back into "civilization" and subdued by ferocious beating, or they were sold farther down South. They were even killed, if they offered resistance. This treatment of Native Americans and African slaves paralleled Euro-American treatment of the "chaotic green growth" in the wilderness. It was either to be subdued by rigorous exploitation and rearrangement, or it was to be destroyed so that the Euro-American pursuit of order could prevail. "Uncultivated land, as an early nineteenth-century report put it, was absolutely useless."[11] To this way of Euro-American pioneer thinking, "uncultivated" Indians and resistant African slaves were also useless. Vestiges of this pioneer way of thinking about the wilderness exist to this day in America due, in part, to the way the Bible, Puritanism and notions of development supported the idea of America as "wilderness condition" and the idea that "savage people" were to be tamed.[12]

However, by the late eighteenth and early nineteenth centuries the Romantic Movement that flourished in Europe had come to life in American culture. Romanticism—denoting fascination and "enthusiasm for the strange, remote, solitary and mysterious"[13]—associated beauty and godliness with the wilderness. As Roderick Nash describes them, the European Romantics rejected the meticulous order the Enlightenment advocated. They "turned to the unkempt forest. Wilderness appealed to romantics bored or disgusted with man and his works."[14] The wilderness offered freedom and solitude. Since exaltation of "the primitive" was a cornerstone in Romantic thought, many Romantics believed the happiness and well-being of humans "decreased in direct proportion to . . . [their] degree of civilization."[15]

For the Euro-Americans in the New World, living daily with what they believed to be the threat of the wilderness and wilderness people, Romanticism was not so purely expressed by the few who began advocating it. In American culture at large, the romantic fascination with the wilderness never completely replaced the distaste for wilderness that existed in the pioneer mind. As Nash stated, "Appreciation [of the ideas advocated in Romanticism] . . . resulted from a momentary relaxation of dominant antipathy [to the wilderness]."[16] But after independence from England in the late eighteenth century, Euro-Americans were searching for a national and cultural identity, for a way of proudly presenting their country's assets in relation to those of England and Europe. It was nation-building time, and building meant more than developing a stable and productive economy. A distinctive American culture had to be created. According to Nash's speculations, "The nation's short history, weak traditions, and minor literary and artistic achievements seemed negligible compared to those of Europe."[17]

So the Americans found one way in which their country was different from Europe, and they built on this difference. "Wilderness had no counterpart in the Old World. Seizing on this distinction and adding to it deistic and Romantic assumptions about the value of wild country," Americans began to claim that the wilderness was not a liability. Rather, it was an asset.[18] Nash makes the point that while Americans continued to have pride in their pioneering experience, by the mid-nineteenth century "wilderness was recognized as a cultural and moral resource and a basis for national self-esteem."[19]

Although there is no definite proof that any of the white American attitudes toward the wilderness (pioneer, Romantic or nationalist) influenced the
American slave's attitude toward the wilderness, it seems that slave attitudes
were often in direct opposition to what mainline culture was projecting about
the wilderness at the time. Perhaps the slaves' own personal experience with
the wilderness helped create their positive attitude toward it. Thus, before
the end of the American Revolutionary War and even before the end of the
American Civil War, the slaves did not share the pioneer's view of the wilderness. To the slave, the wilderness was a friend that often sheltered and fed the
runaway slave. In the wilderness slaves often gathered the plants and herbs
they used for healing. Sometimes when slaves were beaten by their masters,
they ran off and hid several days in the wilderness. The vegetation and fruit
in the wilderness sustained them.

Possibly the slave's positive attitude toward the wilderness was also influenced by various African traditions, which regarded many aspects of nature
as friendly and nature itself as a sustainer of life. Perhaps some of the African
and animistic ways of thinking about nature were, in one form or another,
passed down by generation after generation of slaves. Though many slaves
were familiar with the Bible, apparently they did not take seriously those
parts that told man he had dominion over nature. Nor did they translate this
to mean conquering the wilderness as the American pioneer did. More similar to Romanticism's understanding of the wilderness as good and beautiful,
the slaves—perhaps before Romanticism flourished in America and contrary
to the pioneers' ideas—respected the integrity of nature and the wilderness.

After emancipation, however, the slaves' notion of wilderness took on
added dimension. Their understanding of wilderness was not only of a place
where black men and black women, like Hagar, met God. It was also the wide,
wide world (a hostile place), where black women must go to seek a living for
their families. Thus the black female poet and novelist Frances W. Harper,
writing in the late nineteenth and early twentieth centuries, could speak in
her novel *Iola Leroy* of ex-slave women who, "like Hagar of Old," went into
the wide, wide world to make a living for themselves and their children. Edmonia Lewis, a nineteenth-century black artist, could carve her female statue
"Hagar in the Wilderness," thereby appealing to the sense of wilderness as
an isolated position in a hostile world as well as an actual place in which the
biblical Hagar met God. After the Civil War, this African-American notion of
the world as hostile wilderness was similar to the pioneers' view of the natural wilderness as hostile. Interestingly enough, this was a period in America

when Romantic views about the wilderness had flourished to the extent that there was great public concern for preserving the wilderness. In fact, in 1872 President Ulysses Grant signed papers "designating over two million acres of northwestern Wyoming as Yellowstone National Park."[20]

Immediately after slavery, then, African Americans apparently had two attitudes toward wilderness. One, deriving from antebellum days, emphasized religious experience and projected positive feelings about the wilderness as sacred space. The other sense of the wilderness seemed shaped by new experiences of economic insecurity, social displacement and the new forms of oppression ex-slaves encountered in a "free" world. In her narrative, ex-slave Kate Drumgoold describes the kind of "freedom" the emancipated slaves realized when she said, "There are many doors that are shut to keep us back as a race."[21] Thus wilderness had begun also to carry negative connotations.

Apparently, at some point in African-American consciousness, these two senses of wilderness came together in the appropriation of the biblical Hagar. In African-American culture, this Hagar-in-the-wilderness figure began to represent both the positive antebellum black religious experience of meeting God in an isolated place and the negative postbellum experience of "pioneering" in a wide world hostile to African-American social and economic advancement.

No other biblical image could have been more appropriate than Hagar in the wilderness for representing the African-American past and present. In the two accounts of her story in Genesis, Hagar goes into the wilderness. In the first account (Genesis 16:1–9), Hagar is still a slave. In her pain and misery she meets *her* God for the first time. Her experience with this God could be regarded as positive by African Americans because God promises survival, freedom and nationhood for Hagar's progeny. The African-American community has, all of its life, struggled for survival, freedom and nationhood.

In the second Genesis account (Genesis 21:1–9) Hagar is again in the wilderness. She and her child are no longer slaves, but their freedom has brought them into dire economic straits—just as freedom brought severe economic consequences to newly freed slaves. Like African-American people, Hagar and her child are alone without resources for survival. Hagar must try to make a living in the wide, wide world for herself and her child. This was also the task of many African-American women and the entire community of black freedpeople when emancipation came.

In African-American culture this postbellum symbolic sense of the wilderness experience, with Hagar as its representative figure, is inclusive—just as the black antebellum understanding of the wilderness experience was inclusive. With Hagar (and male child) as its content, the postbellum symbol represented simultaneously black women's experience and the experience of the entire community, female and male. Perhaps because the ex-slave's world was in a state of almost total flux after the Civil War, the community needed something to hold together its historic memory of its past *and* its present imaginative potential for shaping a positive quality of life in freedom.[22] Thus the Hagar-wilderness symbolism held together women's and the community's past history, present situations and intimations of hope for a better future.[23]

This symbolic sense of wilderness held together what the community took to be women's positive body experience (pregnancy, motherhood, nurturehood), the slave's positive religious experience in the antebellum wilderness (which involved the body) and the community's experience as an ethnic body in the free world of postbellum America. This sense of wilderness held together black women's negative experience of oppression (through sexist bondage and the surrogate situation) and the community's negative experience of racial bondage and continuing manhood struggle. It held together black women's positive struggle for autonomy, through resistance and rebellion, and the community's positive struggle for self-determination through resistance, rebellion and being cast out of slavery.

The postbellum notion of wilderness (with Hagar and child as its content) emphasized black women's and the black community's negative economic experience of poverty and social displacement. It held together women's positive encounter with God, which provided hope for the future through survival struggle, and the community's historic and positive encounter with God, which provided hope for the future through the community's liberation struggle. The black postbellum notion of wilderness brought together black women's experience of holding the family together with the community's experience of black male impotence in relation to the economic straits in which his family found itself.[24] This postbellum African-American symbolic sense of wilderness, with Hagar at its center, makes the female figure symbolic of the entire black community's history of brutalization during slavery; of fierce survival struggle and economic servitude after liberation; of children being cheated out of their inheritance by oppressors; of threat to the life and well-being of the family; of the continuing search for a positive, productive quality of life for women and men under God's care.

This postbellum sense of wilderness gave vast and inexhaustible dimensions to the provincial antebellum wilderness, which was once definite space within specific boundaries located in time and easily accessible to the slaves. Wilderness as wide, wide world could not be contained, but wilderness as a specific place could be. Thus in postbellum black consciousness, wilderness as a definite place situated in time became vague in African-American understanding of the fundamentals of the wilderness experience. However, postbellum black people still had a sense that the wilderness experience involved isolating one's self (more especially one's mind) from competing forces and withdrawing in fervent prayer, meditation and fasting. Apparently the belief was that one's troubles in the world and infirmities (caused by troubles in the world) would be ministered to by God. But a special, physical location for the wilderness experience was not necessary. So, while the antebellum wilderness experience was structured by physical isolation in a specific location; relation; personal/spiritual healing; transformation and motivation to return, the postbellum notion of wilderness experience was different. It involved isolation more mental than physical (no specific location); struggle through prayer and/or fasting yielding communication with God; transformation not primarily of a person's more secular bent but primarily transformation of human relationships in a wide world. The motivation to return (one's body) that structured the antebellum wilderness experience diminished in the postbellum wilderness experience, for personal conversion and meeting Jesus no longer necessitated returning one's self bodily from one location (designated as sacred space) to the ordinary world of daily affairs. Rather, suppliants' location for meeting Jesus was wherever they found themselves in the wide, wide world.

### Intellectual Significance of Symbolism

After slavery, the symbolic use of Hagar in the wilderness helped develop African-American conceptual life in two ways. First, Hagar, functioning as symbol *and* signal in this development, brought together the sacred and the secular in postbellum African-American thought. In her symbolic function she stands for the connection between the African-American antebellum heritage of "sacred-space-meeting Jesus" content of the wilderness experience and the postbellum secular and social notion of the wilderness experience in a wide, hostile world where the economic struggle is severe. In her function as signal, Hagar calls attention to the presence and importance of black women's experience in African-American culture, while she simultaneously calls attention to the unity of black males and black females in certain community experiences. This means, then, that black women should not separate "woman-experience" from their experience in the community's survival and liberation struggles involving black men.

Second, the Hagar (and child) content of the wilderness symbolism brings together the spiritual and the political. Thus religious life in the black postbellum Christian community can continue to express itself, simultaneously, in both spiritual and political terms.[25] In the biblical account in Genesis Hagar's experiences in the wilderness are constituted by political and spiritual interconnections.[26] African-American historian Evelyn Brooks sees a similar character in African-American women's experience. Brooks describes organized postbellum black Baptist women revealing "the feminine presence as both a spiritual and political force within the black community."[27] Black women and the African-American Christian community see no contradiction in the black church and its leadership exerting political action in the wide world as they simultaneously affirm the work of God in this activity—thus linking the political and the spiritual.

There were, of course, historical black Hagars, like Harriet Tubman, who modeled this connection for the community during slavery and into freedom. Thomas Wentworth Higginson, a high-ranking Union officer in the Civil War, described Tubman as "the greatest heroine of the age."[28]

Tubman herself believed her success in singlehandedly liberating over three hundred slaves was superintended by God, who had preordained her political action.[29] Benjamin Quarles describes Tubman as

> molded by a deep reservoir of faith in God. . . . [She] felt that Divine Providence had willed her freedom and that a guardian angel accompanied her, particularly in her missions of deliverance.[30]

To African Americans, Tubman, like Hagar, "personified resistance. . . . She symbolized courage, determination and strength."[31] Until her death in 1913, she helped postbellum black people find their way in the "wilderness" of freedom. This spiritual-political connection in black Christian women's experience has continued beyond Tubman's death in the life and work of such women as Ida Wells, Rosa Parks, Fannie Lou Hamer and others.

The later post-Reconstruction black community could continuously accept these females modeling the unity of the political and the spiritual because Hagar, who also modeled this unity, had become firmly rooted in the community's historical memory and imagination. It is no wonder that the twentieth-century African-American anthropologist John Langston Gwaltney could "define" Aunt Hagar as "a mythical apical figure of the core Black American nation" ("mythical" suggesting spiritual and "nation" suggesting political).[32] And in 1992 African-American film maker Julie Dash ("Daughters of the Dust") passes Hagar along in a character bearing that name confronted by some life-situations similar to those confronting the biblical Hagar. In the movie Hagar is a single parent. She is connected to the "tribe" (a Gullah family in the Sea Islands) not by kinship but by marriage, though she is a widow. As the picture ends, Hagar is going out into the wide, wide world—along with other family members—to make a living for herself and her child. It is Hagar who has been most vocal, belligerent and active in family politics on the island. Her spirituality is obvious as she participates in the activities sustaining the family's survival. One can suppose she will be just as vocal and active politically and spiritually wherever she goes.

### Social Significance of Symbolism

If we can assume that symbols have a social effect in the community using them, we can make a suggestion about the effect the Hagar-in-the-wilderness symbolism can have upon African-American women's social identity. This Hagar symbolism provides a historically realistic model of non-middle-class black womanhood. Contrary to Anglo-American ideals about "true womanhood," this African-American notion affirms such qualities as defiance; risk-taking; independence; endurance when endurance gives no promise; the stamina to hold things together for the family (even without the help of a mate); the ability, in poverty, to make a way out of no way; the courage to initiate political action in the public arena; and a close personal relation with God. Her field of activity is both the private and public domain. Affirming this model of womanhood, the black community can celebrate the moral, intellectual, spiritual and emotional strength poor black women have exercised as they withstood trouble and trials in a hostile world.[33] Thus, Hagar in the wilderness models a kind of womanhood compatible with the historical facts of the lives of many rank-and-file African-American women.

There have, however, been other models of womanhood advocated in the African-American community by educated, elite, upper-class black people. In the late nineteenth and early twentieth centuries these educated blacks (some of them women) perpetuated a model of womanhood akin to the Victorian model of "true womanhood" affirmed and advanced in Anglo-American society. The Victorian ideal woman was an exact opposite of the kind of womanhood Hagar-in-the-wilderness and many poor black women modeled. The Victorian true woman was described as one "who, through Christ, blesses man and helps make his home a joy and life a privilege."[34] White ministers described this ideal woman as "pliant . . . adapted [by nature] to meet man's wants . . . feminine . . . soft, tender and delicate." Further, the true (woman's . . . sphere is the home. It is there that she has the opportunity of exercising, to best purpose and in its fullest extent, her distinctive and special gifts."[35] She "stands for home, tenderness, gentleness, unselfish love and sacrificial care."[36] The proper vocation for this idealized woman was motherhood and, of course, "wifehood." The most prominent biblical figure advocated as modeling true womanhood was the Virgin Mary. Through an analogy, the Rev. W. Cunningham voiced the popular sentiment of the age regarding the Virgin Mary as precedent for idealized womanhood:

> There was a woman once who was marked out from all others on earth, and all generations have called her blessed. The Virgin Mary had a wonderful place assigned her, but she was not vain of her privileges. . . . She had no thought of herself at all. . . . She stood by the cross, if her presence might support him in his dying agonies, heedless of her own sorrow, self-forgetful, self-sacrificing. . . . And the women who walk in her footsteps are blessed still, blessed in every generation as it comes and goes.[37]

In the African-American community in the late nineteenth and early twentieth centuries, this Victorian ideal of true womanhood found expression in voices of "race men and race women." These were usually educated black men and women engaged in what was called "racial uplift"; that is, working to elevate newly emancipated (but oppressed) black people through political activism, education, moral reform and economic advancement. Race men Booker T. Washington (championing industrial education and economic uplift) and W. E. B. Du Bois (championing political activism and humanistic/classical education) were conditioned by Victorian social decorum regarding women. Both men subscribed to the social philosophy designating the public arena of political activism as the proper place for themselves as men and the home as the proper place for women as wives and mothers. As Claudia Tate puts it: "Washington and Du Bois, like the other black male intellectuals of their time, would have understood social activism as principally a masculine prerogative and would have felt that it was their right as men to dominate the work of racial uplift."[38]

Linda M. Perkins makes the claim that though black men and black women were both involved in the work of racial uplift immediately after the Civil War, racial uplift gradually became the work of black women.[39] This was primarily because uplift began to be defined exclusively in terms of black people's social needs, like education of children, moral instructions for moral reform, household management, adjustment to American standards of cleanliness (hygiene), community organization and so on. Once the work of racial uplift passed to black women, much of the discourse about it became the occupation of educated black women. Race women such as Anna Julia Cooper, and church women such as Lucy Wilmot Smith, Mary Cook and Virginia Broughton began to discuss the goals of "uplift" for black women.[40] They used language that inadvertently supported elite, educated black men's "Virgin Mary taste" and their preference for the Victorian "true woman," whose place was in the home and not in the arena of political activism. Establishing a context for discussing the needs of black women, Cooper stressed the importance of the home and women's place in it as she made reference to international and national conditions. She cited "impure homelife" as the source of some problems in Turkey.[41] She believed that America's potential for realizing great strides in human relations rested "chiefly on the homelife and on the influence of good women in those homes."[42] Cooper paid tribute to Old Norse legends that "breathe the . . . spirit of love of home and veneration of the pure and noble influence there presiding—the wife, sister, the mother."[43] She believed that many of the benevolent institutions and altruistic motivations in America occurred because a " 'mothering' influence from some source is leavening the nation."[44]

The foundation of her argument for women's rights was her assumption "that there is a feminine as well as a masculine side of truth; that these are related not as inferior and superior . . . but as complements."[45] However, Cooper defined the character of these complements much like the advocates of Victorian true womanhood defined the difference between male and female conceptual endowments. She claimed that "man is more noble in reason, so the woman is quick in sympathy. . . . He is indefatigable in pursuit of abstract truth, so is she in caring for the interests by the way—striving tenderly and lovingly that not one of the least of these 'little ones' shall perish."[46]

Yet we are not to underestimate Cooper's great contribution to black women's struggle against racism in the white feminist movement of the time and black women's struggle against sexism in the black male civil rights movement. She waged a noble battle to move black women, albeit middle-class black women, from invisibility to visibility in both movements as she pressured to secure all black people's rights in white American society. Claudia Tate is correct when she makes the point that by using domestic imagery in her speeches, Cooper "feminized social activism in ways that permitted black women access to activist discourse."[47]

Nevertheless, we cannot overlook the fact that the maternal virtues Cooper advocated in her speeches were those of an educated and elite black womanhood. She, like most educated black women of her time, greatly resented many white people's opinion that no matter what a black woman achieved, "A Negro woman cannot be a lady."[48] Though Cooper argued for the social equality of black women with black men and argued for the equality of all black people with white people, her arguments appealed to and were apparently directed to an educated, upperclass audience. Literary critic Mary Helen Washington states the case well when she confesses "to a certain uneasiness about Cooper's tone in these essays, a feeling that while she speaks for ordinary black women, she rarely, if ever, speaks to them."[49] Therefore, Washington questions how Cooper understood the relation between herself as a highly educated woman and the black women she described as "mute and voiceless." Washington concludes that Cooper's essays lack all indication that poor black women actually "existed in [Cooper's] imagination as audience or as peer."[50]

Cooper's argued positions for black female rights did not translate into rights for all black women. As Linda Perkins claims, most upper-class black women educators finally went along with what their social class expected of a "true woman" in terms of gentility, refinement, education, duty and sacrifice. Most educated, upper-class black women wanted to be recognized as ladies. And in black upper-class society, one was a lady according to the Victorian concepts of the "true woman." Perkins's evaluation of these women's predicament is worth repeating:

> Even though the prevailing economic deprivation of blacks at the end of the nineteenth and early twentieth centuries demanded that black women work, many elite blacks nevertheless embraced the Victorian "true womanhood" ideal of the 1820's and 1830's. . . . As with New England white women of the antebellum period, black women were expected to be self-sacrificing and dutiful. (Prior to emancipation all blacks were expected to do so.) Speeches and articles abound citing black women as the nurturers and the guardians of—not the thinkers or leaders of—the race. Most black women educators accepted the charge.[51]

Evelyn Brooks's important work on some nineteenth-century educated black Baptist women reveals that they too were caught up in the trend of appropriating the Victorian true womanhood ideals to describe the ideal womanhood and proper work for African-American women. Brooks classifies these women—Mary Cook, Lucy Wilmot Smith and Virginia Broughton—as feminist theologians and shows that they obtained many of their ideal models for black womanhood from the Bible. Thus biblical women Dorcas, Phoebe, Deborah and Huldah (wife of Shallumen) were held up by these Baptist women as examples of the kind of womanhood involved in the work of salvation. Black women were encouraged to imitate these biblical women. The Baptist women also referred to ancient civilizations to show that Christianity brought with it a more elevated status for women. Describing what she labels the black feminist theology of Smith, Broughton and Cook, Brooks indicates how their understanding of uplift, of women's status in Christianity and their ideas about Victorian true womanhood came together in their theology. She says:

> Black feminist theology presented woman's uplift within an evolutionary framework that repeatedly referred to the degraded status of women in ancient civilizations and in contemporary non-Christian cultures, thus arguing that the standard of womanhood evolved to a higher plane with the spread of Christianity. This view enhanced the significance of motherhood and domesticity. Since mothers were considered the transmitters of culture, woman's virtue and intelligence within the home measured the level of civilization.[52]

The black Baptist women framed their messages about black womanhood in the context of sexual and racial concerns, and "each of the two categories formed a separate basis for the articulation of a dual gender consciousness." So, says Brooks, "Within the contexts of sex and race, Black women understood themselves equally as homemakers and as soldiers."[53]

These Baptist feminists were clearer about what it meant to be homemakers than they were about what it meant for black women to be soldiers. Nineteenth-century black Baptist feminist theology was clear in its evaluation of the Virgin Mary as "the highest expression of womanhood."[54] Motherhood and the home were primary motifs in its discourse. Home was to be a place wives/mothers made comfortable for their husbands, even though the women might also be engaged outside the home in other work proper for black people's uplift.

Though Cooper and the black Baptist feminist theologians enlarged opportunities for some black women, their Victorian true-womanhood language and categories were not congruent with the social and economic needs of the masses of poor African-American women. While the Virgin Mary image of true womanhood may have appealed to financially secure black women educated enough to know how to use the image to pressure the American power structures, many poor uneducated black women still modeled the characteristics associated with the Hagar-in-the-wilderness image of womanhood. For them, conditions had not changed much since slavery. They were fighting a desperate battle for basic economic—and sometimes physical—survival on a daily basis.

Just as Hagar's sojourns in the wilderness were precipitated by the exploitative and hostile treatment she received from her slave owner, the poor uneducated postbellum black female's difficulties in the world of work were often exacerbated by the treatment she received from white female employers and fellow workers. Dolores Janiewski reports incidents in the work place where white women, often with the aid of white men, came together to persecute black women just as Sarai and Abram were together in their brutal treatment of Hagar. Janiewski reports that even though white men and women had serious labor struggles with each other in Southern factories, the white women and white men together mobilized to keep manufacturers from hiring black women and black men.[55] When an Atlanta textile mill tried to hire black women and black men in 1896, white workers formed a union headed by a white woman. She and her white female supporters forced the ouster of the black workers.[56] "The mere rumor that black workers would be hired in 1919 precipitated mob attacks on black women in Macon, Georgia, which resulted in two deaths."[57] And, "During World War II, white women employed in Danville, Virginia, struck for and won the dismissal of the black women recently hired."[58] All of these incidents threatened the economic survival of poor black women and their families. Hence poor black women in the late nineteenth century (and after) could not affirm black Baptist feminist Virginia Broughton's opinion that there was a " 'general awakening and rallying together of Christian women' of all races."[59]

However, like Hagar in her wilderness experiences, black women used resistance strategies to counteract the persecution aimed at them. Janiewski cites a report from Auburn, Alabama, describing resistance strategies black women used in 1903. The black women took time off or quit work whenever they desired. They refused to stay overnight in the homes of their employers, and they often took breaks during the day to check things at their own homes. They took food and other things from their employers "in the belief that much white property belonged by right to the descendants of the slaves who had produced it."[60] They would not enter their employers' homes through the back or kitchen door. They resisted any kind of discipline their employers tried to exercise.

Today many black women like Hagar, raising families alone, demonstrate courage and personal ingenuity as they struggle to find resources for survival. Sociologist Beverly O. Ford introduces her readers to eight black women who have depended upon their own wits, their kinship ties and each other to survive on the pitifully inadequate welfare stipends they receive each month for their children's care. These women find ways to augment their income, but they do not depend upon men for this. As one woman, Dora, said, "It's okay if and when I get it [money from estranged husband, etc.] but you can't have your chaps (children) depending on something that may never come. When they need something I know it's me that's gotta get it for them."[61] Ford's concluding statement is that for all these eight black women "the dominant conception of womanhood is that of the strong, resourceful Black woman. It has its roots in the Black cultural tradition." This model continues to operate in their lives, Ford says, "because poverty and oppression which caused this model of womanhood to develop is very much a reality for them."[62] These women resemble Hagar in the wide, wide world as they try to make a life for themselves and their children. Apparently Hagar in the wilderness as an image of womanhood—poor, hardworking, strong, self-reliant, autonomous, committed to her family, communicating with God—continues to live and thrive in the African-American world.

I think we can suggest that some of the historic tension that has existed in the African-American community between black men and black women about the nature of black women's femininity[63] may stem from conflict between the Hagar-in-the-wilderness model of black womanhood (emerging from the grassroots of black heritage) and the Victorian "Virgin-Mary/true-woman" model of womanhood imported from the white community through black middle-class channels.

Perhaps what Daryl Dance sees in black literature as the portrayal of the black mother as either Eve or Madonna is, in actuality, a conflict primarily in black male literary consciousness and imagination between Hagar and the Madonna. Perhaps on the part of these male writers to whom Dance refers, what has occurred is a misidentification of biblical women analogous to black women.

In the Bible Eve was never in the position to provide survival strategies for anyone, as far as her story goes. The Hagar stories are those which suggest that an ex-slave mother could, with only God's help, be in complete charge of furnishing her son with survival strategies. There are no other stories like this in the Bible. Dance's evaluation suggests that black male writers represent the black mother as Eve because they are accusing her of repressing their manhood by furnishing them with survival tactics that do not enhance the manifestation of black manhood.[64] Therefore they think black mothers deceive black sons as Eve deceived Adam. This is a skewed analogy.

Black women themselves, as well as many people in the black community, praise black women's emotional and spiritual strength. White people and white sources have attached the label devious to black women's personality. Thus the Eve characterization of deviousness assigned to black women belongs more to white interpretations of black women than to black women's interpretation of their own reality. Most black people would apparently agree with the late George Jackson, who said, "The Black woman has in the past few hundred years been the only force holding us [the Black race] together and holding us up."[65]

Just as the Hagar-in-the-wilderness symbolism helps us see models of black womanhood in a new way, it also helps us gain more insight about America's historic way of governing the African-American community and about the resistance strategies black women and the black community have used to oppose oppression.

### Political Importance of Symbolism: Survival and Resistance

One of the constituent ideas in the Hagar-in-the-wilderness symbolism is Hagar's, black women's and black people's encounter with the threat—and often actuality—of death-dealing circumstances. Alone in the wilderness, pregnant on one occasion and alone with her son in the wilderness on the other occasion, Hagar and child surely would have died had not God intervened. Threatening death and destruction historically has been one of the ways oppressive power structures in America have effected the social control of the African-American community.

For the African-American woman, the wilderness experience—a sojourn in the wide world to find survival resources for self and children—has often involved mourning the death of her children. The end has not been caused by their starvation. Rather, it has been caused by the systematic effort of the

State and some of its white supporters to discourage black progress by a form of destruction African Americans are today labeling genocide. In the large inner-city communities—Harlem, Bedford Stuyvesant, Philadelphia, Detroit and others—many black people are charging that white power structures in America are, and have been through the ages, committing genocide upon black people and their communities.

Recently I heard a Harlem, New York, woman describe what she called "genocide American style." She said,

> You close off opportunities for people through inadequate and inappropriate education, which therefore renders them unemployed and unemployable. You take away their housing and they become beggars on the street. You give them a historical memory of organized white violence breaking into their communities and killing them at will, and the courts not prosecuting white violence against black people. You constantly harass them through police brutality. (Remember the Rodney King incident in California?) You make sure the people in the community cannot accumulate wealth because you shut off their access to financing and to borrowing power from banks. You introduce a system of welfare that breaks up the home and devalues black fatherhood. You control the media so that black people are projected as criminals and the general public gets the idea that black people are morally depraved. You make sure their communities look poor, rundown, and dirty because the city does not clean the streets very often; the dilapidated property in the area is owned by slum landlords (usually wealthy white people). In other words, you render black people hopeless. Then you make available in their communities, in cheap and plentiful supply, what it takes to destroy them—drugs. Black people do not have the money to bring drugs into this country and control the distribution of them—that has to be done by wealthy white people. Hopeless, black people in the poverty-stricken communities take the drugs and gradually destroy themselves. American power structures can then say "black people did it to themselves; they committed suicide." Therefore, the charge of genocide is not made against the State, even though the State has been one of the chief architects of black hopelessness and death.

Though the above definition comes from the grass roots, there are others equally significant. In *Axis Rule in Occupied Europe* Raphael Lemkin, who coined the term genocide, spoke of "a composite of different acts of persecution or destruction" constituting genocide. According to sociologists Chalk's and Jonassohn's account of Lemkin's view, genocide means

> attacks on political and social institutions, culture, language, national feelings, religion, and the economic existence of the group. Even non-lethal acts that undermine the liberty, dignity and personal security of members of a group constitute genocide if they contributed to weakening the viability of the group. Under Lemkin's definition, acts of eth-nocide—a term coined by the French after the war [World War II] to cover the destruction of a culture without the killing of its bearers—also qualified as genocide.[66]

However, of ultimate importance for our discussion is the definition of genocide provided in Article II of the Genocide Convention adopted by the United Nations on December 9, 1948. The adoption of this definition by the UN provided the occasion for African Americans, in 1951, to present a petition to the Fifth Session of the General Assembly of the UN meeting in Paris, charging the United States with genocide in relation to African Americans. Entitled "We Charge Genocide," this petition was also simultaneously submitted by Paul Robeson to the office of the Secretary General of the UN in New York City.[67] The convention designated the following acts as genocide:

1. killing members of a group;
2. causing serious bodily or mental harm to members of the group;
3. deliberately inflicting on the group conditions of life calculated to bring about its physical destruction in whole or in part;
4. imposing measures intended to prevent births within the group;
5. forcibly transferring children of the group to another group.[68]

The petition "We Charge Genocide" provided convincing evidence to show that the character of black people's oppression in America fit every item of the description the UN had given of genocide. The petition showed how lynching of Negroes in the South constituted "killing members of the group." The names and circumstances were given of masses of black victims who had been persecuted in the South from 1945 to 1951. The petition listed names of many innocent black men and women who had suffered serious bodily and mental harm because of the brutality they received at the hands of policemen, law officers and mobs of white people. Economic exploitation, poor health care delivery, ghetto living and disease-breeding housing were some of the evidence given to support the claim that conditions were deliberately inflicted upon the group to weaken its viability. Though black Americans presented an appealing, convincing and well-documented case against the United States, "the UN did not respond to the Petition"—regardless of the fact that Article IV of the UN-adopted genocide convention claimed that persons committing genocide would be punished.[69]

This petition was not the first time the lynching of black people was brought to the attention of the public. In the late nineteenth century a black woman Ida Wells-Barnett devoted much of her life and work to monitoring lynchings. Wells-Barnett reported that in the last three decades of the nineteenth century, "more than ten thousand Negroes have been killed in cold blood, without the formality of judicial trial and legal execution...and for all these murders only three white men have been tried, convicted, and executed."[70] Organizations like the Ku Klux Klan and the Regulators came to life and orchestrated murders to prohibit ex-slaves and all black people from gaining power through their new freedom to exercise the vote.[71]

The definitions of genocide provided by the Harlem woman, by Raphael Lemkin and by the United Nations have a firm point of agreement in their contention that genocide involves inflicting conditions that weaken the viability of the group. Attempting to destroy the cultural identity of black Americans; destroying the language of the African slaves; attacking African-American leaders; preventing the formation of institutions in the community; trying to destroy the national feelings of African Americans; destroying the economic existence of the group—all of this amounts to weakening the viability of the black American community. This aspect of the definition brings to light the fact that black people have experienced genocide during every phase of their history in America. And this kind of genocide has been directly caused or indirectly condoned by the State.

When Africans were brought to these shores as slaves, the fabric of their cultures and their languages was attacked. Much was destroyed. Terribly brutal penalties were imposed upon any slaves caught trying to preserve their African culture and African language.[72] Even the bodies of slaves were not exempt from attack; they were used in medical experiments. Maude White Katz reports an advertisement for sick and disabled slaves made by doctors and medical colleges. According to Katz, the catalogue of a medical college in South Carolina included this paragraph:

> No place in the United States offers as great opportunities for the acquisition of medical knowledge, subjects being obtained from among the colored population in sufficient number for every purpose, and

proper dissections carried on without offending any individuals in the community.[73]

Further, Katz reports that a "Dr. Stillman of Charleston, South Carolina, kept a standing notice in the *Charleston Mercury* similar to that which appeared in the medical catalogue." Dr. Stillman's advertisement was directed to

> planters and others. Wanted, fifty negroes. Any person having sick negroes, considered incurable by their respective physicians, and wishing to dispose of them. Dr. Stillman will pay cash for negroes affected with scrofula or King's evil, confirmed hypochondriacism, apoplexy, diseases of the liver, kidneys, spleen, stomach, and intestines, bladder and its appendages, diarrhea, dysentery, etc. The highest cash price will be paid on application as above.[74]

Not only black bodies, but also black minds have been affected by this American way of trying to weaken the viability of the black community. America's public educational systems have, through the years, made African-American history and culture invisible by keeping them out of the schools' curricula and educational materials, including text books. The presence of the models of achievement bearing black history and culture is minimized by racist hiring practices of boards of education and by racist admission policies of institutions of higher education preparing teachers. Making blacks invisible has been one of the primary tools white power structures use to attack the minds and identity of African Americans. Black school children get no sense of their group's contributions to the nation's history and culture. This destroys children's self-esteem and their ability to imagine themselves as achievers.

The attack upon the *black* nationalist feelings of black people by white power structures was obvious in the early twentieth century in the way the American government dealt with Marcus Garvey and the Universal Negro Improvement Association he headed. Garvey was ultimately imprisoned and the association, which once numbered in the thousands throughout America, lost a lot of its strength. Garvey had successfully planned the moving of masses of black people out of America into Africa. He had obtained ships to execute the move. Had this been allowed to materialize, the foundation of the American capitalist economy would have been severely weakened, because black people constitute that base. As with the lynchings in the South, white power trumped up enough charges (which most black people questioned) to justify the attack upon Garvey and his organization. In more recent times other black organizations that enlarged black nationalistic feelings, especially in the area of counter-cultural politics and economics, have been systematically destroyed. One such organization was the Black Panther Party, which flourished in the African-American communities during the 1960s and 1970s.

A relevant question that has circulated for years among some black people is this: Why is it that when honest, charismatic black leaders emerge who are helping black people obtain a securer life and a more prosperous future in America, they get harassed, run out of town or assassinated? There has been no forum in the community to deal with this question. But perhaps there is truth in the black-folk observation that the American government's unwritten policy regarding black leadership is that the leaders either get bought or get buried. Martin Luther King, Jr., and Malcolm X could not be bought; they were buried. Throughout their careers as leaders, both men were harassed by federal and local law agents. In fact, harassment is still in vogue as a way for the government to try to control black leadership. In the June–July 1992 issue of the NAACP's *Crisis* magazine, David Hatchett reveals the involvement of federal law enforcement officials in the harassment of black politicians today.[75] Hatchett reminds the reader that this kind of harassment has been happening since the end of Reconstruction after the Civil War in the nineteenth century. He reports that "many authorities say that history is repeating itself as black political leaders today are under an assault no less intense than that which swamped black political power 100 years ago."[76]

### Black Women's Resistance Activity

African-American women have not been passive in the face of the threat of destruction and death. The Hagar-in-the-wilderness symbolism directs attention to African-American women's history of resistance, which has been especially rich from the time of slavery until this very day. Like the slave woman Hagar, many African-American slave women had belligerent attitudes expressed in the numerous slave insurrections they instigated. And they were not afraid to let their religion express itself in the rebellious action they caused. Maude White Katz reports that "the Negro women were considered troublemakers on the plantations. On many plantations they kept the rest of the slaves in the state of unrest." She says, "There was a plantation where the slaves refused to work because an old slave called Sinda made a prophecy that on a certain day the world would come to an end."[77]

Almost from the day when they first arrived as slaves in America in 1619, African-American women have rebelled against their plight. They have used a variety of resistance strategies, some subtle and silent, others more dramatic. They petitioned courts for the freedom of themselves and their children; they were accused of burning buildings and of attempting to poison their owners. Like Hagar, they ran away from slavery. They participated with slave men in conspiracies and insurrections. They killed their children to keep them from a life of enslavement. They passed on doctrines of resistance to their children. Consider these rebellious incidents by black women:

- in 1675 a slave woman named Angell petitioned a Virginia court for her freedom because her master promised her she would be free at his death. This freedom did not materialize, so she sued. The court rejected the appeal.
- Jenny Slew, a slave in Massachusetts, sued her owner because he was unlawfully holding her in slavery; finally she won her case, was set free, and her owner was ordered to pay her nine pounds.
- "A slave woman in Kentucky was sentenced to death for 'mixing an ounce of pounded glass with gravy' which was intended for her master and mistress."[78]
- In 1775 a slave woman in Cambridge, Massachusetts, was burned alive "for participating in a plot to poison her master."[79]
- "Negro women seemed to have fanned the flames of revolt in Massachusetts with their resistance to slavery before the Revolution in 1776. Maria, a slave...[in]...Roxbury [Massachusetts],... was sentenced to death by burning on a charge of incendiarism."[80]
- "The chief conspirator in the plot to burn down Charleston, Massachusetts, was a [slave] woman named Kate."[81]
- "A mother on a Georgia plantation killed thirteen of her babies to save them from slavery."[82]
- Two women, Lucy and Charlotte, participated in the revolt led by Nat Turner in Southampton County, Virginia, in 1831.

In their resistance activity slave women's persistence was often uncanny. The following notice posted by a slave owner promises

> $50.00 REWARD. Ran away from the subscriber on the 27th of March ... A Negro woman named Sarah, about 6 feet high and very slim. . . .

Sarah is the biggest devil that ever lived, having poisoned a stud horse and set a stable on fire, also burnt Gen. R. Williams stable and stock yard with seven horses and other property to the value of $1500. She was handcuffed and got away at Ruddles Mills on her way down the river, which is the fifth time she escaped when about to be sent out of the country.[83]

An ex-slave woman told of the doctrine of resistance passed on to her by her slave mother, who refused to be whipped by slave owners. The daughter claimed that

with all her ability to work, she [the slave mother] did not make a good slave. She was too high spirited and independent. The one doctrine of my mother's teaching which was branded upon my senses was that I should never let anyone abuse me.[84]

The heart of the slave mother's doctrine of resistance was this: "Fight, and if you can't fight, kick; if you can't kick, then bite."[85]

After slavery, during Reconstruction, black women continued to manifest a strong resistance posture. Katz tells of an incident in 1876 when an effort was made to steal the vote of the freedmen at an election poll. Black women made a plan to resist this. They filled their aprons with shavings and matches and threatened to set the town on fire. This settled the matter. They followed this course of action again when adversaries threatened to kill a government inspector at the polls. Katz says, "A natural outcome of her political activities was that a Negro woman was the first to cast a ballot in the state of Mississippi [after the Civil War]. Her name was Lucy Tapley."[86]

Since Reconstruction, the black civil rights struggle in America has also been fueled by the bold resistance activity of African-American women. According to Charles Payne's reports about civil rights work in the Mississippi Delta during the 1960s, "Men led, but women organized. . . . Women canvassed more than men, showed up more often at mass meetings and demonstrations, and more frequently attempted to register to vote."[87] Payne accounts for this large-scale participation of black women by the fact that the Mississippi civil rights movement was initiated and supported by the black church. And the church population is from 85 to 90 percent female.

The uncanny stamina of these women was certainly based in what the church provides in the way of sisterhood and community. They themselves describe the source of their courage in the language of black women's faith:

Lou Emma Allen...was often afraid...[but] she was sure the Lord would see her through....Susie Morgan...prayed and prayed over the decision to join [the movement in Mississippi] and finally she saw it was what the Lord wanted her to do....Ethel Gray...[experienced] rattle-snakes...[thrown on her porch by people driving by]. She testified, "We stood up. Me and God stood up."[88]

The similarities between these women's plight and faith and Hagar's is striking. Like Lou Emma Allen, Hagar must have been afraid in the wilderness, pregnant and alone. Like Susie Morgan, Hagar had a word with God, and radical obedience was her response to God's will. Like Ethel Gray, Hagar suffered indignities and abuse from those who had more power than she did, but she defied them by resisting their authority over her movements. These Mississippi women and Hagar had their wilderness experience of courage, fear, aloneness, meeting God and obeying God's will for transformations in their lives. Finally, all the women and Hagar could testify, "Me and God stood up."

# PART II

# WOMANIST GOD-TALK

## Chapter 6

# WOMANIST GOD-TALK AND
# BLACK LIBERATION THEOLOGY

Using some of the issues from the biblical Hagar-Sarah stories as models, the preceding chapters have shown the fabric of Hagar's and African-American women's experience designed by their exploitation, by their faith in God, by positive and negative human relationships and reactions, by motherhood, by fierce survival struggles and by resistance strategies. We have seen how social processes in the African-American community and the Anglo-American community affected black women's lives. We have seen how black women often used their religion to cope with and transform the negative character of some of these processes. We have also seen a collective aspect of black women's experience determined by their shared life-situation with black men in conditions of oppression and in the formation of community symbols.

Now we must determine the theological yield of this womanist focus upon black women's and Hagar's experience. Inasmuch as womanist theology is dialogical in the black community first we pose the question: What does the womanist analysis in this book have to say to black liberation theology? There are at least three areas in which womanist theology can dialogue with black liberation theology: theological method, certain areas of Christian doctrine and ethics. New ethical tasks are identified when black theology takes African-American women's experience seriously.

### Theological Methodology

Much of the womanist analysis in this book raises methodological issues that either enlarge upon or challenge the methodological perspectives contained in some of black liberation theology. The methodological issues with which we will be concerned are the use of the Bible, the understanding and function of experience in black liberation theology and the notion of the theological task in the same theology.

### *The Bible and Black Liberation Theology*

A womanist rereading of the biblical Hagar-Sarah texts in relation to African-American women's experience raises a serious question about the biblical witness. The question is about its use as a source validating black liberation theology's normative claim of God's liberating activity in behalf of *all* the oppressed. James Cone asserts that

> the biblical witness...says...God is a God of liberation, who speaks to the oppressed and abused and assures them...divine righteousness will vindicate their suffering...[and that] it is the Bible that tells us that God became human in Jesus Christ so that the kingdom of God would make freedom a reality for all human beings.[1]

The Hagar-Sarah texts in Genesis and Galatians, however, demonstrate that the oppressed and abused do not always experience God's liberating power. If one reads the Bible identifying with the non-Hebrews who are female and male slaves ("the oppressed of the oppressed"), one quickly discerns a non-liberative thread running through the Bible. In the Genesis stories about Hagar and Sarah, God seems to be (as some Palestinian Christians today suggest about the God of the Hebrew testament) "partial and discriminating."[2] God is clearly partial to Sarah. Regardless of the way one interprets God's command to Hagar to submit herself to Sarah, God does not liberate her. In Exodus God does not outlaw slavery. Rather, the male slave can be part of Israel's rituals, possibly because he has no control over his body as Hagar had no control over her body. Thus "the Lord said to Moses and Aaron, 'this is the ordinance of the passover: no foreigner shall eat of it; but every slave that is bought for money may eat of it after you have circumcised him' " (Exodus 12:43–44);[3] but "no sojourner or hired servant may eat of it" (12:45). The sojourner and hired servant can refuse to be circumcised, but the slave cannot because the slave master owns the slave's body.

In the covenant code (Exodus 20:22–23:33) God identifies the rights of the Hebrew male slave. After six years of enslavement, the male slave gets his freedom in the seventh year. God does not object to Hebrew men selling their daughters as slaves. But the daughters shall not be given their freedom (except under special circumstances) as the male slaves are. God says the slave's wife (if given him by his master) and his children belong to the slave master. Therefore, even if the slave husband is emancipated, the slave wife and her children remain in bondage. The only way the family can stay together is for the father to remain a slave.

In the holiness codes (for example, Leviticus 19) God's commandments to the people of Israel show differences God makes with regard to slave women. Leviticus 19:20–22 states, "If a man lies carnally with a woman who is a slave, betrothed to another man and not yet ransomed or given her freedom, an inquiry shall be held." The text says, "They shall not be put to death, because she was not free; but he shall bring a guilt offering for himself to the Lord, to the door of the tent of meeting, a ram for a guilt offering." Further, "The priest shall make atonement for him with the ram of the guilt offering before the Lord for his sin which he has committed; and the sin which he has committed shall be forgiven." The suggestion here is that the law regards a slave woman and a free woman differently. If the man had slept with a free woman, they both would have been put to death. "The reason for this legal clemency is that the slave-woman is regarded as another man's property, i.e., his concubine."[4] He is guilty because he has "sinned against" another man, not because he has cohabited with the slave woman. Slave women are not as valuable under the law as free women.

While God tells ancient Israelites that "if your brother becomes poor beside you, and sells himself to you, you shall not make him serve as a slave" (Leviticus 25:39), God also says, "you may buy male and female slaves from among the nations that are around about you . . . you may bequeath them to your sons after you, to inherit as a possession for ever; you may make slaves of them, but over your brethren the people of Israel you shall not rule one over the other, with harshness" (Leviticus 25:46).

Later renderings of the law in Deuteronomy with regard to slaves also stress lenient treatment for the Hebrew slave. And run-away slaves should not be returned to their masters (Deuteronomy 23:15); they must be given asylum and are not to be oppressed. There is no indication in the text whether "not to be oppressed" means not to be enslaved. In 1 Samuel 8:16 God tells the people of Israel, through Samuel, that the king will take the best of their male and female slaves and put them to work in his service. But God does not denounce these instances of enslavement. In Jeremiah 34:8–22 God tells the Israelites that "every one should set free his Hebrew slaves, male and female, so that no one should enslave a Jew." There is no mention of freedom for non-Jewish slaves.

The point here is that when non-Jewish people (like many African-American women who now claim themselves to be economically enslaved) read the entire Hebrew testament from the point of view of the non-Hebrew slave, there is no clear indication that God is against their perpetual enslavement. Likewise, there is no clear opposition expressed in the Christian testament to the institution of slavery. Whatever may be the reasons why Paul advises slaves to obey their masters and bids Onesimus, the slave, to return to his master and later advises the master to free Onesimus, he does not denounce the institution of slavery. The fact remains: slavery in the Bible is a natural and unprotested institution in the social and economic life of ancient society—except on occasion when the Jews are themselves enslaved. One wonders how biblically derived messages of liberation can be taken seriously by today's masses of poor, homeless African Americans, female and male, who consider themselves to be experiencing a form of slavery—economic enslavement by the capitalistic American economy. They may consider themselves outside the boundaries of sedentary, "civilized" American culture.

Womanist theologians, especially those who take their slave heritage seriously, are therefore led to question James Cone's assumption that the African-American theologian can today make *paradigmatic* use of the Hebrews' exodus and election experience as recorded in the Bible. Even though Cone sees that for the Hebrews "election is inseparable from the event of the exodus," he does not see that non-Hebrew female slaves, especially those of African descent, are not on equal terms with the Hebrews and are not woven into this biblical story of election and exodus.[5] One might agree with Cone that Jesus had liberation of the oppressed on his mind when he was reported to have said,

> The Spirit of the Lord is upon me, because he has anointed me to preach good news to the poor. He has sent me to proclaim release to the captives and recovering of sight to the blind, to set at liberty those who are oppressed, to proclaim the acceptable year of the Lord. (Luke 4:18–19)

But the non-Jewish person of slave descent may question what Jesus had in mind in Matthew 10:5–6, where he is reported to have charged his disciples, saying, "Go nowhere among the Gentiles, and enter no town of the Samaritans, but go rather to the lost sheep of the house of Israel." This suggests a kind of bias against the non-Jew that accords well with Paul's way of situating Hagar, the female slave, and her progeny outside the promise of freedom he describes in Galatians 5.[6] Biblical scholars may give various interpretations of the Matthew 10 texts derived from their historical critical or literary critical methodology. Nevertheless, the non-liberative strand in the Bible and the tension it apparently places upon black liberation theology's norm for interpreting scripture (i.e., God's liberating action on behalf of all the oppressed) make it difficult to understand how the Bible can function today in the way that James Cone suggests: "It matters little to the oppressed who authored scripture; what is important is whether it can serve as a weapon against oppressors."[7] Equivocal messages and/or silence about God's liberating power on behalf of non-Hebrew, female slaves of African descent do not make effective weapons for African Americans to use in "wars" against oppressors.

Though there may be problems with his view of the overwhelmingly liberative work of God demonstrated in the Bible in relation to *all* the oppressed, James Cone is right to emphasize the significance of the community of faith for influencing the way the community's theologians use the Bible. He reminds the reader that "the theologian brings to the scripture the perspective of a community," and

> ideally the concern of that community is consistent with the concern of the community that gave us the scriptures. It is the task of theology to keep these two communities (biblical and contemporary) in constant tension in order that we may be able to speak meaningfully about God.[8]

Cone's use of the word *ideally* suggests that such consistency might not always be able to be maintained, and he is also right to suggest that the "reality" of the matter exists in the tensions. The African-American community's identification with the non-Hebrew, female slave Hagar (rather than with Abraham and Sarah), is not consistent with the community that gave us the scriptures. Yet the African-American community has also seen a relation between its life of bondage and that of the ancient Israelites in Egypt. At this point the consistency between the two communities is maintained. Black people, and black liberation theologians, have in this instance identified strongly with the Hebrews and not with other people whom the former slaves (the Israelites) are reported to have destroyed, like the Canaanites.[9]

However, black theologians—in order to present a true rendering of the faith of the African-American Christian community—must not be concerned only about the tensions between the contemporary black community and the biblical community. They must also reveal the tensions in the community's faith, so that the African-American Christian community can become aware of how these tensions affect its theology and life. The community will see, on the basis of its way of appropriating the scripture, that it expresses belief in a God who liberates (the God of the enslaved Hebrews) and a God who does not liberate (the God of the non-Hebrew female slave Hagar). It may be that spasmodic participation of the African-American denominational churches in the African-American struggle for social change stems as much from unconscious tensions in their faith as from the growing bourgeois attitude of many of their congregations.

If black liberation theology wants to include black women and speak in behalf of the most oppressed black people today—the poor homeless, jobless, economically "enslaved" women, men and children sleeping on American streets, in bus stations, parks and alleys—theologians must ask themselves some questions. Have they, in the use of the Bible, identified so thoroughly with the theme of Israel's election that they have not seen the oppressed of the oppressed in scripture? Have they identified so completely with Israel's liberation that they have been blind to the awful reality of victims making victims in the Bible? Does this kind of blindness with regard to non-Hebrew victims in the scripture also make it easy for black male theologians and biblical scholars to ignore the figures in the Bible whose experience is analogous to that of black women?[10]

This study suggests that if black liberation theologians want to respond to these questions about black liberation theology's bias against black women, they must assume an additional hermeneutical posture—one that allows them to become conscious of what has been made invisible in the text and to see that their work is in collusion with this "invisibilization" of black women's experience. Therefore, in the use of scripture theologians should initially engage a womanist hermeneutic of *identification-ascertainment* that involves three modes of inquiry: subjective, communal and objective. Through an analysis of their own faith journey with regard to its biblical foundations, theologians discover with whom and with what events they personally identify in scripture. Through an analysis of the biblical foundation of the faith journey of the Christian community with which they are affiliated, Christian theologians determine the biblical faith, events and biblical characters with whom the community has identified. Biblical aspects of the community's faith-journey are revealed in sermons, songs, testimonies by the people, liturgy, ritual and in its socio-political-cultural affiliations in the world. This subjective and communal analysis acquaints theologians with the biases they bring to the interpretation of scripture. Then theologians engage the objective mode of inquiry that ascertains *both* the biblical events, characters and circumstances with whom the biblical writers have identified *and* those with whom the biblical writers have not identified, that is, those who are victims of those with whom the biblical writers have identified.

By engaging this womanist hermeneutic of *identification-ascertainment,* black liberation theologians will be able to see the junctures at which they and the community need to be critical of their way of using the Bible. Engaging this hermeneutic also allows black theologians to see at what point they must be critical of the biblical text itself, in those instances where the text supports oppression, exclusion and even death of innocent people.

Womanist theologians, in concert with womanist biblical scholars, need to show the African-American denominational churches and black liberation theology the liability of its habit of using the Bible in an uncritical and sometimes too self-serving way. This kind of usage has prohibited the community from seeing that the end result of the biblical exodus event, begun in the book of Exodus, was the violent destruction of a whole nation of people, the Canaanites, described in the book of Joshua. Black liberation theologians today should reconceptualize what it means to lift up uncritically the biblical exodus *event* as a major paradigm for black theological reflection. To respond to the current issues in the black community, theologians should reflect upon exodus from Egypt as *holistic story* rather than *event.* This would allow the community to see the exodus as an extensive reality involving several kinds of events before its completion in the genocide of the Canaanites and the taking of their land. The community would see the violence involved in a liberation struggle supposedly superintended by God.

In the exodus story there are the violent acts of God against Israel's oppressors, the Egyptians. There is the pre-exodus event of the Hebrews obtaining economic resources (reparations?) from the Egyptians before they left Egypt. There is God's violence against the Egyptians as they attempted to subdue the Israelites crossing the Red Sea. There are the violent acts of the Hebrews, sanctioned by God, as they killed every person in the land of Jericho except Rahab and her family. God is supposed to have sanctioned genocide in the land of Makkedah, in Libnah and in the Promised Land of Canaan. This kind of reflection upon exodus as a holistic story rather than as one event allows black theologians to show the black community the awful models of God projected when the community and theologians use the Bible so that only Israel's or the Hebrews' understanding of God becomes normative for the black community's understanding of how God relates to its life. On the basis of this holistic story, the black community and black theologians must explore the moral status of violence in *scripture* when the violence is mandated and/or supported by God.

What is suggested here is *not* that black theologians in their use of scripture ignore the fact of black people's identification with the exodus of the Israelites from Egypt. This is part of African-American Christian history and should be remembered by the community. Neither do I mean to suggest that black theologians should refrain from referring to the texts in the book of Exodus and to Jesus' words in Luke 4 in ways that are meaningful for the exposition of the gospel in our time. Nor should liberation language and liberation ideas be lost to black theology. However, I suggest that African-American theologians should make it clear to the community that this black way of identifying with God *solely* through the exodus of the Hebrews and Jesus' reported words in Luke belongs to the black historical period of American slavery. Apparently this was the time when God's liberation of the Israelites or the exodus was the subject and "predicate" of the biblical ideas undergirding African-American Christian theology. Such is not the case today. To build contemporary systematic theology only on the exodus and Luke paradigm is to ignore generations of black history subsequent to slavery—that is, to consign the community and the black theological imagination to a kind of historical stalemate that denies the possibility of change with regard to the people's experience of God and with regard to the possibility of God changing in relation to the community. Obviously I do not agree with Cecil Cone's argument that "the post–Civil War black religious expressions are grounded in the same black religious experience as the pre–Civil War expressions."[11] By not qualifying this statement, Cone suggests that black religious experience has not changed since slavery.

However, I cannot deny that exodus has been a prevalent theme in African-American history. After slavery, when some blacks fled oppression in the South and went into new western territory, they were called the Exodusters. Through his Universal Negro Improvement Association, Marcus Garvey advocated a kind of exodus for Afro-Americans that would end in their return to Africa. And in the social revolution of the 1960s in America, black people used the language of liberation to voice their discontent. But it may be difficult to prove that the biblical model of the Hebrews' exodus out of Egypt or that Jesus' words in Luke were a guide for the actions of all these groups.

Pointing out these problems with the use of the Bible in black liberation theology might also show theologians that in order to respond to the tensions in African-American faith and to suggest woman-inclusive correctives, they might have to rely upon non-Christian and non-Jewish sources to interpret texts and shape their talk about the community's understanding of how God relates to its life. Some black theologians have intimated that African sources might be helpful for shedding light on the way the African-American Christian community's African heritage has historically informed its understanding of God's relation to its life. Theologian Cecil Cone makes this kind of suggestion when he claims that the primary sources of black religion are "the African tradition, the American experience of slavery, biblical Christianity."[12] Then, in his discussion of the African-American slave's use of scripture, Cone says,

> The slaves' appropriation of the Bible was made easier by the fact that certain parts of Scripture, especially in the Old Testament, were in keeping with the slave's African religious tradition. Slaves already possessed the concept of a Supreme Being who created, sustained, and ruled the world. This meant, of course, that the Old Testament's Almighty Sovereign God did not seem unfamiliar to him. What this God did for the children of Israel was in harmony with the slaves' own understanding of the divine. Gradually through this conversion of Christianity, slaves accepted and utilized the Bible as one of the sources of black religion.[13]

This certainly suggests that for a more precise understanding of the African concept of Supreme Being that slaves may have brought with them, theologians should consult sources dealing with the religions of West Africa during the slave period in America. These sources could also help in the interpretation of scripture.

As the scholarship of Cain Hope Felder and Robert Bennett has shown, there is much to be gained by using such sources to enlighten our understanding of the place of Africa in the Bible. Black people can begin to see their roots in the biblical story. The rereading of the Hagar-Sarah text in this study shows how the work of the Egyptologists helps us enlarge our understanding of who Hagar might have been. Though African Americans have a long way to go in shaping their understanding of Hagar, they are encouraged to believe that the use of non-Christian and non-Jewish sources in biblical interpretation can provide insights that help black theologians speak more meaningfully about African roots and Christian gospel. But these African sources will be of little value to African-American theologians if they are basically androcentric and female-exclusive.

Equally as important as the use of the Bible in black liberation theology is the issue of the nature and function of experience. Something called the black experience is the point of departure for the anthropology in the liberation theology focused upon in this study. An African-American cultural designation for the character of black existence in the United States, the black experience is a controlling influence in the design of James Cone's systematic theology. By reviewing the understanding of black experience in the works of James and Cecil Cone and James Deotis Roberts, we begin to see the limitations of this naming of experience as far as black women are concerned. When we bring the insights of the preceding chapter regarding the wilderness experience into relation with the notions of the black experience in black liberation theology, we begin to see how the introduction of black women's experience expands our knowledge of the character of black people's existence in North America.

### *Black Experience, Wilderness Experience, Theological Task*[14]

The works of the black liberation theologians used in this study agree that racial oppression helped create what they refer to as the black experience. Black liberation theology presents blackness as an important qualitative, symbolic and sometimes sacred aspect of the black experience.[15] It portrays the experience as a holistic reality with four active constituents.

1. *The Horizontal Encounter.* This is interaction between black and white groups in a socio-historical context. The interaction results in negative and/or positive relationships and sociopolitical situations. Most often the encounter between blacks and whites is described negatively in black liberation theology. From this encounter, suffering has become a characteristic of African-American community life.

2. *The Vertical Encounter.* In this category black liberation theologians speak of the meeting between God and oppressed people. This meeting not only results in the creation of sustaining and nurturing cultural forms, like black religion, but the oppressed also achieve positive psychological and physical states of freedom and liberation.

3. *Transformations of Consciousness.* These can occur in both a positive and negative sense. They are positive when oppressed people arrive at self- or group-identity through awareness of self-worth and through the appreciation of the value of black people and black culture. Transformations of consciousness are negative when black people give up positive black consciousness and identify with alien and destructive forms of consciousness.

4. *An Epistemological Process.* This is a special way the mind processes data on the basis of action in the three categories above. The socio-

historical context plays an important role in this process. (Theologian James Cone emphasizes the significance of this process for the black theological task.)

In their various writings, black liberation theologians discuss the black experience in accord with the effects of one or more of these active constituents. On the basis of negative effects in horizontal encounters, in his early works James Cone describes the black experience

as a life of humiliation and suffering...the totality of black existence in a white world where babies are tortured, women are raped and men are shot. The black experience is existence in a system of white racism.[16]

Relying on the creators of black art for part of his understanding of the social effects of horizontal encounters between black and white people, Cone recalls the poet Don Lee's claim that the black experience refers concretely to black people sleeping in subways, "being bitten by rats, six people living in a kitchenette."[17] In his later work Cone recognized a redeeming character of this experience when he describes black people, in the midst of hostile relationships, trying to shape life and "to live it according to their dreams and aspirations."[18]

James Deotis Roberts, on the other hand, alludes to the black experience in terms of the positive and negative effects of the horizontal encounter between black and white people. He expresses an "appreciation for the Euro-American contributions to black culture in this country."[19] Nevertheless, Roberts communicates his understanding of the black experience as a negative sociopolitical reality where dehumanizing relationships exist between black and white people.

While the history and character of black/white relations are important, the Cones and Roberts suggest that the vertical encounter between God and humans constitutes the most salient feature of the black experience. This encounter occurs in history and empowers black people to transform negative, oppressive social forces into positive life-sustaining forms. Theologian Cecil Cone most graphically describes the powerful action in this encounter. He emphasizes the positive psychological benefits black slaves derived from meeting God:

The power of God...provided creative possibilities in a noncreative situation. Recognition of one's sinfulness was merely the first step in the dynamics of the black religious experience. It was followed by what has commonly been known in black religion as saving conversion. The character of conversion was marked by the suddenness with which the slave's heart was changed. It was an abrupt change in his entire orientation toward reality; it affected every aspect of the slave's attitudes and beliefs. . . . The new level of reality . . . caused the slaves to experience a sense of freedom in the midst of human bondage.[20]

On the basis of this encounter and the ensuing conversion, many slaves gained strength to oppose the social and political structures enslaving black people. Cecil Cone cites black slave preachers (Nat Turner, Denmark Vesey, Gabriel Prosser) who connected their slave rebellions with their encounters with God. Richard Allen, another slave, gained strength in his encounter with God and proceeded with his efforts to establish the African Methodist Episcopal Church.

While Cecil Cone suggests that the God-human encounter conditions black experience, James Deotis Roberts suggests that black experience is affected by certain transformations in black consciousness. James Cone emphasizes a special epistemological process as foundational for the black experience. Roberts declares that knowledge of the transformations in black consciousness is vital for understanding god-talk in the black community. He says the theologians can choose how to interpret the black experience, but they are obligated to show the character of black consciousness transformed so that the black person "moves from color blindness to color consciousness" and becomes aware of the implications of Black Power.[21]

Transformations of consciousness, horizontal and vertical encounters and epistemological processes happen in a socio-historical context. Hence the socio-historical context of actions and ideas is important in black liberation theology. In accord with a sociology of knowledge perspective, James Cone claims that consciousness is created by the social context, and so epistemological realities are different for black and white people. Therefore, black theologians and white theologians have different mental grids. For Cone, "the social environment functions as a mental grid deciding what will be considered as relevant data in a given inquiry."[22] These different mental grids determine the sources and the method each theologian uses in the construction of theological statements.

Apparently Cone is suggesting an epistemological screening process created by a people's history, cultural patterns, political realities, socioreligious values and patterns of action. This mental grid becomes a way of knowing which determines modes of action. On the basis of James Cone's discussion of the social context of theology, it is obvious that the black experience—with its horizontal encounters, vertical encounters and transformations of consciousness—is also an epistemological screen through which black people perceive, respond to and help create their reality.

For James Cone, James Deotis Roberts and Cecil Cone, the black experience determines the task of black theology. However, each of these theologians emphasizes a different aspect of this experience in his understanding of the theological task. James Cone emphasizes the church's vertical encounter with God in relation to God's liberating work in the world. Theology concerns revelation, and revelation is described as "the liberating character of God's presence in Jesus Christ as he calls his people into being for freedom in the world."[23] The task of theology is confessional, for the theologian (as exegete, prophet, teacher, preacher and philosopher) must clarify the church's faith in relation to its participation in God's liberating activity in the world.

James Deotis Roberts suggests that the theological task involves healing the negative relations in horizontal encounters. Thus theologians must minister to both blacks and whites. They speak the message of liberation to the victims of oppression. Yet, if theologians speak the Christian message, they must speak reconciliation regardless of the risks and the personal costs.

Cecil Cone apparently understands the theological task not only to involve the black theologian's attempt to acquaint the community with the meaning at the heart of black religion, that is, the community's radical encounter in history with the "almighty sovereign God." Since, for Cecil Cone, "Black religion is . . . [the] only appropriate point of departure" for black theology, the task of black theologians is also to explicate this religion so that all of its dimensions are seen and understood by the community. Of special importance is the theologians' task of emphasizing and assessing the conversion experience, which results from black people's encounter with the almighty sovereign God.[24] Thus Cecil Cone also stresses the vertical encounter in relation to the black theological task.

This notion of black experience and the theological tasks associated with it are determined by the black liberation theologians' view of black history. James Cone, Cecil Cone and James Deotis Roberts, in the works used here, present the anthropological side of black history as a continuous social and political struggle between black and white people over the issues of enslavement and the dominance and prevalence of racial oppression in white-black relations. This struggle has informed the creation of black art, religion and culture. But language about the struggle assumes an androcentric black history. Therefore a masculine indication of person and masculine models of victimization dominate the language and thought of black liberation theology.[25] Therefore one can conclude, as theologian Jacqueline Grant did some years ago, that black women have been left out of black liberation theology and its understanding of historical agency.[26] The black experience and theological tasks described therein (as well as the view of history) presuppose and perpetuate black androcentrism.

Womanist analysis in the preceding chapters suggests another kind of history to which black theology must give attention if it intends to be inclusive of black women's experience. This is "women's re/production history." It involves more than women birthing children, nurturing and attending to family affairs. Though the events and ideas associated with these realities do relate, "women's re/production history" has to do with whatever women think, create, use and pass on through their labor for the sake of women's and the family's well-being. Thus black women's resistance strategies belong to black women's re/production history—just as the oppressive opposition to these strategies from dominating cultures belongs to this history. Through the lens of black women's re/production history we can see the entire saga of the race. We see the survival intelligence of the race creating modes of resistance, sustenance and resurrection from despair. We see the exploitation of the community's spiritual, material and intellectual resources by extra-community forces met by the uncanny, redemptive response of the religion black women created in the African-American denominational churches.

Black women's re/production history provides the context in which the black experience is appropriated as a female-and-male inclusive wilderness experience. The movement from black experience to wilderness experience expands the content and merges some of the categorical constituents described above as making up the notion of black experience reflected in black liberation theology. For example, the wilderness experience can also be said to be composed of horizontal encounters and vertical encounters. However, the content enlarges. Whereas the horizontal encounter in the black experience involved interaction "between black and white groups in a socio-historical context" and primarily presupposes encounters between males, in the wilderness experience the horizontal encounter presupposes female-male and female-female encounters. The black experience assumes that the suffering characteristic of the African-American community has resulted only from the horizontal encounter between blacks and whites. The wilderness experience suggests that this characteristic suffering has also resulted from black women's oppression in society and from the exploitation of black women in family contexts. Whereas the vertical encounter in the black experience in black liberation theology involves the meeting between God and oppressed people (read men) resulting in the creation of androcentric cultural forms and hierarchical relational patterns, the encounter between God and women in the wilderness experience does more than strengthen women's faith and empower them to persevere in spite of trouble. The meeting between God and enslaved women of African descent also provides these women with new vision to see survival resources where they saw none before.[27] And black women understand these resources to be for the sustenance of a family-centered rather than an androcentric or fema-centric black culture.

In the vertical encounter between black women and God in the wilderness experience, transformation of consciousness and epistemological process come together in the new great faith-consciousness this meeting bestows upon black women. This faith-consciousness guides black women's way of being and acting in the wide, wide world. Their stories tell of their absolute dependence upon God generated by a faith-consciousness incorporating survival intelligence and visionary capacity.[28] This survival intelligence and vision shape the strategies black women and the black community use to deal with or resist difficult life-situations and death-dealing circumstances.[29] Without this female faith-consciousness and its constituent parts basic to the African-American community's wilderness experience, black political history in America would be less rich and less productive.[30]

Hence, I suggest that in black theology today, the wilderness experience is a more appropriate name than the black experience to describe African-American existence in North America. This is so because:

1. wilderness experience is male/female/family-inclusive in its imagistic, symbolic and actual content; black experience has been described with an androcentric bias in theology, and its perimeters are narrowly racial;
2. wilderness experience is suggestive of the essential role of human initiative (along with divine intervention) in the activity of survival, of community building, of structuring a positive quality of life for family and community; it is also suggestive of human initiative in the work of liberation; black experience says very little about black initiative and responsibility in the community's struggle for liberation, and nothing

about internal tensions and intentions in community building and survival struggle;

3. wilderness experience is African-American religious experience that is simultaneously African-American secular experience; thus wilderness experience—especially in its symbolic dimension—signals the unity of the sacred and the secular in African-American reality; black experience does not function or signal this way;

4. indicating more than the negative reality the name black experience has come to typify in both the African-American and Anglo-American world, wilderness experience extends beyond being bitten by rats and living six people in a kitchenette; wilderness experience indicates female-male intelligence and ingenuity in the midst of struggle, creating a culture of resistance;

5. wilderness experience in its symbolic manifestation in African-American consciousness lifts up and supports leadership roles of African-American women and mothers;

6. in a Christian theological context wilderness-experience, more than black experience, provides an avenue for black liberation theologians, feminist theologians and womanist theologians to dialogue about the significance of wilderness in what each identifies as the biblical tradition most conducive to the work of his or her theological enterprise. While black liberation theologians lift up the exodus/ liberation tradition as foundational, they have forgotten to give serious attention to the wilderness experience in the exodus story, in which the ex-slaves grumbled against God and wanted not to bear responsibility for the work, consciousness and struggle associated with maintaining freedom. While some feminist theologians claim the prophetic tradition significant for the biblical foundations of feminist theology, they give little or no attention to the way in which the wilderness figures into the work of making the prophet and making a people. Womanist theologians can claim the biblical wilderness tradition as the foundation of their enterprise and as a route to discourse not only because Hagar's, black women's and black people's experiences with God gained dimension in the wilderness, but because the biblical wilderness tradition also emphasizes survival, quality of life formation with God's direction and the work of building a peoplehood and a community. Womanist theologians can invite feminist, black liberation and other interested theologians to engage with them in the exploration of the question:

What is God's word about survival and quality of life formation for oppressed and quasi-free people struggling to build community in the wilderness?

Womanist theology, as it takes woman-inclusive wilderness experience seriously, must examine the ways in which Christian doctrine affects black women. Though space will not allow more than a surface treatment of this issue in this book, it will serve our purposes to take a look at a few doctrinal realities in relation to black women's surrogacy experience, described at length earlier. Then we can consider the kind of dialogue this assessment causes us to have with black liberation theology on this matter of doctrine and black women.

### Doctrine: Surrogacy and Redemption

One of the results of focusing upon African-American women's historic experience with surrogacy is that it raises serious questions about the way many Christians, including black women, have been taught to image redemption. More often than not the theology in mainline Protestant churches (including African-American ones) teaches believers that sinful humankind has been redeemed because Jesus died on the cross in the place of humans, thereby taking human sin upon himself.

In this sense Jesus represents the ultimate surrogate figure; he stands in the place of someone else: sinful humankind. Surrogacy, attached to this divine personage, thus takes on an aura of the sacred. It is therefore fitting and proper for black women to ask whether the image of a surrogate-God has salvific power for black women or whether this image supports and reinforces the exploitation that has accompanied their experience with surrogacy. If black women accept this idea of redemption, can they not also passively accept the exploitation that surrogacy brings?

I recognize that reflection upon these questions causes many complex theological issues to surface. For instance, there is the issue of the part God the Father played in determining the surrogate role filled by Jesus, the Son. For black women, there is also the question of whether Jesus on the cross represents coerced surrogacy (willed by the Father) or voluntary surrogacy (chosen by the Son) or both. At any rate, a major theological problem here is the place of the cross in any theology significantly informed by African-American women's experience with surrogacy. Even if one buys into the notion of the cross as the meeting place of the will of God to give up the Son (coerced surrogacy?) and the will of the Son to give up himself (voluntary surrogacy?) so that "the spirit of abandonment and self-giving love" proceeds from the cross "to raise up abandoned men,"[31] African-American women are still left with the question: Can there be salvific power for black women in Christian images of oppression (for example, Jesus on the cross) meant to teach something about redemption?

As the history of classical Christian doctrine reveals,[32] theologians since the time of Irenaeus and Origen have been trying to make the Christian idea of atonement believable by shaping theories about it in the language and thought that people of a particular time understood and in which they were grounded.[33] For instance Origen (A.D. 183–253), capitalizing on the current beliefs in devils and spirits, advocated and affirmed what had come to be known as a ransom theory of atonement. This theory claimed that Jesus' death on the cross represented a ransom God paid to the devil for the sins of humankind. The ransom theory was the orthodox position of the church for nearly a thousand years. But it declined when another age dawned. Anselm emerged in the eleventh century and spoke of atonement using the chivalric language and sociopolitical thought of his time. His theory of atonement described sin as the human way of dishonoring God. People owed honor to God just as medieval peasants and squires owed honor and loyalty to their overlords. However, humans had no power to give satisfaction to God for disloyalty to God through their sin. According to the codes of chivalry in Anselm's time, one atoned for a crime either by receiving punishment or by providing satisfaction to the injured person. Since God did not want to punish humans forever (which the sin deserved) and since humans had no means to render satisfaction to the injured honor of God, the deity, Godself, made restitution for humanity. God satisfied God's own violated honor by sending God's Son to earth in human form ultimately to die on the cross.

There were also the theories of atonement associated with Abelard, who lived from 1079 to 1142. Since the church in the Middle Ages put great stress upon the penitential life of believers, it was reasonable for Abelard to see Calvary as "the school of penitence of the human race, for there men of all ages and races have learned the depth and power of the love of God."[34] Often referred to as the moral theory of atonement,[35] this idea emphasized God's love in the work of atonement and claimed that when humans look upon the death of Jesus they see the love of God manifested. The cross brings repentance to humankind and shows simultaneously God the Father's love and the suffering inflicted upon that love by human sin. This moral theory of atonement taught that the cross was "the most powerful moral influence in history, bringing to men that repentance which renders them able to be forgiven."[36]

As the Renaissance approached and the medieval worldview collapsed, the Anselmian and Abelardian way of understanding the atonement began to decline. The Renaissance was a time of great interest in the revival of ancient law. So, it was reasonable to expect the reformers to work out their theories of atonement in legal terms grounded in the new political and legal thought of the sixteenth century. Thus Calvin spoke of the justice of God, of the divine law of punishment that could not be overlooked, of the infinite character of human sin that deserved infinite harsh punishment. But, according to the reformer, God is both just and merciful. Therefore, God with infinite mercy provided a substitute who would bear the punishment of human sin. Jesus Christ came to offer himself as a substitute for humans. He took their punishment upon himself. Thus the reformers advocated a substitution theory of atonement.

While these ransom, satisfaction, substitution and moral theories of atonement may not be serviceable for providing an acceptable response to African-American women's question about redemption and surrogacy, they do illustrate a serviceable practice for theologians attempting today to respond to this question. That practice (as shown by the theologians above) is to use the language and sociopolitical thought of the time to render Christian ideas and principles understandable. So the womanist theologian uses the sociopolitical thought and action of the African-American woman's world to show black women their salvation does not depend upon any form of surrogacy made sacred by traditional and orthodox understandings of Jesus' life and death. Rather their salvation is assured by Jesus' life of resistance and by the survival strategies he used to help people survive the death of identity[37] caused by their exchange of inherited cultural meanings for a new identity shaped by the gospel ethics and world view. This death of identity was also experienced by African women and men brought to America and enslaved. They too relied upon Jesus to help them survive the forging of a new identity. This kind of account of Jesus' salvific value—made compatible and understandable by use of African-American women's sociopolitical patterns—frees redemption from the cross and frees the cross from the "sacred aura" put around it by existing patriarchal responses to the question of what Jesus' death represents.

The synoptic gospels (more than Paul's letters), also provide resources for constructing a Christian understanding of redemption that speaks meaningfully to black women, given their historic experience with surrogacy. Jesus' own words in Luke 4 and his ministry of healing the human body, mind and spirit (described in Matthew, Mark and Luke) suggest that Jesus did not come to redeem humans by showing them God's "love" manifested in the death of God's innocent child on a cross erected by cruel, imperialistic, patriarchal power. Rather, the texts suggest that the spirit of God in Jesus came to show humans *life*—to show redemption through a perfect *ministerial* vision of righting relations between body (individual and community), mind (of humans and of tradition) and spirit. A female-male inclusive vision, Jesus' ministry of righting relationships involved raising the dead (those separated from life and community), casting out demons (for example, ridding the mind of destructive forces prohibiting the flourishing of positive, peaceful life) and proclaiming the word of life that demanded the transformation of tradition so that life could be lived more abundantly. Thus, Jesus was quick to remind his critics that humans were not made for the Sabbath; rather, the Sabbath was made for humans. God's gift to humans, through Jesus, was to invite them to participate in this *ministerial* vision ("whosoever will, let them come") of righting relations. The response to this invitation by human principalities and powers was the horrible deed the cross represents—the evil of humankind trying to kill the *ministerial* vision of life in relation that Jesus brought to humanity. The resurrection does not depend upon the cross for life, for the cross only represents historical evil trying to defeat good. The resurrection of Jesus and the flourishing of God's spirit in the world as the result of resurrection represent the life of the *ministerial* vision gaining victory over the evil attempt to kill it. Thus, to respond meaningfully to black women's historic experience of surrogacy oppression, the womanist theologian must show that redemption of humans can have nothing to do with any kind of surrogate or substitute role Jesus was reputed to have played in a bloody act that supposedly gained victory over sin and/or evil.

Black women are intelligent people living in a technological world where nuclear bombs, defilement of the earth, racism, sexism, dope and economic injustices attest to the presence and power of evil in the world. Perhaps not many people today can believe that evil and sin were overcome by Jesus' death on the cross; that is, that Jesus took human sin upon himself and therefore saved humankind. Rather, it seems more intelligent and more scriptural to understand that redemption had to do with God, through Jesus, giving humankind new vision to see the resources for positive, abundant relational life. Redemption had to do with God, through the *ministerial* vision, giving humankind the ethical thought and practice upon which to build positive, productive quality of life. Hence, the kingdom of God theme in the *ministerial* vision of Jesus does not point to death; it is not something one has to die to reach. Rather, the kingdom of God is a metaphor of hope God gives those attempting to right the relations between self and self, between self and others, between self and God as prescribed in the sermon on the mount, in the golden rule and in the commandment to show love above all else.

Though space limitations here prohibit a more systematic reconstruction of this Christian understanding of redemption (given black women's surrogacy experience), there are a few things that can be said about sin in this kind of reconstruction. The image of Jesus on the cross is the image of human sin in its most desecrated form. This execution destroyed the body, but not before it mocked and defiled the Jewish man Jesus by publicly exposing his nakedness and private parts, by mocking the *ministerial* vision as they labeled him king of the Jews, by placing a crown of thorns upon his head mocking his dignity and the integrity of his divine mission. The cross thus becomes an image of defilement, a gross manifestation of collective human sin. Jesus, then, does not conquer sin through death on the cross. Rather, Jesus conquers the sin of temptation in the wilderness (Matthew 4:1–11) by resistance—by resisting the temptation to value the material over the spiritual ("Man shall not live by bread alone"); by resisting death (not attempting suicide that tests God: "if you are the son of God, throw yourself down"); by resisting the greedy urge of monopolistic ownership ("He showed him all the kingdoms of the world and the glory of them; and he said to him, all these I will give you, if you will fall down and worship me"). Jesus therefore conquered sin in life, not in death. In the wilderness he refused to allow evil forces to defile the balanced relation between the material and the spiritual, between life and death, between power and the exertion of it.

What this allows the womanist theologian to show black women is that God did not intend the surrogacy roles they have been forced to perform. God did not intend the defilement of their bodies as white men put them in the place of white women to provide sexual pleasure for white men during the slavocracy. This was rape. Rape is defilement, and defilement means wanton desecration. Worse, deeper and more wounding than alienation, the sin of defilement is the one of which today's technological world is most guilty. Nature (the land, the seas, the animals in the sea) are every day defiled by humans. Cultures and peoples (Native Americans, Africans, Jews) have been defiled and destroyed by the onslaught of Western, Christian, patriarchal imperialism in some of its ugliest forms. The oceans are defiled by oil spills, and industrial waste destroys marine life. The rain forest is being defiled. The cross is a reminder of how humans have tried throughout history to destroy visions of righting relationships that involve transformation of tradition and transformation of social relations and arrangements sanctioned by the status quo.

The resurrection of Jesus and the kingdom of God theme in Jesus' *ministerial* vision provide black women with the knowledge that God has, through Jesus, shown humankind how to live peacefully, productively and abundantly in relationship. Jesus showed humankind a vision of righting relations between body, mind and spirit[38] *through an ethical ministry of words* (such as the beatitudes, the parables, the moral directions and reprimands); *through a healing ministry of touch and being touched* (for example, healing the leper through touch; being touched by the woman with an issue of blood); *through a militant ministry of expelling evil forces* (such as exorcising the demoniacs, whipping the moneychangers out of the temple); *through a ministry grounded in the power of faith* (in the work of healing); *through a ministry of prayer* (he often withdrew from the crowd to pray); *through a ministry of compassion and love.*

Humankind is, then, redeemed through Jesus' *ministerial* vision of life and not through his death. There is nothing divine in the blood of the cross. God does not intend black women's surrogacy experience. Neither can Christian faith affirm such an idea. Jesus did not come to be a surrogate. Jesus came for life, to show humans a perfect vision of ministerial relation that humans had very little knowledge of. As Christians, black women cannot forget the cross, but neither can they glorify it. To do so is to glorify suffering and to render their exploitation sacred. To do so is to glorify the sin of defilement.

### Re-Enter Black Liberation Theology

Most treatments of redemption in black liberation theology do not raise questions about Christian notions of atonement. The black theologian Olin P. Moyd merely states that black religion affirms that "the atonement took place on the Cross of Calvary."[39] He goes on to claim that "black religion has grown out of a childlike faith."[40] It has not expended

> any extended theological debate on the matters of how one man
> could atone for the sins of all or to whom the ransom was paid, or

why it was necessary that a human life be sacrificed in order that God might redeem humanity from sin and guilt if God is all powerful and thus could have wrought human salvation by some other means.... [41]

The critique of atonement views by womanist theology invites black liberation theologians to begin serious conversations with black females about the black Christians' understanding of atonement in light of African-American women's experience of oppression. Perhaps such a conversation can begin with the incarnation and the cross. By removing their sexist lens, black theologians can see that though incarnation is traditionally associated with the self-disclosure of God in Jesus Christ, incarnation also involves God's self-disclosure in a woman: Mary. The angel Gabriel tells her, "The Holy Spirit will come upon you, and the power of the Most High will overshadow you; therefore the child to be born will be called holy, the Son of God" (Luke 1:36). Translated in terms of African-American heritage from traditional African religions, one can say, "The Spirit mounted Mary." The word was first made flesh in Mary's body. Incarnation, in a womanist understanding of it in the Christian testament, can be regarded as a continuum of the manifestation of divine spirit beginning with Mary, becoming an abundance in Jesus and later overflowing into the life of the church.

Womanist theologians and black liberation theologians can also discuss the meaning of the cross in their theologies. The centrality of the cross in James Deotis Roberts's christology is especially unsettling for the womanist theologian conscious of the way in which images of redemption associated with the cross support a structure of domination (surrogacy) in black women's lives. For Roberts, it is through the cross that revelation and reconciliation are understood. He says:

> No one can fully understand the revelation of God if he does not know the meaning of the cross not merely as unmerited suffering but also as a healing balm. Others may have to seek the cross, but as for the black man, the cross finds him—it follows and haunts him.... The black man shoulders a cross at birth and never emerges from its burden.... In an understanding of the cross from the vantage point of black consciousness, the black Christian experiencing the revelation of God through the black Messiah bears an existential cross.... But the cross is also revelatory of the love of God.... It is through the window of the cross that we see the face of God.[42]

Connecting the black Messiah, the cross and reconciliation, he says:

> When we discover Christ as the black Messiah, as the one who enters into our black experience, the meaning of his cross and our suffering are reconciliation. The reconciliation of man to man, through the reconciliation of man to God, releases the healing power of the cross of Christ into this anxious, broken, and bitter world. Only redeemed men can serve as agents of reconciliation.... On the cross Christ gives himself to mankind. Black men and women, reconciled to God through the cross of Christ, but who through their suffering, their own cross-bearing, share the depth of his suffering, are purified, mellowed, and heightened in sensitivity and compassion.[43]

Women must question Roberts's way of seeing such positive value in oppressed black women identifying with Christ through their common suffering wrought by cross-bearing. Black women should never be encouraged to believe that they can be united with God through this kind of suffering. There are quite enough black women bearing the cross by rearing children alone, struggling on welfare, suffering through poverty, experiencing inadequate health care, domestic violence and various forms of sexism and racism.

Obviously, black liberation theology's understanding of incarnation, of revelation, Jesus Christ and reconciliation holds very little promise for black women. A complete revisionist approach in these areas of black liberation theology is needed if black women are ever to be included. Womanist theology informed by woman-inclusive wilderness experience must, in the final analysis, lead black male liberation theologians to see in their theological thinking the "male bond" between them and white males whom they identify as oppressors.

Black liberation theologians and womanist theologians will perhaps agree on one thing; that is, that their black theological projects have some common ethical tasks. The work of this study suggests that one task is and always has been to encourage black people and the African-American denominational churches to be continuously engaged in a process of "revaluing value."[44] Black male liberation theologians have apparently engaged the process so that black male consciousness will not be lost in theological discourse. Womanist theologians, who dialogue on the basis of woman-inclusive wilderness experience, engage the process so that black women's experience can become visible and be included in the discourse in theology. Black liberation theologians and black womanist theologians would no doubt disagree about the principles that should guide this process. It is to the matter of "revaluing of value" and the principles associated with it that we now give attention as we bring some of the ethical insights in this book into dialogue with black liberation theology.

### Ethical Task, Ethical Principles

The "revaluing of value" done in the works of James Deotis Roberts, James Cone and in this book has been guided by ethical principles shaped by the gender and racial identity, historical reality and biblical tradition with which each writer's work identifies.

The ethical principle guiding James Deotis Roberts's work is the importance of reconciliation in the black struggle for liberation under the guidance of God's wrath, love and mercy. Black and male, Roberts advocates a kind of reconciliation in race relations history in America that is only authentic if whites have taken seriously the black man's struggle to be liberated from racial oppression. Roberts relies upon the prophetic tradition to provide the biblical foundations for his revaluing process. It is this ethical principle that has helped Roberts to determine the value to be revalued—the historic goal of black/white race relations in America. According to Roberts, integration as a goal should be replaced by what he identifies as the goal of interracialism in black/white relations. He says:

> I do not advocate integration as a goal. Integration is a goal set by whites and is still based upon the superordination-subordination principle of whites over blacks, even blacks with superior education and experience to whites under whom they must live and serve. In any situation where whites write the agenda for integration . . . this is what integration means. The slave-master, servant-boss, inferior-superior mentality underlies all integration schemes in which whites write the agenda. This is the reason why I am against integration.[45]

Then Roberts goes on to revalue the goal of black/white race relations as he names a new value, that is, *interracial.*

> Black and white relations should be interracial. This allows for two-way participation in the interaction between the races. It overcomes the self-hate implicit in the belief that all whites are superior to all blacks just because white is inherently better than black. . . . It enables blacks

to appreciate their own heritage to the extent that they consider it a worthy commodity to be shared with others. In this manner liberation leads to reconciliation between equals. This position is productive of the psychological and sociological health of blacks. It is needed for a right perspective for better race relations. It is consistent with an understanding of God as lovingly just, the dignity of all men, and sinfulness of all men, and their reconciliation with God.[46]

With this new goal as the object of black/white race relations, blacks—in activities also involving whites—"must operate on the basis of interracial equity." And equity "implies the natural and God-given; it is rooted in both nature and grace and is shared by all men. Thus, what is equitable cannot be given or taken away by whites." For, says Roberts, "to think and act on this principle [of equity] is the only means to liberation and the only proper basis for black/white reconciliation."[47]

It is, of course, the biblical prophetic tradition carried forth in such prophets as Amos and Hosea to which Roberts appeals.

Amos presents a just and angry God who looks with disdain upon the rich exploiting the poor. Hosea speaks of a just God who condemns his people for their infidelity but nevertheless loves and forgives them. God's wrath, God's love and God's forgiveness are the foundations upon which liberation and reconciliation can be built in black/white race relations seeking the interracial goals.

It is Roberts's attempt to revalue "means" that puts his ethical task of revaluing in conflict with James Cone. Roberts claims that the question of "means" is a serious dilemma facing black Christians in their relations to whites:

> While certain revolutionary theologians advocate violence or counter-violence in Latin America and South Africa, the "by whatever means necessary" ethic needs careful examination by black theologians and ethicists. It may be loudly applauded by black militants who have an ear for inflammatory rhetoric, but it can hardly do for a sound Christian basis for ethics in the area of race.[48]

Instead of the "by whatever means necessary" as a value in the black liberation struggle, Roberts revalues "means" so that massive, black participation in the political process in America becomes the "means" valued for its ability to put blacks in important leadership roles. This focus upon revaluing "means" leads Roberts to take a strong stand against violence, which the "by whatever means necessary" method might value as appropriate strategy in securing the liberation of black people.

Addressing his work to the same historical problem as Roberts, that is, to the character of black/white race relations in America, black male theologian James Cone engages a process of revaluing of value in accord with an ethical principle at the heart of his work. And that principle is the "liberation of black people from racial oppression by whatever means, necessary in a liberation struggle superintended by God." Unlike Roberts, Cone, in *God of the Oppressed*, champions neither violence nor nonviolence as the proper strategy for black people to use in their liberation struggle against racial oppression. However, he does say:

> When I hear questions about violence and love coming from the children of slave masters whose identity with Jesus extends no further than that weekly Sunday service, then I can understand why many black brothers and sisters say that Christianity is the white man's religion, and it must be destroyed along with white oppressors. What many white people fail to realize is that their questions about violence and Christian love are not only very naive, but are hypocritical and insulting. When whites ask me, "Are you for violence" my rejoinder is: "Whose violence?" "Richard Nixon or his victims?" "The Mississippi State Police or the students at Jackson State?" "The New York State Police or the inmates at Attica?"[49]

Cone validates his ethical principle by calling attention to what he thinks ought to have been the inseparable relation between the Bible's word about liberation and the church's theological and ethical positions on oppression throughout its history. Had the early church and the church fathers been faithful to the biblical portrayal of the revelation of God in Jesus as the oppressed one whose gospel was concerned with the poor and oppressed of the earth, Christian theology and ethics would have developed in a different way. And the church would never have forgotten that to live the Christian life means to join the oppressed in their struggle for liberation. For, says Cone, "whatever else the gospel of Jesus might be, it can never be identified with the established power of the state. . . . It can never be identified with the actions of people who conserve the status quo." Consequently, "This was the . . . error of the early church. By becoming the religion of the Roman state, replacing the public state sacrifices, Christianity became the opposite of what Jesus intended."[50]

So Cone's ethical principle of "liberation by whatever means necessary in the liberation struggle superintended by God" guides his process of revaluing the discipline of Christian ethics as he responds to the question: What am I to do?[51] The implication of Cone's revaluing is that the traditional Christian response of "love" to questions concerning "living the Christian life" is inadequate. The traditional way white Christians have described Jesus' love is not the criterion for Christian ethical judgement. Rather, says Cone:

> We begin answering this question [What am I to do?] by stating once more: because the oppressed community is the place where one encounters God's liberating deed, it is also the only place where one can know the will of God. We cannot be what we are apart from what God has done and is doing in the oppressed community. Thus the criteria of ethical judgment can only be hammered out in the community of the victims of injustice.... For Christians, Jesus is the source for what we do.... Jesus is the criterion of our ethical judgment.[52]

This means, then, Christians must revalue the value of law and morality in the society on the basis of the liberation needs of the oppressed. When ethics is grounded in the oppressed community, "oppressors cannot decide what is Christian behavior." Cone says African-American slaves knew this; therefore, they rejected the white oppressors' laws but they did not reject law and morality. "They formulated a new law and a new morality that was consistent with black strivings for freedom."[53]

Thus Cone advocates that Christian ethics be revalued so that it becomes Christian liberation ethics—"What we are to do, therefore, is not decided by abstract principles but is defined by Jesus' liberating presence in our community." Hence "the oppressed community is the place where we are called to hammer out the meaning of Jesus' presence for Christian behavior. ... We can create our ethic only in dialogue in the struggle of freedom."[54]

Cone revalues the negative value put upon violence not by indicating that violence is a value for oppressed people to adopt. Rather, he suggests that our value judgments and questions about violence must be shaped by our examination of the violence that brought America into being as a country and the violence that white oppressors have inflicted upon black Americans throughout history. An ethic of liberation "arises out of [a new sense of] love, for ourselves and for humanity. This is an essential ingredient of liberation without which the struggle turns into a denial of what divine liberation means."[55] What a liberation ethic seeks, according to Cone, is not vengeance for the oppressed. "Our intention is not to make the oppressors slaves but to transform humanity. Hatred and vengeance have no place in the struggle of freedom."[56] As far as reconciliation is concerned, Cone is convinced that it is only possible after black people have been liberated from their racial oppression. And the equity he mentions is the equity between male and female. As one would expect, his strong liberation emphasis is grounded in the biblical exodus traditions telling about the power of God in Israel's liberation struggle in the Hebrew testament and about Jesus' liberating power in relation to the oppressed in the Christian testament.

Just as certain ethical principles guided the ethical task of revaluing value in the work of Roberts and Cone, an ethical principle came to life in this womanist book and suggested that the task of revaluing value is absolutely essential for theological and ethical works dealing with black women's reality. This is so because most values in the black and white world related to black women are oppressive and have caused black women to be engaged in a most fierce survival struggle that seems to have no end. This black female survival struggle becomes a source informing what we focus upon in our theological and ethical treatment of black women's experience. But the difference between the female ethical effort and that of the black male liberation theologian is that the black female theologian, in her ethical task of revaluing, must also reconstruct and redeem from invisibility the life-world of African-American women. On the basis of the reconstruction and redemption in this book, an ethical principle emerges as a guide in identifying what is to be revalued. The ethical principle yielded is "survival and a positive quality of life for black women and their families in the presence and care of God." So that which womanists (or black women) are to revalue are the spiritual, religious, political, educational strategies and values Western culture urges black women to use for survival and for developing a quality of life for the community.

While the ethical principles in Roberts's and Cone's works were shaped by male identity and by the historical realities associated with black/white race relations, the ethical principle for revaluing that came to life in this book depended upon female identity and the historical realities associated with black women's re/productive history. Thus it was intimated that black and white values associated with black female role-functioning around the notion of motherhood had to be revalued. Perhaps sometimes unconsciously, both black and white people have valued the mammy or surrogacy aspect of black women's motherhood role. Of course, clues about how this revaluing could be done come from Alice Walker in *The Color Purple,* where it is suggested that motherhood as a role of caretaker for children must become a community role shared by males and females.

Theologically, this ethical task of revaluing the value of oppressed motherhood is essential for deriving a woman-inclusive notion of biblical incarnation and revelation (especially Christian testament revelation). As this chapter revealed in the section on doctrine, the notions of incarnation (and revelation) prevalent in black liberation theology leave black women of African-slavewoman descent in the outsider-position to which Paul relegated Hagar in the book of Galatians. Therefore, if the incarnation in and the revelation of God in the oppressed mother is ignored, it is of very little significance to black women that black male liberation theologians (in the execution of their ethical task of revaluing value) connect the revelation of God in Jesus, the Oppressed Son, with liberation and reconciliation. The conclusion here is that this task of revaluing the value of black motherhood has important social and theological implications for understanding the character and practice of religion in the African-American community.

Some black male liberation theologians and some womanist theologians may have a great deal to say to each other about the meaning of *means* in ethics supporting a liberation struggle and ethics supporting women's survival and quality of life struggle. The discussion in this chapter indicated that some black male liberation theologians have, on occasion, advocated that an ethical principle of "liberation by any means necessary" be exercised in liberation struggle. This suggests, of course, that the oppressed are free of all predetermined moral constraints as they design liberation strategies.

However, black women's sources used in this study suggest that a more nuanced understanding of *means* might be operative in black women's struggle for survival and positive quality of life. While their means might be free of moral constraints imposed by alien social forces, the design and character of the means of the struggle are governed by black women's communication with God through prayer, by their faith in God's presence with them in the struggle, by their absolute dependence upon God to support resistance and provide sustenance. Like Hagar's means, African-American religious women's means in survival and quality of life struggle develop in accord with their radical obedience to what they understand to be God's word speaking to their struggle. God becomes the element of necessity in the emergence of black women's survival and quality of life strategies. Thus, in accord with this female understanding, womanist theologians might suggest ethical perspectives emphasizing woman-God-communication-action as "necessary means" rather than "by any means necessary."

This shade of difference between the meaning of *means* in their respective theologies suggests that some black male liberation theologians and some womanist theologians should begin to talk seriously about the black ethical task of revaluing value. For it is through their joint work that the black community will see not only some of the tensions between liberation ethics and survival/quality-of-life ethics, but also how these tensions can provide resources for the work of revaluing. The community will also see how a liberation ethic and a survival/quality-of-life ethic work together for the creation of freedom, peace and well-being in the African-American community.

This chapter has tried to show the possibilities for discourse when womanist issues and presuppositions challenge black liberation theology. In the areas of methodology, doctrine and ethics new insights emerged that demonstrate that black theology will only grow to the extent that black women's perspectives are brought into its hermeneutical circle. I hope that black theologians will be wise enough to encourage the discipline to grow.

We turn now to another question: What are the possibilities of dialogue between womanist and feminist theologians, given the analysis in this book?

## Chapter 7

# WOMANIST-FEMINIST DIALOGUE: DIFFERENCES AND COMMONALITIES

It is presumptuous to speak of "theology" as if there were only one and as if theology were an objective science. . . . Theology is . . . acceptable only as a heuristic device that provides a "space" in which different theologies can meet to discuss their commonalities and differences in order to deepen their understanding. This conversation is an important one for the different theologies to engage in because the struggles to which they relate are interconnected.

—Ada María Isasi-Díaz and Yolanda Tarango, C.C.V I.
*Hispanic Women: Prophetic Voice in the Church*

Just as womanist theology has an organic relation to black liberation theology, so does it also have an organic relation to feminist theology in its various strands: Hispanic, Asian, Jewish and Anglo-American. This means that black male liberationists, womanists and feminists connect at vital points. Yet distinct and sometimes hostile differences exist between them precipitated, in part, by the maladies afflicting community life in America—sexism, racism and classism. Consequently, womanist god-talk often lives in tension with its two groups of relatives: black male liberationists and feminists. The preceding chapter has indicated the areas in which womanist theology and black male liberation theology have cause for discourse. Now the task is to turn to the feminist theological enterprise to discover how the content of this book suggests a basis upon which womanists and feminists can dialogue about their differences and commonalities.

### The Differences

There are at least four areas where difference in womanist and feminist conceptualizations can give birth to dialogue that might enlighten both groups of women. These areas are:

1. in various cultural contexts, understanding the meaning of "what is acceptably female";[1]

2. the scope and definition of the term *patriarchy*;

3. different and sometimes opposing hermeneutical positions;

4. different responses to the question: What can we say about God's relation to the oppressed in history?

By focusing upon each area of difference separately, we become aware of some of the specific feminist and womanist theologians whose work can help begin dialogue with the womanist analysis in this book.

### *What Is Acceptably Female?*

Some Asian Christian women respond to this question by lifting up the Virgin Mary, reconstituted. Chung Hyun Kyung's treatment of Asian women's new idea of Mary, the mother of Jesus, accords in some ways with African-American women's response to the Virgin Mary image. But there are also differences. Like Asian women, black women today are apt to find the androcentric church's rendition of Mary "alien . . . because she is either too clean, too high, and too holy or she is too sweet, too passive and too forgiving."[2] Within the context of North American culture where white disdain of black permeates almost every idea and image advanced in the mainstream, African-American women must contend with the way the social appropriation of the Virgin Mary has contributed to the advancement of white supremacy. The Virgin Mary as a social construct has stood for purity and innocence, which were qualities assigned to white women. Black women were construed by white social mythology to be loose, immoral, incapable of either innocence or purity. Thus the Virgin Mary can be a negative symbol for black women: "too white" and "too false" to represent "what is acceptably [black] female." There is no denying the compatibility of African-American women's reality with Chung's statement that "when Mary is placed as a norm for 'ideal womanhood' outside of Asian women's everyday, concrete, bodily experience, she becomes a source for disempowerment for Asian women."[3]

Yet there are some questions the womanist content in this book poses to the appropriation and feminist dress of Mary in Chung's book. Asian women, according to Chung, "view the virginity of Mary, not as a *biological* reality, but as a *relational* reality. . . . Virginity lies in her true connectedness to her own self and to God. It is an inner attitude, not a psychological or external fact." Chung continues, stating that Asian women claim "when a woman defines herself according to her own understanding of who she really is and what she is meant for in this universe (and not according to the rules and norms of patriarchy), she is a virgin."[4] Finally, says Chung, reporting Marianne Katoppo's views:

> Her virginity persists "in spite of sexual experience, child bearing and increasing age." Actually her virginity, her ability to be a self-defining woman, grows because of her full range of life experience.
>
> Virgin is "the symbol for the autonomy of women." Virgin primarily means not "a woman who abstains from sexual intercourse" but a woman who does not lead a derived life, as "daughter/wife/mother" of men. She is a "woman who matures to wholeness within herself as a complete person, and who is open for others."[5]

A question here, it seems to me, is whether this feminist position on virginity plays into the hands of the patriarchy it claims to reject as Asian women assign value and virtue to virginity—just as patriarchal biblical and cultural traditions assign value and virtue to virginity. Why is the term virgin needed at all to describe women's independence and maturity, since the term is "scared to the bone" with male handling? Are a new language and new adjectives needed? In the context of non-Christian Asian cultures is there something inherently positive about the terms *virgin* and *virginity* that makes Asian Christian women want to claim these terms in their descriptions of femaleness? Does this definition of these terms facilitate dialogue in Asia between Christian and non-Christian women?

Given African-American women's sexual exploitation and their experience with social-role surrogacy, there would be a reluctance to articulate an understanding of virgin as "a woman who is open for others" without qualifying what that means. And since womanist theologians claim the importance of family (female, male and children) for women's liberation and survival, there would be concern about the loss of Joseph in the working out of the Christian story about Jesus and his mother. The African-American family has for generations been under attack by white and colonial power structures that have been especially brutal toward black men. The loss of Joseph as an active participant in the unfolding of this story amounts to a breakdown in the portrayal of family. We ask our Asian sisters to teach us their meaning of "virgin ... [as] a woman who does not lead a *derived life* as daughter/wife/mother of men [and of women?]. Can there be such a thing

as an un-derived life for Christian feminist women who are daughters/
wives/mothers of men and women, but who do not want their femaleness
defined by the virgin/virginity language?

There is also the question of whether class distinctions among women
in the various Asian cultures make a difference in how (or if) the particular
Asian woman appropriates the virgin and virginity language. Is the Virgin
Mary "a model of full womanhood and liberated humanity" for all Christian Asian women irrespective of class position?[6] The issue of class looms
large in African-American cultural criticism and womanist theology, which
probes the social, cultural, political and religious significance of the more-
than-one-hundred-year-old appropriation of the biblical Hagar by African
Americans. Earlier, reference was made to the class realities that figured into
the appropriation of the Virgin Mary as a model of true womanhood in the
African-American community. Apparently some rank-and-file black people
(along with artists and some professionals) continue to recognize Hagar's African heritage and the congruence of her experience with African-American
women's and the community's history. Therefore Hagar has been for many
African Americans a model of full womanhood. Dialogue would allow womanists and Asian feminists to discover what these two models of womanhood
have to say to each other when they are put to work in contemporary Christian women's freedom struggles.

Womanist theology would be reticent to designate either Hagar or the
Virgin Mary as models of liberated human beings since both women are always powerless and never able to take care of *their own* business or set *their
own* agenda for their lives. Throughout most of the biblical story about her,
Hagar was a slave. And when she was freed, she was freed into poverty and
what looked like an impossible life-situation. In Matthew's account of Mary's
pregnancy, she is not presented as a free adult consenting in the matter of
bearing the child Jesus. Matthew 18:1 (*RSV*) claims, "Now the birth of Jesus Christ took place this way. When his mother Mary had been betrothed
to Joseph, before they came together she was found to be with child of the
Holy Spirit." Neither is Joseph's consent considered before the fact. Rather
the angel of the Lord makes pronouncement after pronouncement (18:21)
to Joseph in a dream. No conversation occurs between Mary and the angel of
the Lord. Mary is voiceless, without speech in this Matthew text.

Though Luke—in his account of Jesus' birth—is generous enough to
allow a conversation between the angel Gabriel and Mary, the story is full of
male pronouncements and mandates for Mary's life: "You *will* conceive...."

You *shall* call his name Jesus. . . . The Holy Spirit *will* come upon you. . . . The power of the Most High *will* overshadow you. . . . The child *will* be called holy" (Luke 1:31–35). Mary's response—"Behold, I am the handmaid of the Lord: let it be done to me according to your word" (1:38)—suggests that she agrees because she is a servant of the Lord. Can servants disagree or refuse the jobs their masters assign them and still stay in relation and favor with their employers/masters? Does the language Mary uses to describe herself as servant suggest free womanhood? Did Mary have a real choice? Could she have said no, given the command language used by Gabriel? Is there danger of this female servanthood language being appropriated socially in the male-dominated societies in which most women live, so that women's "servanthood" is made to look like "women's choice"?

I am uneasy with the claim that "Mary suffered most of her life due to her *choice* of giving birth to the Messiah."[7] Does this kind of faith give sacred validation to women suffering on behalf of men? Chung's reference to Mary's "social motherhood" is apt to appeal to those areas of African-American culture where black mothers are also "mothers of the church" and "community mothers." This is, however, a heavily burdened "motherhood." And given the kind of critique the content of this womanist book directs to Christian notions of atonement, womanist theology cannot affirm the suffering of "social motherhood" or the suffering of any other kind of motherhood. Nevertheless, Asian women's recognition of the key role of Mary in the work of redemption resonates with the thought in this book that *both* Mary and Jesus are active in the work of redemption. The womanist claim is that the work of redemption is possible because they both experience the incarnation. (Perhaps womanists and Asian feminists can have lengthy discussion about women's choice and autonomy in relation to womanist and feminist notions of redemption and incarnation.)

It seems to me that Christian womanists and Asian, Hispanic, Anglo-American and Jewish feminists have a lot to say to one another about this issue of "what is acceptably female" in their cultures. This dialogue can lead to a real critique of the biblical texts' provision of female models and the limitations of female appropriation of these models in various cultural contexts. The question of "acceptable female identity" in culture is important because its exploration often reveals what a society regards as good and beautiful. We get to the heart of the culture's oppressive aesthetic values, and we see the great tragedy in women's lives when they try to live up to these values.

Among womanists and feminist theologians, heterosexual women and lesbian women can come together for serious dialogue to discover if there are ways heterosexual female culture oppresses lesbian women on the basis of homophobic responses to the question of what is "acceptably female."

Womanists, Anglo feminists, Hispanic feminists, Asian feminists and Native American feminists need much conversation about this issue, because many incentives exist in various cultures to pressure women of color to shape images of themselves as closely as they can to those of white women. It is no secret that in American culture white Hispanic women are more favored than dark-skinned Hispanic women by the society's power structures, that is, the distributors of goods and services. Some Asian-American women are undergoing surgery to remove "the slant" from their eyes. Many black women change their hair, bleach their skin and "pinch" their noses in order to look more like white women. Not only in America but also in Africa black women are confronted with this problem.[8]

In dialogue, American womanist and feminist theologians can assess their theological anthropologies to discover whether this notion of "white acceptable female" is either inferred or assumed or even ignored. Feminist theologians have devoted much creative energy exposing the way the Western theological tradition has denied the full humanity of women and has denied that women are in the image of God.[9] Now female theologians must ask if their own anthropological positions forget that in many cultures, for women to be assumed to have any humanity at all, it must be white-woman humanity. If this issue of white women as exclusive model of female humanity is not addressed in feminist and womanist theological anthropology, does the theology—by its silence on the issue—not perpetuate the idea of white-woman humanity as the model of all female humanity? Does silence on this issue amount to serious female involvement in the roots of domination?

In addition to the above concerns, the differences in their understandings of the foundations of women's oppression can inaugurate lively discourse between womanists and feminists. African-American women's historic experience, as well as the community's appropriation of the Hagar-Sarah stories, makes visible the conflict and brutal treatment women with upper-class privilege can inflict upon women of lower classes. Most white feminists station this female behavior under the umbrella of patriarchy and therefore give very little *serious* attention to assigning some of the responsibility to women for this historical phenomenon of women oppressing other women.[10]

### *Scope and Definition of Patriarchy*

True enough, most Anglo-American women live only with the illusion of authority and power, which is mostly derived from powerful males. Nevertheless, white males and white females together often administer the mainline social systems in America that oppress black women and the black family. Though many white feminists speak of multilayered oppression (usually meaning racism, sexism and classism), they do not give serious attention to the ways they participate in and help perpetuate the terrible social and cultural value systems that oppress all black people. Very few if any discussions of patriarchy give full and serious attention to women's oppression of women.

Obviously African-American women need to devise their own terms, express their own ideas, garner their own support for describing black women's reality so that their oppression by black men, their oppression by white men and their oppression by white-male-white-female-dominated social systems can be seen clearly. Reading, reflecting upon and analyzing African-American women's sources for this book have taught me that womanist scholarship in theology needs to do more than borrow the vocabulary of white feminism to describe black women's world of relations. Womanists must search deeply in the hidden "underlays" of African-American language and culture to find the "female-stuff" with which to craft a world of meaning. Womanist words and descriptions must be true to the reality they claim to represent—black women's lived experience in the everyday world.

*Patriarchy*—as a term to describe black women's relation to the white (male and female) dominated social and economic systems governing their lives—leaves too much out.[11] It is silent about class-privileged women oppressing women without class privilege. It is silent about white men and white women working together to maintain white supremacy and white privilege. It is silent about the positive boons patriarchy has bestowed upon many white women, for example, college education; the skills and credentials to walk into the jobs the civil rights movements obtained for women; in some cases the *choice* to stay home and raise children and/or develop a career—*and* to hire another woman (usually a black one) "to help out" in either case.

This is not to say that most women in male-centered societies have unlimited choices; they do not. Neither is this to say that white women should refrain from using the concept of patriarchy to describe *their* relation to their fathers, brothers and other white males governing their world. But for *patriarchy* to be inclusive of black women's experience in white society, there needs to be discussion between womanists and feminists about revision of the term. Black and white women need to become conscious of the negative effect of their historic relations. When this is clearly seen and anticipated, perhaps white feminists will become more conscious of the ways in which their life-work perpetuates the oppressive culture of white supremacy. Then womanists can perhaps desist in questioning the sincerity of white feminism about the liberation of *all* women. Perhaps womanists can then forget the words of southern white feminist Belle Kerney, spoken in 1903. Black women can quit construing these words to be the unspoken policy of contemporary white feminism, North and South. Kerney said:

> Just as surely as the North will be forced to turn to the South for the nation's salvation, just so surely will the South be compelled to look to its Anglo-Saxon women as the medium through which to retain the supremacy of the white race over the Africans.[12]

It must be stated emphatically here that the intention of womanist-feminist dialogue in theology is not for any group of women to "whip up" on another group. Rather, the purpose is for all feminist-womanist women to exchange ideas, enlarge definitions and concepts and plan political strategies. Women must learn to help each other see when and how they are instruments of their own and other people's oppression. Just as white feminists are invited to dialogue with womanists about their definitions, womanist theologians (who are among the educated elite) must dialogue with poor, uneducated women of all colors in order to discern where womanist definitions, concepts and practices oppress poor women. Womanist biblical scholar Renita Weems, in her retelling of the Hagar-Sarah story, reminds womanists of their potential power to exploit women poorer and less educated than themselves. Weems admits that though she is the child of domestics and the great-granddaughter of a slave,

> yet through freak circumstances and the grace of God, I am an educated and employed black woman upon whom, from time to time, capital-ism confers the opportunity to exploit other women—both black and white. My potential victims are those who are neither educated nor employed.[13]

Weems is correct: "None of us [women] is safe from the ravages of a society which makes room for only a chosen few and keeps at bay the vast major-ity."[14] But if we come together in compassion and concern for each other, womanists and feminists can build bridges over which future generations of women can cross from bondage to freedom.

Feminists have, nevertheless, done solid and substantial theological work, which can inform some of the efforts of womanist theologians. The feminist identification of what they describe as the patriarchal character of the Bible has done a great service in showing the world that many portions of this book support the oppression of women.[15] Yet both feminist and womanist Christian women agree that the Bible cannot be "scrapped" because it has been and continues to be fundamental in the life, faith and hope of many women. Most feminists and womanist Christian theologians agree with liberation theologian Letty Russell that there is liberating word in the Bible.[16] But women have to turn over many layers to get to this liberating word, and in the process, they may have opposing views about how biblical interpretation (hermeneutics) should be approached. It is about hermeneutics that womanists, theologians and scholars in religion need to be in conversation with each other.

### Womanist/Womanist Dialogue in Hermeneutics

Womanist hermeneutics must take seriously the assumption that the Bible is a male story populated by human males, divine males, divine male emissaries and human women mostly servicing male goals, whether social, political, cultural or religious. Thus, when they probe the Bible for meanings relevant to African-American women's experience and faith, contemporary womanists engage a hermeneutical posture of suspicion, just as their feminist sisters do. That said, another truth must be articulated.

Womanists have a slave cultural heritage of which to be mindful. This cultural heritage, patterned by biblical motifs, is the context of the early Christian origins of African Americans. It was this cultural heritage and its biblical patterning that transmitted to slaves the hope for liberation and the belief that God's power sustained their survival struggle. This slave way of using the Bible must be affirmed. Thus the womanist also engages a hermeneutical posture of affirmation as she attempts to discern both the Bible's message to black women and the meaning for black women of the biblically derived black cultural patterns.[17]

African-American slaves, female and male, created an oral text from a written text (the King James Version of the Bible).[18] They composed this oral text by extracting from the Bible or adding to biblical content those phrases, stories, biblical personalities and moral prescriptions relevant to the character of their life-situation and pertinent to the aspirations of the slave community. They took from the Bible those things that assured them that they were under God's care, that God would eventually bring justice to their cause because "He had the whole world in *his* hand." This oral text was passed along from generation to generation of black people in songs, tales, rhymes, stories and sermons. Its content was a curious mixture of female-inclusive statements and androcentric faith-claims. Thus the oral text could speak of God as mother, father, sister and brother while it simultaneously claimed that "*he* has the whole world in *his* hand," "My God *he* is able," or "My God don't come when you want *him*, but he always comes on time."

Womanist sociologist of religion Cheryl Townsend Gilkes illustrates slaves structuring this oral text when she shows how they augmented a fragment from Psalm 68 (God as "father to the fatherless") with God as "mother to the motherless." As lines in a spiritual song, these "fatherless . . . motherless" phrases were also united by the slaves with phrases about God being "sister to the sisterless," and "brother to the brotherless." In this way, Gilkes says black people created an "Afrocentric biblical tradition."[19]

Gilkes claims that what she refers to as "the Afrocentric usage of this psalm [adding female meaning to the psalm] . . . points to the importance of gender."[20] There is also another way to account for what this tradition pointed to. I suggest that these additional fragments emphasized the importance of family and reaffirmed African-American kinship ties, which the institution of slavery broke at will. This adding of mothers, brothers, sisters proclaimed that there was power in family and kinship because God took the place of whoever was missing from the relation. God provided the function the missing person would have provided, such as nurture (mother to the motherless, father to the fatherless) and peer relationships (sister to the sisterless, brother to the brotherless). Even though kinship ties were torn asunder by the slavocracy, God restored the function.

However, Gilkes is correct to assert that this African-American way of extracting material from the biblical canon and shaping it to fit into a black life context represented a technique of fashioning "a biblical tradition relevant to the black condition."[21] She shows that the strategy has continued to the present and that this "Afrocentric biblical tradition" was fundamental for the creation of African-American culture. Some of this language is, as Gilkes claims, female inclusive. But I would not go as far as Gilkes when she suggests that since Africans in Africa also prayerfully [?] recognized the motherliness of God in Christ through Jesus's lament, "O Jerusalem, Jerusalem, thou that killest the prophets, and stonest them which are sent unto thee, how often would I have gathered thy children together, even as a hen gathereth her chickens under her wings, and ye would not!," it is not unreasonable to assume that the Africans in the New World grasped its importance also. It is quite possible that the spiritual "Rocking Jerusalem" reflects imaginatively on this text and indirectly links the discipleship of Mary and Martha to the role of God the Mother in Jesus, an interesting argument for the necessity of women's ordination to the priesthood.[22]

It seems to me that there are problems to be dealt with in the spiritual songs before we can identify specific biblical texts and speculate about the slave's reflection and interpretation of these texts in their songs. What about the masked meanings Frederick Douglass and others reported the language of spiritual songs contained? We have as yet devised no instrument to break the masks. We may therefore be locked out of substantial meanings. But I think Gilkes is within reason to suggest that the slaves' creation of the spiritual songs was definitely related to the way in which they interpreted the Bible. However, I am less convinced that what Africans in Africa "prayerfully" did in terms of motherliness and God related directly to the African-American slaves' creation of female references in the spiritual songs.

Womanists, writing after Gilkes's article was published in 1989, must now take seriously the critique and analysis of the historic motherhood role by contemporary African women themselves. Buchi Emecheta's *The Joys of Motherhood* comes to mind. She depicts the reality of African motherhood as anything but joyful and free for African women. Also Awa Thiam, an African feminist, has written *Black Sisters, Speak Out*, containing the voices of African women speaking out against the oppression in such social institutions affecting motherhood as institutionalized polygamy.

In addition to Emecheta's and Thiam's books, other critiques are coming out by African women. Several African female theologians are adding their voices to this chorus of women. Mercy Oduyoye is among them.[23] Many African women are discovering that some African culture (even precolonial) has both negative and positive effects for women and mothers. Nigerian theologian Rosemary N. Edet—in her discussion of rituals devoted to women's puberty, birthing and widowhood—speaks words that should definitely affect the way that African-American women romanticize African motherhood:

Rituals...have both positive and negative aspects and so promote as well as hinder women's growth and development. The oppressive aspects of childbirth ritual...are: it imparts ritual impurity and guilt to the act of bringing forth new life; it deprives the women of nutritious means which they need after giving birth, and thus creates health hazards; the segregation [of women from the community during menstruation and after childbirth] deprives women of rights of movement and of the ability to seek medical or other help; and the rites create a sense of inferiority and self-deprecation—they subjugate women and deprive them of self-worth. On the positive side, childbirth rituals are occasions of thanksgiving, joy and celebration.[24]

Josephine Olagunju of Nigeria speaks of cultural practices reflecting the attitude "that women are subordinate to men." Her description of the fate of widows in some parts of Nigeria is instructive when African-American women try to assign complete liberative value to our African heritage about motherhood. Olegunju reports that

a woman is not allowed to cleanse herself, or she must sit by the mountainside until her husband is buried. After the burial, his property is divided among the children; if she's found favor in her husband's family, she will be cared for, otherwise she's entitled to nothing. If she should die before him, he doesn't go through the same treatment.[25]

This means, then, that womanists must be careful not to romanticize African sources of motherhood or African-American appropriations from Africa regarding women's freedom.

I wonder if Gilkes, in her discussion of an Afrocentric biblical tradition, does not idealistically accept the egalitarian strain in black sources without asking some vital questions. For instance, Gilkes claims:

Such an extension of the text [that is, Psalm 68] to incorporate God's motherly omnipotence not only opposes the oppressive utilization of gender within the community—perceptions in tension with the dominant culture. AfroAmerican culture remembered the heroism of its mothers along with that of its fathers and therefore constructed its myths, by extending the biblical materials provided, "in memory of her."[26]

Questions emerge here. How do we account for the rampant sexism in the African-American denominational churches? Did it come from the dominant culture? Why has this female-mother-God aspect of African-American culture not been efficacious enough historically to make *unnecessary* the arguments black women have had to wage for women's ordination and for women to be put on deacon boards? Nineteenth-century black women Jarena Lee and the ex-slave Old Elizabeth—themselves closer to the slave era than we are—told of sexism among black churchmen and preachers.[27] Why is it that not a single likeness of "God or Jesus as Mother" (that is, as female image) appears on the stained glass windows in black churches where pictures of white male and sometimes black male Jesuses do appear?

Apparently womanist scholars must be very critical of this Afrocentric biblical tradition. We must ask if African Americans created an oral text (or biblical tradition from the Bible) that functioned socially and politically in opposing ways; that is, it granted mothers (not all women) power but denied *all* women authority? Did our African heritage, our American heritage and our African-American strategies for establishing a black biblical tradition *together* create a split-consciousness granting power to mothers but investing *all* the authority in males? We must ask: Is this emphatic association of God with the mother role oppressive to those black women who are not mothers and cannot be or do not choose to be?[28]

Questions notwithstanding, Gilkes demonstrates brilliantly in her article how the Bible contributed to the African-American community's creation of cultural patterns reaching back to Africa but incorporating material from a slave present, while reaching into the future toward liberation and the promised land.

There is no denying that I, like Gilkes, have discovered that apparently for hundreds of years black *folk culture* has tried to appropriate the Bible so that black women's experience as well as black men's experience is included and vital in the community's Christian consciousness. African-American appropriation of the biblical Hagar stories and the symbolic use of Hagar's experience in the community seem to support what both Gilkes and I have seen in the sources. Nevertheless, sexism abounds in the black world. Neither Gilkes nor I have as yet ferreted out the source(s) of this sexism. Perhaps womanist Christian ethicists will, in the future, provide us with an in-depth scientific study of the male-female power and authority dynamic operating in the African-American denominational churches. This may shed light on what looks like opposing attitudes toward black women: one egalitarian and one oppressive.

There is a difference, though perhaps slight, in the conclusions Gilkes and I reach about what we have noticed in common. Whereas Gilkes concludes that this woman-inclusive strain among the Christian folk is part of the formation of an Afrocentric biblical tradition, I suggest that this egalitarian strain has to do with the interpretative principles (hermeneutics) the folks used in their interpretation of the Bible. And these interpretative principles derived from their life-situation and community aspirations.

The deposits of African-American culture suggest that liberation and survival were vital issues in slave consciousness. Thus the slave's questions with regard to scripture were: What has God to say and do about our community's liberation? What has God to say and do about our community's survival? Put simplistically, my womanist claim is that, for the slaves, Moses and Jesus (and God's action through them) was the answer to the former question. And Hagar and Ishmael (and God's response to them) was the way the slaves answered the latter question. While we cannot romanticize it, we cannot forget the influence that African heritage must have exerted upon the African slave's interpretation of both the Bible and the new culture (American white) into which the slave was thrown with no preparation whatsoever. We can speculate that it was altogether consistent with some African consciousness for African slaves in America to appropriate a female and her child (Hagar and Ishmael) in relation to survival. This is because some of the slaves came from matrilineal cultures where survival and progeny were counted through the female.

Of course, Hagar's and Ishmael's life-situation was like that of black female slaves and their children. Like Hagar they experienced harsh treatment from slave mistresses. Slave women were raped by slave masters. Slave masters fathered children by slave women, and then often disclaimed and sold them away to other plantations. Like Hagar and Ishmael when they were finally freed from the house of bondage, African-American ex-slaves were faced with making a way out of no way. They were thrown out into the world with no economic resources. The issue for Hagar and Ishmael and for the newly freed African-American slaves was quality of life. The question was and still is today, how can oppressed people develop a positive and productive quality of life in a situation where the resources for doing so are not visible?

Black liberation theology is providing the theological explication of the liberation principle of black biblical interpretation. Womanist survivalist/ quality-of-life theology (at least in this book) is beginning to provide the theological explication of the survival principle of African-American biblical interpretation. When our hermeneutical principle is God's word of survival and quality of life to oppressed communities (or families) living in a diaspora, we put different emphasis upon biblical texts and identify with different biblical stories than do black liberation theologians.

However, some womanist theologians are more committed to the liberation hermeneutic while other womanist theologians may be more committed to the survival/quality-of-life hermeneutic. Though both groups would perhaps agree that these two hermeneutical principles should be employed simultaneously in the interpretation of biblical texts, they obviously need to dialogue. The subjects of their conversation might be the different images of God issuing from the application of the two hermeneutical principles *and* the different responsibility (in the survival modality) put upon the community for the formation of a positive, productive quality of life. It could well be that some Hispanic feminist theologians and some Jewish feminist theologians, who understand survival to be a primary issue in their communities, might also join this dialogue."[29]

In the survival modality God's word is not always compatible with what feminist and womanist liberationists might want to hear. For example, the story of the Babylonian Captivity is useful for black American descendants of slaves trying to survive in economic captivity in North America. Parts of this story tell people how to survive bondage and how to secure their quality of life. In Jeremiah, God's word to Jews (who are free) is that some of them will be taken into captivity into Babylon. Then, when they are in exile in Babylon, Jeremiah sends a letter containing God's word to the exiles. This word is a female-male inclusive "survival and quality of life" word. In Jeremiah 29:4–7 God, having promised survival to the exiled Jews, sends these commands to the captives:

> Build houses and live in them; plant gardens and eat their produce. Take wives and have sons and daughters; take wives for your sons, and give your daughters in marriage, that they may bear sons and daughters; multiply there, and do not decrease. But seek the welfare of the city where I have sent you into exile, and pray to the Lord on its behalf, for in its welfare you will find your welfare.

While extensive womanist exegesis is required to gain in-depth meaning here, some surface remarks can be made about this text. We can respond to the question of how the womanist survival/quality-of-life hermeneutic initially interprets the text. First of all, community responsibility is commanded in the work of survival of the group. Whereas the promises of the survival of the progenies of Abram and Hagar were the responsibility of the God they knew (or who knew them), these exiles in Jeremiah apparently have the choice of multiplying or decreasing. Oppressed black Americans, female and male, will understand this text to be advice about how to oppose the genocide they experience from time to time in America. Sons and daughters are to be involved in this work of guarding against and opposing genocide. Both sons and daughters are to be involved in and produced by this group's re/production history. In addition to the production of humans, this re/production history includes an economic dimension: building houses (producing homes for themselves) and planting gardens (producing food for themselves).

Then there is God's advice that black Americans might not want to hear: "Seek the welfare of the city where I have sent you into exile, and pray to the Lord on its behalf, for in its welfare you will find your welfare." In other words, seek the welfare of your oppressors? African Americans in the diaspora can perhaps hear the silence in the text reiterate what their experience in America has taught: when the white-controlled power structures and ordinary white people are prospering, then black people are at least not brutalized as badly. When the white-controlled power structures and ordinary white people are suffering economically and when the white population decreases, black people are brutalized and scapegoated in every possible way. While oppressed people live in territories controlled by their oppressors, the welfare of the oppressed is tied into the welfare of oppressors. Therefore, black people may hear this text suggesting that the oppressed should become engaged in politics and prayers as a way of seeking the welfare of the city, as well as their own welfare.

But what womanist survival/quality-of-life hermeneutics cannot forget about this exile of Jews told in the book of Jeremiah is God's promise that one day they will be free to return to their country. When they did return they were, like the newly freed African-American slaves and like Hagar and Ishmael, faced with the issue of survival without proper economic resources. Not only God, but also the community must work in behalf of its survival and the formation of its own quality of life. The womanist survival/quality-of-life hermeneutic means to communicate this to black Christians: Liberation is an ultimate, but in the meantime survival and prosperity must be the experience of our people. And God has had and continues to have a word to say about the survival and quality of life of the descendants of African female slaves.

## *God and the Oppressed in History*

When womanist theologians engage a survival/quality-of-life hermeneutic in the interpretation of biblical texts, an image of God emerges different from the liberator God championed in some liberation theology. Dialogue is needed here.

Latin American biblical scholar Elsa Tamez rereads the Hagar-Sarah texts[30] from the context of "Christians immersed in the process of liberation"[31] and sees liberative impulses in God's actions in relation to Hagar and Ishmael. But my womanist reading does not see God's action in this text as particularly liberative. I come to the text from a Christian context of concern for poor black women, children and men immersed in a fierce struggle for physical, spiritual and emotional survival and for positive quality of life formation. Thus, while Tamez sees in the text God's word of liberation to the slave woman of African descent, a black American womanist reading from the context of a survival/quality-of-life struggle, sees God responding to the African slave Hagar and her child in terms of survival strategies.

The two times that God relates directly to Hagar are in the context of helping her come to see the strategies she must use to save her life and her child's life. The first strategy is to go back to her oppressor and make use of the oppressor's resources. The second survival strategy not only has to do with the woman and child (family) depending upon God to provide when absolutely no other provision is visible, but also includes, upon God's command, the woman Hagar lifting up her child and "holding him fast with your hand" (Genesis 21:18, *RSV*). According to some biblical scholars this literally means "make your hand firm upon him . . . which is idiomatic for lending support and encouragements"[32] to the child. The assurance of the survival of mother and child comes from God, who reiterates the promise "for I will make him a great nation" (Genesis 21:18b). In the Hebrew testament world-view, one survived through one's progeny and ancestors.

The feminist "liberation lens" and the womanist "survival lens" can, on occasion, provide a common vision. A case in point is Genesis 16:9, when God tells the run-away slave Hagar to return and submit herself to Sarah, who has physically abused Hagar in a most brutal way. Though the interpretation of this text has been an issue in biblical scholarship, Tamez interprets it in a way consistent with what a womanist survival/quality-of-life hermeneutic would yield:

> What God wants is that she and the child should be saved, and at the moment, the only way to accomplish that is not in the desert, but by

returning to the house of Abraham. Ishmael hasn't been born. The first three years of life are crucial. Hagar simply must wait a little longer, because Ishmael must be born in the house of Abraham to prove that he is the first-born (Deuteronomy 21:15–17), and to enter into the household through the rite of circumcision (Chap. 17). This will guarantee him participation in the history of salvation, and will give him rights of inheritance in the house of Abraham.[33]

While God is concerned about Ishmael's and Hagar's survival, there are some questions womanists must ask about God's relation to the terms of survival upon which Hagar lives in Abraham and Sarah's household. Does God care more about the oppressor Sarah than about the oppressed Hagar? When Sarah becomes jealous of Ishmael and decides that he—though firstborn—will not inherit along with her son Isaac, she demands that Hagar and Ishmael be thrown out of the house. Abraham opposed this, but God intervened telling him to do as Sarah asks. What are we to say about God's action here? Can we conclude that what looks like God favoring the oppressor female is just the way the story is told in the Bible, that it is not necessarily the way God actually behaves with regard to oppressed-oppressor relationships? If we answer this question affirmatively, do we not discredit all biblical descriptions of God's actions in relation to humankind?

Tamez does not question God's favoring the oppressor Sarah over the oppressed Hagar. Rather, in a liberation mode she concludes: "God let her [Sarah] act that way because he had other plans for Hagar, a better future than in the house of Abraham."[34] But there is nothing in Hagar's story in the Bible to suggest a better future for her. In fact, Hagar's and Ishmael's future seems highly precarious and more threatened than their existence in Abraham's house.

Nevertheless, African-American women as well as African-American people in general have through the years found hope in Hagar's story. I believe the hope oppressed black women get from the Hagar-Sarah texts has more to do with survival and less to do with liberation. When they and their families get into serious social and economic straits, black Christian women have believed that God helps them make a way out of no way. This is precisely what God did for Hagar and Ishmael when they were expelled from Abraham's house and were wandering in the desert without food and water. God opened Hagar's eyes and she saw a well of water that she had not seen before. In the context of the survival struggle of poor African-American women this translates into God providing Hagar [read also African-American women] with *new vision* to see survival resources where she saw none before. God's promise to Hagar throughout her story is one of survival (of her progeny) and not liberation. In Hagar's story liberation is self-initiated and oppressor-initiated. Human initiative "sparks" liberation—not divine initiative. In Genesis 16 Hagar liberates herself; she is a run-away slave. In Genesis 21 Sarah, her oppressor, initiates Hagar's liberation. God merely agrees with Sarah. In both instances Hagar is liberated into precarious circumstances.

On the basis of the Hagar-Sarah texts the feminist and womanist liberationist and the womanist survival/quality-of-life advocates may provide different responses to the question, How does God relate to the oppressed in history? The liberationist may say God relates primarily to liberation efforts. The survivalist may say God relates primarily to survival/quality-of-life efforts. Some feminists and womanists may say God relates to the oppressed both ways at different times or at the same time. Again, the issue is not who is right or wrong. The issue is an understanding of biblical accounts about God that allows various communities of poor, oppressed black women and men to hear and see the *doing* of the good news in a way that is meaningful for their lives.

The truth of the matter may well be that the Bible gives license for us to have it both ways: God liberates and God does not always liberate all the oppressed. God speaks comforting words to the survival and quality-of-life struggle of many families. The biblical stories are told in a way that influences us to believe that God makes choices. And God changes whenever God wills. But African-American Christian women are apt to declare as Hagar did, "Thou art a God of Seeing" (Genesis 16:15). And seeing means acknowledging and ministering to the survival/quality-of-life needs of African-American women and their children.

### There Are Commonalities

Though differences exist in their cultural contexts, social locations and experiences, feminists and womanists hold in common a belief that sexism exists in most institutional expressions of the Christian religion in North America. Many feminists and womanists agree that a serious and critical review of Christian symbols, doctrines and practice is necessary in order to determine precisely how and if women's oppression can be supported by the religion. With regard to the concern and the content of *Sisters in the Wilderness*, common ground exists between some feminists and womanists who are reviewing Christian doctrine.

Just as the womanist view of black women's experience in this book led to serious questions about Christian notions of redemption, some Anglo-feminist analysis has also led to questioning the Christian theories of atonement on the basis of the abuse of women and children. Feminist scholars Joanne Carlson Brown and Rebecca Parker take a critical look at the idea of suffering developed in Christian theories of atonement.[35] Though some of their ideas are vastly different from what *Sisters in the Wilderness* projects,[36] Brown and Parker claim, as I do, that most of the history of atonement theory in Christian theology supports violence, victimization and undeserved suffering. The earlier discussion of atonement in Chapter 6 above agrees with Brown and Parker's assertion that "the central image of Christ on the cross as the savior of the world communicates the message that suffering is redemptive."[37]

Their critique of Martin Luther King, Jr.'s idea of the value of the suffering of the oppressed in oppressed-oppressor confrontations accords with my assumption that African-American Christian women can, through their religion and its leaders, be led passively to accept their own oppression and suffering—if the women are taught that suffering is redemptive. Brown and Parker quote Martin Luther King, Jr.'s words about suffering which he saw as

> a most creative and powerful social force....The non-violent say that suffering becomes a powerful social force when you willingly accept that violence on yourself, so that self-suffering stands at the center of the non-violent movement and the individuals involved are able to suffer in a creative manner, feeling that unearned suffering is redemptive, and that suffering may serve to transform the social situation.[38]

Brown and Parker's critique of this theology "is that it asks people to suffer for the sake of helping evildoers see their evil ways. It puts concern for the evildoers ahead of concern for the victim of evil. It makes victims the servants of the evildoers' salvation."[39]

Here, Brown and Parker unconsciously conjure up for me an ancient African-American civil rights strategy that some highly visible young black activists are today criticizing. This strategy, used by Frederick Douglass, Martin Luther King, Jr., and others is called moral suasion.[40] It assumed that black people could obtain their rights by appealing to the moral conscience of their white oppressors. And, of course, undeserved black suffering at the hands of white people has been fodder for the moral suasion argument. Today, some young civil rights activists deny that white America has a moral conscience with regard to black people.[41] Therefore it is useless for black people to make this appeal.[42]

Some of Brown and Parker's conclusions to their critique of Christian theories of atonement resonate with what the womanist god-talk here affirms about Jesus. Brown and Parker claim Jesus did not choose the cross. He "chose to live a life in opposition to unjust, oppressive cultures.... Jesus chose integrity and faithfulness, refusing to change course because of threat."[43] Womanist god-talk speaks in terms of a ministerial vision of righting relations as the center of Jesus' mission. And it can be claimed that these right relationships he advocated challenged the injustice characterized by oppressed-oppressor relations. Jesus' ministerial (or pastoral) vision brought justice and care to relationships. Brown, Parker and the womanist god-talk in this book apparently agree: People do not have to attach sacred validation to a bloody cross in order to be redeemed or to be Christians. "To be Christian means keeping faith with those who have heard and lived God's call for justice, radical love and liberation; who challenged unjust systems both political and ecclesiastical."[44]

A womanist addendum to this would declare that to be a Christian also means to be tangibly related to the survival/quality-of-life struggle of suffering black people—the homeless, the people with AIDS, people living in dire poverty, the poverty-stricken single parent trying to raise children. To be a Christian is to share one's skills and economic resources with victims. To be a Christian is to affirm the life of black Americans and other threatened groups by joining their survival struggle against genocide. Thus the Christian allows the threatened ones to educate him or her about the many forms genocide can take in a "democracy." To be a Christian in North America is to wage war against the white cultural, social and religious values that make the genocide of black people possible. To be a Christian is to wage this war in the name of Jesus and his ministerial vision of relationship, which involved whipping the money changers (read those in charge of genocidal values) out of the Temple.

There are also commonalities among some of the ideas in *Sisters in the Wilderness* and some of the god-talk of womanist theologian Kelly Delaine Brown. This is especially noticeable in Brown's article "God Is As Christ Does: Toward a Womanist Theology."[45] Brown believes that womanist theologians must reflect upon at least two aspects of black women's experience: "the complexity of their distinctive oppression," and "their ability to survive and achieve in spite of that oppression."[46]

The research I did in black women's sources revealed to me the complexity of black women's oppression and the simplistic way in which that experience has been reduced to race, gender or class categories. When I viewed black slave women with regard to every activity and relation in which they were involved to make the slavocracy work, it became clear to me that black women's bodies had been exploited to a degree matched by no other group in the society.

White women, as a group, did not experience such a complete exploitation of their bodies as did black women. Black women's labor, their nurturing capacities, their sexuality was made available to any powerful white person who wanted to *use* black women. Like Brown, I realized the *distinctive* complexity of black women's heritage of oppression. From this kind of realization the surrogacy language came into the womanist god-talk in this book. Certainly *Sisters in the Wilderness* is in agreement with Brown's contention that black women's survival and achievement record, achieved in spite of complex oppression, is a vital source for womanist theology.

And the story of black Christian women's fortitude cannot be accurately told without Jesus, whom these women have historically regarded as their helpmate on their journey. While *Sisters in the Wilderness* does not explore christological questions, but rather briefly provides a response to questions surrounding redemption and atonement, there is an assumption here that womanist theology must, in many theological areas, render an understanding of Jesus Christ. And I agree with Brown's statement that "womanist theology must be very selective in the language and symbols used to describe and point to Christ's particular meaning for black women."[47] But I would add that we womanists must reshape the christological question so that our consideration of the issue does not just speak to and have relevance in the academy. For instance, we must ask if the classical christological distinction between the Jesus of history and the Christ of faith is the proper emphasis if black Christian women's experience is shaping the content of our talk about Jesus Christ. My research tells me that Brown is correct when she says

[womanist theology] must always make it clear that the ultimate significance of Christ is not predicated on skin color or gender but on sustaining and liberating activity. Regardless of how tempting it may be to describe Christ in biological likeness of a black woman, as a quick and easy means to allow black women to see themselves in Christ and Christ in themselves, to do such a thing is theologically misleading. Although Christ can certainly be embodied by a black woman, it is more in keeping with black women's testimonies to Jesus and Jesus' own self-understanding if womanist theology describes Christ as being embodied wherever there is a movement to sustain and liberate the entire black community, male and female.[48]

Black women are, then, more apt to see Jesus/Christ as spirit sustaining survival and liberation efforts of the black community. Thus black women's question about Jesus Christ is not about the relation of his humanity to his divinity or about the relation of the historical Jesus to the Christ of faith. Black women's stories in the first part of this book and Cheryl Gilkes description of an Afrocentric biblical tradition in this chapter attest to black women's belief in Jesus/Christ/God involved in their daily affairs and supporting them. Jesus is their mother, their father, their sister and their brother. Jesus is whoever Jesus has to be to function in a supportive way in the struggle. Whether we talk about Jesus in relation to atonement theory or christology, we womanists must be guided more by black Christian women's voices, faith and experience than by anything that was decided centuries ago at Chalcedon.

Our black communities are engaged in a terrible struggle for life and well-being. All of our talk about God must translate into action that can help our people live. Womanist theology is significant *only* if it contributes to this struggle. We must, like Hagar, obtain through our God-given faith *new vision* to see survival and quality-of-life resources where we have seen none before. Since feminists and womanists come from many cultures and countries, womanist-feminist dialogue and action may well provide some of the necessary resources. Recognizing and honoring our differences and commonalities can lead in directions we can perhaps both own.

*Chapter 8*

# WOMANIST REFLECTIONS ON "THE BLACK CHURCH," THE AFRICAN-AMERICAN DENOMINATIONAL CHURCHES AND THE UNIVERSAL HAGAR'S SPIRITUAL CHURCH

Any attempt to discern the meaning of African-American women's faith and action would be incomplete without reflection upon "The Black Church" and the African-American denominational churches in which African-American women have, through the years, invested much care, commitment, time and money. It is therefore appropriate at this point to provide womanist reflections on the black church, the African-American denominational churches and the Universal Hagar's Spiritual Church, given some of the insights in this book.

## *"The Black Church" Invisible*

The black church does not exist as an institution. Regardless of sociological, theological, historical and pastoral attempts, the black church escapes precise definition.[1] As many discussions of it as there are, there will be that many (and more) different definitions. Some believe it to be rooted deeply in the soul of the community memory of black folk. Some believe it to be the core symbol of the four-hundred-year-old African-American struggle against white oppression with God in the struggle providing black people with spiritual and material resources for survival and freedom. Others believe it to be places where black people come to worship God without white people being present.

I believe the black church is the heart of hope in the black community's experience of oppression, survival struggle and its historic efforts toward complete liberation. It cannot be tampered with or changed by humans to meet human expectations and goals. The black church cannot be made respectable because it is already sacralized by the pain and resurrection of thousands upon thousands of victims. It cannot be made elite because it is already classless. In America it came first to the community of slaves. It cannot be made racial because it is too real for false distinctions. It cannot be made more male than female because it is already both, equally. It cannot be made heterosexist because it is a "homo-hetero" amalgam. It cannot be made political because it is perfect justice.

We cannot confine the black church to one special location because it can move everywhere faster than a bird in flight, faster than a rocket soaring, faster than time—but slowly enough to put spiritual songs in our burdened souls—slowly enough to put love in our broken lives—slowly enough to bring moments of liberation to our troubled people.

The black church is invisible, but we know it when we see it: our daughters and sons rising up from death and addiction recovering and recovered; our mothers in poverty raising their children alone, with God's help, making a way out of no way and succeeding; Harriet Tubman leading hundreds of slaves into freedom; Isabel, the former African-American slave, with God's help, transforming destiny to become Sojourner Truth, affirming the close relation between God and woman; Mary McLeod Bethune's college starting on a garbage heap with one dollar and fifty cents growing into a multimillion dollar enterprise; Rosa Parks sitting down so Martin Luther King, Jr., could stand up. The black church is invisible, but we know it when we see oppressed people rising up in freedom. It is community essence, ideal and real as God works through it in behalf of the survival, liberation and positive, productive quality of life of suffering people.

It has neither hands nor feet nor form, but we know when we feel it in our communities as neither Christianity, nor Islam, nor Judaism, nor Buddhism, nor Confucianism, nor any human-made religion. Rather, it comes as God-full presence to our struggles quickening the heart, measuring the soul and bathing life with the spirit from head to toe. It comes as moral wisdom in the old folks saying, "You give out one lemon, God gonna give you a dozen back!" It comes as folk-analysis in the old people claiming, "White folks and us both Christians, but we ain't got the same religion." It comes as folk-faith nevertheless believing that *"all* God's children got wings to soar." The black church gave us spiritual songs and blues and gospel and rap and a singing way to justice, fighting. It is invisible, but we know when we see, hear and feel it quickening the heart, measuring the soul and bathing life with the spirit in time.

### *Then There Are African-American Denominational Churches*

The womanist thought in this book makes a distinction between the black church as invisible and rooted in the soul of community memory and the African-American denominational churches as visible. Contrary to the nomenclature in current black theological, historical and sociological works, in this book *the black church* is not used to name *both* the invisible black church and the African-American denominational churches. To speak of the African-American denominational churches as the black church suggests a unity among the denominations that does not consistently exist.

The fallacious merging of the black church and African-American denominational churches hides a multitude of sins against black women prevalent in the African-American denominational churches on a daily basis. Some of these sins are:

- The sexism that denies black women equal opportunity in the churches' major leadership roles. Such action opposes God by denying God's call to black women to preach. This sin has existed in the African-American denominational churches and among black male leadership in the denominations for more than one hundred years. Jarena Lee, whose narrative appeared in 1836, tells of Richard Allen's refusal to ordain her. Allen founded the African Methodist Episcopal Church. Old Elizabeth, a former slave whose narrative appeared in 1863, tells of black men prohibiting her from preaching.[2]

The sin of sexism dies slowly in some African-American denominational structures and hangs on tenaciously in others. The male-dominated black Baptist ministerial association, which has met on Mondays for years at Convent Baptist Church in New York City, only last year voted to accept black female ministers. But a female minister working as an associate pastor at one of the most prominent and prosperous Baptist churches in Brooklyn, New York, tells of other male associate ministers (her colleagues) who put obstacles in her way by trying to refuse her even the space in which to work. She tells of not receiving her paycheck on time and feeling as if she has to beg to be paid for the work she has done. Finally, the major minister of this famous African-American Baptist church told her she was a "pain in the bu-" and fired her when she asked for the pay that was due her at Christmas time.

Another fully ordained black woman says her incentive to pastor would die were she not called by God who supports her courage to stay in ministry. Having grown up in Baptist churches associated with the National [black] Baptist Convention, she has received no support for her ministry from that convention while black males receive much support. In fact, some black Baptist women, whose memberships were in denominational churches associated with the black National Baptist Convention, have had to seek ordination in the denominational churches connected with the American Baptist Convention, an integrated convention where white power is obvious. This means that black males, through the sexist practices in their churches, have left it to white men to affirm black women and to acknowledge black women's call from God while they (black male ministers) reject both black women and the women's call from God. Time and again, black women have told me some of their male colleagues try to "set them up" to fail in their ministries.

- The immoral models of male leadership at the helm of too many of the black denominational churches[3] (even in the nineteenth century, Ida B. Wells spoke of "corrupt" black ministers);[4]
- Collusion that often exists between some black male preachers and the political forces in America oppressing black women and all black people;[5]
- The sexual exploitation of black women in the denominational church by some preachers;[6]
- The tendency of the proclamation and teachings of the denominational churches to be so spiritualized and "heaven-directed" that women parishioners are not encouraged to concentrate on their lives in this world and to fight for their own survival, liberation and productive quality of life. They are not encouraged to develop a self-concept and build female self-esteem. Rather they are indoctrinated to be self-sacrificing and emotionally dependent upon males including male gods sacralizing the male image and making the feminine in Jesus invisible. They are encouraged to disregard and even work against freedom movements afoot in the culture to secure the rights of women;
- The failure of African-American denominational churches on a consistent and large scale, to pool their resources (across all denominational and class lines) in order to deal effectively with the poverty, drug-addiction, homelessness, hunger and health problems such as AIDS sweeping through the black communities in the United States;
- The leadership in the denominational churches encouraging homophobia;
- Responding to the AIDS crisis with denial;
- The emotional exploitation of black female parishioners as ministers

provoking emotional reactions to proclamation and ministry rather than thoughtful questions and responses;

- Building and purchasing elaborate church edifices while thousands of black people live in dire poverty—buildings that are often open only on Sunday and for prayer meeting or Bible study during the week—buildings without viable programs to meet the needs of black women and the black community;
- Failure of the denominational churches to pool their resources in order to develop a powerful, effective and extensive prison ministry working in both female and male prisons on a consistent basis to help black prisoners shape goals and begin to make and realize dreams for their lives—a prison ministry that works as effectively to rehabilitate the health, consciousness and lives of prisoners as the Black Islamic forces often do.[7]

However, it must be pointed out here that some African-American denominational churches are providing outstanding work in some of these areas. Among them are Glide Memorial United Methodist Church in San Francisco, California; Allen A.M.E. Church in Queens, New York; Bridge Street A.M.E. Church in Brooklyn. In *The Black Church in the African American Experience,* C. Eric Lincoln and Lawrence H. Mamiya mention several churches in different parts of the country with effective ministries in the black communities.[8]

Though problems in the church regarding women's freedom, faith and self-concept are old and legion, there have been moments in African-American history when some of the denominational churches have been effective instruments of freedom, survival and positive quality of life formation for all black people. This is when the black church emerges from the soul of community memory.[9] For the black church—having neither denominational commitment nor religious bias—acts as the great judging, healing, fighting, holy Godforce. It breathes compassion and power in the black community as community groups strip systems of oppression down to the core human essential of justice-bearing in the midst of oppressed people's economic, educational, freedom and survival struggles.

Out of the black church Godforce, the black denominations have founded schools for black people; built housing for the poor; birthed great civil rights movements; birthed black salvation-bearers like Harriet Tubman, Sojourner Truth, Milla Granson, Ida Wells Barnett, Fredrick Douglass, Martin Luther King, Jr., Medgar Evers and many other ordinary black women and men. The black church has been the holy Godforce holding black people together body, soul and spirit as the perpetrators of genocide tried to exterminate the community.

Both in slavery and shortly after they came out of bondage, African Americans survived and were welded together as a community by the black church in solidarity with the mutual aid societies and the black extended family.[10] As African Americans became more and more "Americanized" by appropriating white American values of individualism, capitalist economics and classism, the solidarity between the black church, the mutual aid societies and the extended family disappeared.[11] The mainline African-American denominational churches[12] supported the adoption of these white values, and the black church retreated to the deep recesses of the soul of community memory. Many mutual aid societies went out of existence or changed to organizations of lesser importance in the economic structure of the African-American denominational churches. Black people were duped into believing that their economic interests could be served by a white-dominated American capitalist economy and capitalist institutions. The black extended family passed away. Black people, in their effort to be "Americanized," began to believe that the white model of the nuclear family could more adequately service the bonding and the wisdom-transmitting tasks absolutely necessary for the survival of generations of black people: women, men and children. Nothing, of course, could have been farther from the truth. In actuality, the old folks (the grandmothers, grandfathers, great aunts and great uncles: the ancestors) were the carriers of the wisdom and traditions effective for survival and community building. The old folks were alienated from the nuclear family structure. They were isolated from black children who needed, along with their parents, the wisdom of the ancestors. They needed this wisdom in order to learn the strategies in black everyday life, which had worked over time for survival, liberation and for developing a positive, productive quality of life.

The Reverend Patricia Reeberg, Executive Director of the Council of Churches of the City of New York, makes important and supportive evaluations about the work of some of the African-American churches. For instance, there is the problem of the lack of funds to finance important projects some of the churches want to undertake. In an interview in the publication *Routes,* Reverend Reeberg, a Baptist minister, says that small and middle-sized churches have difficulty getting money from traditional sources because they lack the sophistication it takes to go after these funds. So, "many times cake sales, fish fries and bus rides fund most, if not all their projects."[13] Reverend

Reeberg illustrates the grassroots creativity with which these small and middle-sized churches devise ways to meet the urgent needs in the community. She points to St. Paul's Church in Harlem, where the congregation met its goal of feeding hungry members of the community by pooling its finances within the church to increase its capacity for feeding sixty people to feeding two hundred persons.

Reeberg sees three common characteristics of the African-American denominational churches that sustain their leadership in the African-American community:

> 1) The mothering instinct . . . that is always present: if a member is sick or needs assistance, a church "family" adopts them. 2) The enormous commitment to volunteerism: 92 percent of the members volunteer their services; sweat equity is a vital element in the success of the church. 3) The last, but equally important as the others, is the philanthropic nature of the . . . church.[14]

The interviewer of Reverend Reeberg concludes that "the holistic philosophy of integrating the spiritual, the carnal, and the political, enables the African-American church to be an influential force in the community."[15]

But it is also gratifying to learn that some black preachers in America are beginning to see that vast changes must take place in the denominational churches before these groups can work effectively to secure survival, foster liberation and generate a positive, productive quality of life for all African Americans. At the Martin Luther King, Jr., Forum held in New York City in December 1992 at the Schomburg Center for Research in Black Culture, four African-American ministers responded to Martin Luther King, Jr.'s question that titles his book: *Where Do We Go from Here, Chaos or Community?* The four ministers were Jamil Abdullah Al-Amin (formerly known as H. Rap Brown), Imam at the Community Mosque in Atlanta, Georgia; Reverend Calvin O. Butts, pastor of the Abyssinian Baptist Church in New York City; Reverend James Forbes, pastor of the Riverside Church in New York City; and the Reverend Jeremiah Wright, Jr., pastor of Trinity United Church of Christ in Chicago.

Their analyses of the problems facing the churches were full of relevant insights for African-American women, men and children living in today's world. Reverend Butts spoke of the black community and churches as culturally barren. Without knowledge of African roots and the meaning of black American experience, the people lack an adequate black consciousness, which is necessary for the community's self-understanding and advancement. He spoke of the need for black competency. He gave attention to the economic situation in the African-American communities and said the churches could help in this area by accessing public funds for private use. The churches could obtain the funds that could set up employment situations in which black people could hire other black people. Butts pointed to the work of Marcus Garvey and Booker T. Washington as models from the past illustrating that black people can efficiently manage economic resources for the good of black people.

While Reverend James Forbes spoke of the need for a new order among black people, one that would necessitate spiritual revitalization, Reverend Jeremiah Wright spoke of the black community being in a state of confusion. He said black people are confused about identity—hence the constant changing of names from Negro to Afro-American to African-American. "We are confused about our culture," he said. "We have little or no knowledge of our African heritage. We are confused about our history because we have forgotten *our* story. We have confused unity with uniformity. Hence we think that in order to be unified we all have to think alike." Reverend Wright gave at least three ways the African-American denominational churches could alleviate the situation as they responded to Martin King, Jr.'s question—Where do we go from here? First the churches must break with their bourgeoisism and connect with poor, grassroots people. Second, the churches must build strong Christian education programs with an Afrocentric perspective. An Afrocentric perspective teaches self-knowledge. "You cannot love yourself," Wright said, "if you do not know yourself." He was careful to remind the audience that "you cannot be sexist and be Afrocentric." He spoke against homophobia as his third point emphasized a ministry of liberation for the churches. This ministry of liberation would also include vibrant celebration in black worship consisting of preaching, music and the holy spirit.

Confining most of his remarks to what the Koran has to say about moral living, Jamil Abdullah Al-Amin presented a clear and convincing discourse on Allah's intent for the physical, mental and moral well-being of all people, including black people.

The Christian ministers apparently agreed on at least one point. Vast changes must happen in the black community and in the African-American denominational churches if black people are ever going to get out of the throes of oppression. Butts's and Wright's emphasis upon putting an Afrocentric perspective in the center of African-American consciousness is a fine corrective as long as the churches continue to emphasize that *there is neither sexism nor homophobia* in the non-romanticized Afrocentric perspective the churches teach. Since many of the African-American denominational churches are presently sponsoring forums on Afrocentrism, this perspective is gaining a strong foothold in some black communities among the rank-and-file population.[16] Nevertheless, black women, who compose the majority population in these churches, must refuse to accept any perspective (African or not) that does not take seriously black women's experience as a source—that does not take seriously African-American women's oppression and their intellectual, social and spiritual history.

Regardless of these positive features of the African-American denominational churches, there are questions about black women to which all the African-American denominational churches need to respond. What is being done in the churches to motivate self-love and self-esteem among black women? How many times does the preacher's sermon have as its subject the oppression prevailing in the black community—especially the oppression of black women? How many times does the preacher address the emotional and sexual exploitation of black women by black men? How many times has domestic violence been the subject of the sermon? How many times does the sermon advise black men about being positive and responsible parents to their children? How many times does the preacher's sermon tell black men to erase white aesthetic values from their minds and love and respect black-skinned, broad-nosed, beautiful black women *who look like black women?* Are there study groups in the church and outreach programs into the community that are devoted to dealing with these issues? Are there classes on parenting now that there are so many teen-age parents? Is the church supporting the kind of parenthood that accommodates the liberation of women and children as well as that of men? How much attention are the denominational churches giving to discussions and classes on sexuality so that young people can begin sex education early? How much attention is given to young black women coming to terms early with career goals, so that they realize they can have a productive future unburdened by teen-age pregnancies? Are teen-age parents getting the kind of support they need from the churches?

Black women, themselves, must realize that black men may disagree with and fight white men over racism, but far too many black men and white men (preachers included) are thoroughly bonded in their affirmation of the subordination of women. Even W. E. B. Du Bois, who on occasion spoke about women's need for freedom, believed that black women should abide by the status-quo rule: "Men are primary wage-earners and women are mothers and keepers of the home." Black women were to fit into the roles that a "civilized, progressive society" (read white) ordained for women in order to propagate the race. In an address to women at Spelman College Du Bois said black people would not advance like "the virile races of the world . . . unless the Negro women . . . are prepared to assume the responsibility of healthy families, of two or three children."[17] Apparently Du Bois did not believe that black women should play a dominant role in the political life of black Americans. The civil rights struggle was to be controlled by black males.

When black women accept the realization that far too many black men and white men in power agree on the subordination of black women, perhaps they will begin a serious women's movement within the denominational churches—a movement to free women's minds and lives of the androcentric indoctrination and the exploitative emotional commitments that cause many women to be tools of their own oppression and that of other women. Often in the classes I have taught in seminary, black women ministers have lamented the oppression they experience from females as well as from males in the church. Black female pastors say that some women in the churches do not support female ministers. No doubt this lack of support of women by women is tied to the male-dominated and androcentric character of the liturgy and to the thoroughly masculine character assigned to the deity the church women have been taught to worship and celebrate.

Elaborating upon the task of womanist theology, womanist theologian Kelly Delaine Brown addresses African-American women's difficulty in imagining femaleness assigned to the deity the parishioners worship. Brown says, "There are several instances that illustrate understandings of Jesus which are oppressive for black women." She cites the equation often made in African-American faith between Jesus and God: "Black church people have consistently understood Jesus as God; they make little distinction between the two." Thus she asks the question: "Given Jesus' maleness, is such an equation evident when a black church woman says that calling God 'she' just doesn't sound right?"[18] Then Brown poses these questions: "Does a male Jesus imply to black women that God is also male? Does the lack of distinction between the male Jesus and God prevent black women from exclaiming, 'I found God in myself and I loved her / I loved her fiercely'?"[19]

The African-American denominational churches' sin against women exists partly because none of them has engaged a task much needed for the freedom struggle of black people, female and male. That task is a thorough examination of the doctrines to which they subscribe. Most mainline African-American denominational churches derived from white Baptist, Methodist, Presbyterian, Episcopal and other denominations. Though the style of worship in an African-American denominational church may differ greatly from that of its respective white counterpart; though the members of the black denominational churches may believe that the ethical posture of the black denominations, with regard to human rights, is far superior to their white counterparts' ethical posture; though community life in the black and white denominational churches may be organized differently, the doctrinal foundations of the black and the white denominational churches are apt to be the same. Though many African-American denominational churches emerged because of the racism black people experienced when they attended white churches, no African-American denomination has *seriously* examined its doctrinal beliefs to discover whether they support racial, sexual and class oppression.

Obviously, on the basis of black women's surrogacy oppression described in this book, such an examination is needed to explore the understanding and teaching of atonement in the African-American denominational churches. Certainly many African-American male preachers and theologians have seen the need to color Jesus black, thereby attaching sacred meaning to the black male image. But none has seen the need also to question the androcentric bias contained in the denominations' (or the Christian religion's) concept of Jesus. Womanist theologians Jacqueline Grant and Kelly Brown are notable exceptions.[20] Yet all black theologians, male and female, have as far as I know presented the meaning of Jesus for the African-American community by using the analytical theological and doctrinal category called christology to examine the deposits of black Christian culture. The question is this: Is the subject of the christological inquiry, that is, the meaning of the person of Jesus,[21] broad enough or relevant enough to serve as an analytical tool for assessing *all* the African-American Christian understanding of Jesus or God? African-American theologians apparently have not asked the related question: What are the appropriate tools for exploring the meaning of Jesus in an Afrocentric American context rather than an "Afro-Saxon," Eurocentric American context? (This suggests that womanist theologians should begin raising questions about the analytical appropriateness of *all* traditional doctrinal categories for interrogating African-American women's experience—questions that trouble the theological waters [black and white] just as Cain Hope Felder's exploration into the African content in the Bible troubled the biblical waters. Our purpose is not to trouble the waters just for the sake of raising a fuss. Our purpose is to present more precisely what African-American women and the African-American community have and do believe and to exercise a prophetic womanist theological task in relation to this belief.)[22]

Neither have the African-American denominational churches examined their doctrinal affirmations to determine whether their teachings are compatible with and supportive of the African-American four-hundred-year-old (and continuing) struggle for freedom and justice—a struggle in which African-American slaves believed God spoke to them as a community providing good news more powerful and more real than anything white masters and white churches taught.

Some slave mothers taught their daughters a doctrine of resistance. It seems to me that if oppressed people in the African-American denominational churches need any doctrine, they need doctrines of resistance that are taught to the people over and over again. These doctrines could be based upon the experience of African-American people in dialectical relation with the resistance stories and patterns from the Bible and from other African cultural sources. But rigorous methods of criticism must be applied to biblical stories before they can be used to validate the creation of resistance doctrine. These biblical stories must be "decoded" of sexism and of any tendency they might have to support racism, colorism, elitism, homophobia and Eurocentric domination of black people's minds. Any aspect of African-American people's experience and of African cultural sources used to shape resistance doctrine must also be "de-coded" of *all* androcentric, gender, homophobic, class and color bias. To implant this resistance doctrine firmly in the minds of the people and to create memory, resistance rituals would have to be created by the community and enacted as regularly in the African-American denominational churches as the eucharist.

Whereas some liberation theology (especially feminist theology) shies away from affirming the need for doctrinal systems, African-American Christians need doctrine in their churches. But they need *doctrine that emerges from African-American people's experience with God,* not doctrine "inherited" from oppressive Eurocentric forms of Christianity, not female-exclusive doctrine formulated centuries ago by male potentates. It is the unromanticized, egalitarian African heritage and the slaves' experience with God articulated in their narratives, tales and songs that begin to provide materials for the construction of African-American Christian doctrines of resistance. It is God's continuing work in the African-American community's ever-present struggle for economic justice, for physical and emotional survival and for positive quality of life that forms "the stuff" of black Christian doctrines of resistance. Black women in the denominational churches especially need a doctrine of resistance and resistance rituals. They must pass on to generations of their female and male children the memory of African-American women's rich resistance history, some of which has been recounted in this book.

Black American Christians have, in a woeful way, turned their backs on God. They have ignored the wonderful work of God in black people's survival and freedom struggle. After slavery African Americans did not write their story into black scripture that would tell future generations about the people's historic life struggle and about God's wondrous way of dealing with them during bondage and in liberation. The particulars of the community's great faith story have been ignored. Instead black Americans have tried to validate their experience, their way of believing and their way of living a spiritual life only on the basis of the faith-story of the Jews contained in the Bible. We black people do not record for our children our current faith-stories demonstrating God's involvement in black people's lives today. In the African-American denominational churches' liturgies, these stories should be scripture just as vital as the Bible. It is no wonder that the African-American denominational churches are, in their doctrinal structures, little more than pale imitations of white denominational churches, which are, in far too many instances, racist, sexist and homophobic.

The work of the African-American denominational churches' theologians, *in consultation with the ministers and congregations,* should be constantly to develop new principles for interpreting African-American people's history and the Bible—principles taking seriously the faith-experience of African-American people rooted in Africa, in America and in resistance. It would no doubt be helpful for black religious scholars, along with ministers and congregations, to be involved constantly in the task of "revaluing value" so that black people can root out of the African-American denominational churches the alien sexist, capitalist, class and color values black people have internalized in their process of becoming "Americanized" and "Christianized." Instruments for revaluation should be shaped by a nonsexist, nonhomophobic, noncolorist, nonelitist Afrocentric perspective.

Black women in the denominational churches should be especially vigilant in order to guard against the churches' making gender oppression invisible as they "revalue value" to attack the effects of racial oppression on the black community. Too long have black women in the churches taken a back seat and not pushed ahead for female leadership to be visible in the major and financially benefiting roles in the churches. Many black women in the African-American denominational churches have been duped to believe that first black people must expend all of their effort getting rid of racial oppression. They have been told that *later* the community can work on the oppression of women. However, nineteenth-century black women like Sojourner Truth have warned black women that "if the men get their rights and women don't, things will be no better for black women than they were during slavery." Said another way: sexism affords as much bondage as racism.

Among the African-American denominational churches there are some that have never spurned female leadership and female content at the highest levels of the churches' organization and liturgy. Given the advocacy for black women's freedom and leadership in this book, these churches deserve attention. One is especially important because its name reminds black people of the significance of Hagar in the development of African-American religious consciousness.

### *Background for the Universal Hagar's Spiritual Church*

The Universal Hagar's Spiritual Church is not a mainstream church. It belongs to the black spiritual tradition that has been labeled a sect by some black scholars.[23] To understand the Universal Hagar's Spiritual Church one needs to understand the nature and development of the spiritual tradition among African Americans.

The black spiritual churches seem to have first appeared in several large cities in the northern United States and in the South in the first quarter of the twentieth century. Most of the early black spiritual churches were of the storefront variety. Many of them were established by black people who migrated to the cities from the rural areas but did not find acceptance or were not comfortable in the established mainstream African-American denominational churches. While some black rural migrants to the cities did adjust to the large black denominational congregations, others who had been leaders in the churches in their originating territories could not find leadership roles in the city churches. Many of the larger mainstream black churches were catering to the more secular values of the growing black middle class. So the rural newcomers to the city founded their own small churches.[24]

This spiritual church movement among African Americans is unique because women have held major leadership roles from the beginning. Mother Leafy Anderson, a woman of black and Indian ancestry, was at the forefront of the establishment of spiritual churches. Sociologist Hans Baer, referring to the work of Andrew Kaslow and Claude Jacobs, indicates that Mother Anderson established the Eternal Life Christian Spiritualist Church in Chicago in 1913.[25] She later played a major role in the development of the spiritual religion in New Orleans, where the present content of much of the black spiritual movement was determined.[26] She is credited with starting the Eternal Life Spiritualist Church, the first black spiritual church in New Orleans. Though scholars disagree on the date when this church was started, they agree that the overwhelming majority of the founders of the spiritual churches in New Orleans were women. These women were addressed as Mother, and Mother Leafy Anderson—the major forebear of this tradition in New Orleans—trained several other women, who established congregations of their own. Eventually Mother Anderson became "head of an association that included the New Orleans congregations plus others in Chicago, Little Rock, Memphis, Pensacola, Biloxi, Houston and some smaller cities."[27]

The list of women founders of black spiritual churches in New Orleans is extensive. In 1922 Mother Catherine Seals founded the Temple of the Innocent Blood. Mother C. J. Hyde started the St. James Temple of Christian Faith in 1923. Mother L. Crosier started the Church of the Helping Hand and Spiritual Faith in 1923 because of instructions she said she received from the Virgin Mary. Some of Mother Hyde's female disciples received subcharters under her city charter and founded new congregations. One of these disciples was Mother Keller, who organized St. James Temple of Christian Faith, Number 2. Mother Shannon founded the St. Anthony Daniel Helping Hand Divine Chapel. Mother Katherine Francis established St. Michael's Church.

Though the majority of the founders of the black spiritual churches in New Orleans were women, some men also organized churches. Aided by the support of his sister Mother Kate Frances, Father Daniel Dupont established St. Michael's Church, Number 9, in 1932 in New Orleans. Bishop Thomas, who had been a schoolteacher and was a graduate of Xavier University, headed the Spiritualist Church of the South. Many of these spiritualist churches are still thriving in New Orleans, which Hans A. Baer claims has maintained its position of "Mecca of the Spiritualist movement."[28]

The black spiritual tradition—sometimes called the spiritualist tradition—is one of the most syncretistic traditions in African-American christendom. Baer describes the early stages of this syncretistic phenomenon as containing elements of "Spiritualism, Roman Catholicism and Voodooism or hoodoo, as well as other esoteric belief systems." The way in which these various elements were put together in the spiritual churches often depended upon the point of view of the church's pastor and inner circle. According to Baer, "Religious syncretism in the Spiritual Movement is a dynamic process susceptible to a number of structural, cultural and psychological factors." He identifies these factors as "the social composition of the local congregation, the prevailing religious patterns of the Black Churches in its geographical area, and the predilections of the founder or a prominent leader of a particular church or association."[29]

American spiritualism (primarily white), originating in America in 1848, seems to have been the source of some of the black spiritual churches' overwhelming emphasis upon the life and efficacy of spirits. They both understand God as spirit and believe it is possible to communicate with the spirits of deceased loved ones. Whereas American spiritualism fosters seances, the contemporary black spiritual movement in the main is not associated with seances. However, there are some notable exceptions within the black spiritual movement. Apparently seances do occur in some of the congregations of the Universal Hagar's Spiritual Churches. Baer claims that "in addition to believing that one may communicate through dreams or visions with loved ones who have passed into the spiritual plane,... the Hagar's Churches occasionally resort to a seance for making such contact."[30]

At one time in America, blacks and whites were together in the National Spiritualist Association of Churches. But this organization was white dominated. The black numbers increased, and finally in 1922 many of the black people withdrew from this association and formed the National Colored Spiritualist Association with headquarters in Detroit, Michigan. Nevertheless, the National Colored Spiritualist Association seems to have adhered to the beliefs and practices advocated by the National Spiritualist Association of Churches.[31]

While some of the black spiritual churches may have much in common with the white spiritual movement with regard to belief in communicating with spirits, the African heritage of black Americans must be taken into account. Many African slaves came to the new world with a highly developed spiritual consciousness fortified by their belief that they could communicate with the spirits of the ancestors and these spirits could have an effect upon daily life. This may be part of the bedrock of the black spiritual movement, inasmuch as cultural patterns and accustomed ways of thinking are passed on from generation to generation.

Some of the most notable syncretistic elements in the practices and beliefs of the black spiritual churches are based in the Catholic faith. In nearly all the black spiritual churches there are votive candles. People often make the sign of the cross and genuflect when passing before an altar. Some of the churches bear the names of Catholic saints, as do Catholic churches. The minister of one spiritual church identified St. Martin de Porres as the favorite saint in her church.[32] Many of the spiritual churches engage in cultic practices lifting up certain Catholic saints. Some churches believe that if one's faith is not strong enough for one to beseech God directly, one must ask the saints to take the petition to God.

While the black spiritual churches, in general, seem proud of the Catholic content in their belief and worship, most of them adamantly deny the voodoo "stigma" that has been associated with black spiritual churches. Apparently they have accepted the stereotypical (and erroneous) widespread concept that voodoo is evil and is a form of sorcery. In actuality, voodoo—as practiced in places like Haiti—is a credible folk religion originating in the African religion from Dahomey. A voodoo element in the black spiritual movement may be more readily detected in the churches in New Orleans than in other parts of the country. Baer makes the point that "an interesting link connecting Voodoo, Catholicism, and Spiritual religion in New Orleans is St. Expedite." Many people in New Orleans believe this saint is the one to contact when something must be done quickly. "St. Expedite is usually compensated for his services by burning a candle and saying a prayer before his statues 'but at other times, if you're a genuine Voodoo, by leaving a slice [of] poundcake, a new penny or a sprig of green at his feet.' "[33]

There are other esoteric elements in the syncretistic composition of some of the black spiritual churches. In a few churches, people believe in reincarnation. This belief could have come from a minor expression within American spiritualism or it could be an African retention, because some of the traditional African religions taught reincarnation. There are also instances of American Indian elements, especially in New Orleans. According to Baer and Tallant, "The Indian chief Black Hawk is probably the most renowned spirit guide in American Spiritualism. Mother Leafy Anderson was reportedly responsible for introducing Black Hawk into the 'spiritualist' churches in New Orleans as the patron of the South."[34]

We are not to suppose that all of these syncretistic elements in the black spiritual churches separate them from a basic Protestant identification. Baer rightly declares that the syncretistic "elements from these diverse traditions seemed to have been grafted onto or merged with a black version of Protestantism." He goes on to identify this Protestantism as one "that began in antebellum times and came to maturity in a wide array of Baptist, Methodist, Holiness and Pentecostal denominations and sects."[35]

Regardless of this multitude of syncretistic elements, most of the African-American spiritual churches are similar in organization to many black Protestant churches. Like other Protestant churches, the black spiritual churches are organized into hierarchies consisting first of an inner circle of pastors and other ministers, then deacons and trustee boards, missionaries, mothers, nurses and ushers. But unlike most other black Protestant churches, some of the African-American spiritual churches also recognize the role of the mediums who are taught to communicate with the spirit world. Some of the spiritual churches, unlike mainstream black Protestant churches, use exalted titles to address their leaders. They may be referred to as "King, Queen, Prince, Princess, Royal Elect Ruler, Reverend Doctor and Reverend Madam."[36]

Although women can fill leadership roles in every phase of the activities in the black spiritual churches, there are some roles that have been primarily filled by women. These are the roles of missionaries, mothers of the church and nurses. Missionaries help with the teaching of the gospel. In a Sunday morning worship service, they may pray, offer short sermons or direct the testimony period. In addition, missionaries might also give attention to the sick and the needy members in the church. Mother of the church is an honorific title that carries with it the task of assisting with church services if called upon. Mothers of the church, like the missionaries, are not part of the primary power structure in the church, but they are usually given a highly visible spot in the church services. Pews are reserved in the Sunday service for the mothers, who can be distinguished by their attire and headdress. Middle-aged or elderly, the mothers wear long white robes. Usually they wear some kind of white covering on their heads.

Like professional nurses, the nurses in the church wear white uniforms. Their function is to attend to people who go into some kind of ecstasy in the church services. The nurses make sure the ecstatic ones do not injure themselves or anyone else in proximity to them. There is no policy prohibiting men from being nurses.

Within the black spiritual churches there is no exclusivity with regard to gender roles except the mothers of the church. Though the language used in the churches to describe church offices and beliefs may be androcentric, women's leadership is encouraged and supported. For instance, in the Universal Hagar's Spiritual Churches the Wiseman Board is the primary executive structure in the churches. According to Baer, "Many women have served on the board, sometimes constituting the majority of its members. . . . A standard joke in the Hagar's church is the proposal that it should be called the 'Wisewoman Board.' "[37] Many, many black spiritual churches have female ministers. This has been the case since the initial organized churches in the African-American spiritual tradition came into existence.

Yet it must be pointed out that in some of the spiritual churches' belief systems, male images and male deeds appear to be given higher status than female images and deeds. Much more research needs to be done on black women's contribution to the development of the theology of the African-American spiritual tradition. Without this vital information, conclusive assessments of black women's work and contributions within the spiritual movement cannot be provided.

Focus upon one of the African-American spiritual churches can demonstrate the apparent contradiction between strong female leadership roles in the church's administration and the strong androcentric bias in some of the language and objects of worship in the church. With regard to female/male leadership, the Universal Hagar's Spiritual Church represents one of the most egalitarian traditions in African-American christendom.

### The Universal Hagar's Spiritual Church[38]

In the early 1920s George Willie Hurley associated himself with the International Spiritual Church and became a spiritualist preacher. One day he had a vision in which a brown-skinned woman turned into an eagle. He understood this vision to be directing him to found a church. So, on September 23, 1923, Hurley—who would come to be known as Father Hurley to his followers—established the Universal Hagar's Spiritual Church in Detroit, Michigan. Hurley associated the brown-skinned woman in his vision with Hagar, Ishmael's mother.[39] The Universal Hagar's Spiritual Church, under Hurley's direction, grew into a national association composed of many churches in various parts of the United States. Today there are upward of thirty-five congregations located in New Jersey, New York, Illinois, Indiana, Ohio, Pennsylvania, Connecticut, South Carolina, Florida and California. Although it may have been overstatement, Father Hurley referred to this conglomeration of churches as the largest spiritual association in the world.[40]

The Universal Hagar's Spiritual Association of Churches is a complex organization that once had spiritual heads (Father and Mother Hurley) and still has a Supreme Prince (or Princess). The Supreme Prince or Princess serves as business manager and president of the Wiseman Board, the chief executive organ of the churches. The Hagar's churches are organized at the national, district and local levels. The Wiseman Board is composed of seven regular members with two alternate members, usually Princesses and Princes from state or district locations of the Hagar's churches. There are supporting auxiliaries, like the Knights of the All Seeing Eye, the Mediums' League, the Hagar's Young People's Union and the Sacred Sisters, also known as the Universal Hagar Spiritual Association's Virgins. Most of these auxiliaries also function at the national, state/district and local levels. In most churches there is a deacons' board, a deaconesses' board, a mothers' board, a nurses' guild, an ushers' board, a choir, a Sunday School, a feast club and the pastor's aid club.[41]

The Mediums' League "is probably the most prestigious auxiliary in the Hagar's association."[42] The mediums themselves are trained in the School of Mediumship and Psychology established by Father Hurley in 1924. These schools later became part of the congregational structures of the Universal Hagar's Spiritual Churches. Attendance in the mediumship schools is selective; only those who are chosen to do so may attend. Training lasts for several years. Participants are taught how to communicate with the spirit world. When a student successfully completes the school's program, that student becomes an "uncrowned medium and is given a wand, bearing hieroglyphic inscriptions, which is used in certain rituals."[43] Upon finishing the master's program, the student becomes a "crowned medium" or "adept," prepared to be a spiritual advisor or a reader.[44] According to Baer, on special occasions students and uncrowned mediums wear blue "caps for males and robes for females. . . . Adepts wear purple. Students and graduates are not permitted to discuss the specific content of lessons and activities occurring in the School."[45] Women have never been barred from the school or the medium roles. There are female students who are uncrowned mediums and adepts in the Universal Hagar's Spiritual Association. But the school's injunction—

"Man, Know Thyself"—is expressed in androcentric language. No doubt the congregations understand *man* in a generic sense. (Yet I wonder if the school's curriculum would be different if the injunction were "Woman, Know Thyself.")

The Knights of the All Seeing Eye "is a secret Masonlike auxiliary of the Universal Hagar's Spiritual Church. Unlike most Masonic organizations, which are sexually segregated, the K. of A.S.E. [Knights of the All Seeing Eye] is open to both men and women."[46] At the national level, the heads of the K. of A.S.E. are called the Most Royal Exalted Master and the Royal Noble Mistress. There are chapters of the auxiliary in the local congregations. Each of these local chapters is served by an Exalted Knight and an Exalted Scribe. These leaders may be either male or female.

An interesting and unique auxiliary in the Hagar's churches is the Sacred Sisters. They are an association of young women between the ages of eleven and eighteen. Father Hurley established this association "for the purpose of lifting the burdens from our race at home and abroad."[47] Baer describes them as "Sacred Sisters [who] dedicate their lives to prayer. . . . They are not permitted to date boys or to have boy friends." Baer goes on to say that "one pastor told me that although she remained a member of the Sacred Virgins until she was twenty-two years old, she did not find it difficult to obey the rules of the auxiliary because it kept her extremely busy in attendance at various church functions."[48] Several questions emerge here. Does the stated purpose of this auxiliary suggest that black women's sexuality contributes to the burdens of the race at home and abroad? Is this an obvious attempt to control women's sexuality without putting any constraints upon men's sexuality? If the establishment of this organization of Sacred Virgins is an effort to limit teenage pregnancy, ought there to be a parallel organization for young men emphasizing prayer and male virginity?

Apparently Father Hurley was concerned about strengthening the black family. Models of leadership in the Hagar's churches often projected family images. For example, Father Hurley established the office of Supreme Mother, the first of whom was his wife. Baer provides a description of this role and of the assistant that also includes Father:

> The Assistant Supreme Mother serves in place of the Supreme Mother if she cannot be present at a particular event. Each district or state association also has a special Mother, as does each temple. The Temple Mother is in charge of the Altar Staff, a group of altar girls and altar boys who assist in various rituals during the religious services. She, along with the

deaconesses, is also responsible for the general housekeeping activities of the temple. Many Hagar's congregations also have a Temple Father, whose duties roughly parallel those of the Temple Mother.[49]

Many women have been at the very top of the leadership posts of the Universal Hagar's Spiritual Association of Churches. When Father Hurley passed into the spirit realm in 1943, he was succeeded by his wife, Mother C. B. Hurley. She operated in this capacity until 1960, when she died. While no one has been elected to the office of Spiritual Head of the Hagar's Churches since Mother Hurley's death, women have been elected to the major leadership role on the Wiseman Board. The following women have been president of the Wiseman Board: Reverend Ronnie Tatum (elected 1955); Mother Mary Hatchett (elected 1960); and the Reverend Latimer, daughter of Father and Mother Hurley. It is in the theological teachings, not the practice, of the Universal Hagar's Spiritual Church that androcentrism becomes obvious.

### Christ According to Father Hurley

Though the Universal Hagar's Spiritual Churches contain the same kind of syncretistic elements as other churches in the African-American spiritual tradition, Father Hurley made significant departures with regard to the identification of Christ. His understanding was informed by *The Aquarian Gospel of Jesus Christ,*[50] astrology and some of the teachings of messianic nationalism. About ten years after he founded the Universal Hagar's Spiritual Churches, Father Hurley began teaching that his own "carnal flesh" was transformed into the flesh of Christ. He identified himself as "Christ, the God, the Saviour, the Protector of this seven thousand year reign of the Aquarian Age."[51] According to several issues of *The Aquarian Age,* the official newspaper of the Universal Hagar's Spiritual Churches, Father Hurley had a religious experience which convinced him that he was the Christ for the time he identified as the Aquarian era.

He claimed the Holy Spirit came to him when he was thirteen years old and told him to fast for forty days (just as Jesus had fasted). During this time he was only permitted to eat one graham cracker and a glass of milk each day. After the fast, "God told Father Hurley that the existing religions of the world were not congruent with His will. Instead, His doctrines as they were originally taught through Zoroaster, Brahma, Buddha, Mohammed, the major and minor prophets of the Old Testament period, and Jesus had been altered by unbelievers who created segregation, hatred, jealousy, rape, robbery, murdering, and stealing."[52] In order to "reform the religions of the world," God told Hurley, "the Spirit of God was dwelling within his body." Further, God said, "The Spirit of God had at various times occupied the office of the Christ in the form of mortal men. Just as Adam had been the God of the Taurean Age, Abraham the God of the Arian Age, and Jesus the God of the Piscean Age, George Hurley, a black man of humble birth in the deep South of racist America, was born to be the God of the Aquarian Age—a period of peace and social harmony."[53]

Father Hurley identified the essence of the Christ not as a person but as the "wisdom and power of God love" that abided in the male Gods of the Taurean, Arian, Piscean and Aquarian ages. Though Father Hurley considered Mary the Goddess of the Piscean Age, he did not identify Hagar as the Goddess of the Arian age in which Abraham was supposed to be "endowed" with the "wisdom and power of God Love."

He was specific about the duration of the Aquarian Age as well as about the meaning of his reign in it. The Aquarian Age, coming into existence after World War I, is to last for seven thousand years. During this age Protestantism will end, as will segregation and the domination of powerful men over less powerful men. Father Hurley believed his gospel would be the last preached on earth, even though "minor prophets" would emerge after his death. In the year 6953 the name of Father Hurley would be known over all the earth. He taught his followers that in each person the Spirit of God abides. He thought if black people believed in God as spirit and believed that this spirit was in every man and woman, they would gain the self-esteem, the positive thinking and the faith in themselves that it takes to achieve success in this life.

Traditional eschatological themes that many Christians associate with the person and work of Jesus Christ are denied in the teachings of Father Hurley. For instance, he taught his followers there is no such thing as an afterlife of heaven and hell. Rather, heaven and hell are here on earth within every man and woman. Heaven is a state of peace, joy, happiness and success one experiences in this earthly life. Hell has to do with "hatred, jealousy, segregation, lying, robbery, stealing, disease and poverty." A state of sin is indicated by "hatred, prejudice, jim-crowism and segregationism."[54] He warns the Universal Hagar's Spiritual Church members not to seek their salvation in "gentile" Protestant religion. Rather, he advises them to nurture their own "innate forces, to think, to will and to imagine."[55]

Some of the androcentric elements in the belief system of the Universal Hagar's Spiritual Churches appear in the churches' rendition of the ten commandments—especially the fourth commandment.

1. Thou shall believe in Spirit (God) within matter.

2. Thou shall ignore a sky heaven for happiness and a downward hell for human punishment.

3. Thou shall believe in heaven and hell here on earth.

4. Thou shall believe in the fatherhood of God and the brotherhood of man.

5. Thou shall believe in what you sow, you shall also reap.

6. Thou shall believe that the Ethiopians and all Nations will rule the world in righteousness.

7. Thou shall believe that the Universal Hagar's Spiritual Church was revealed to Father G. W. Hurley for the blessing of all nations that believe in him.

8. Thou shall not pray for God to bless your enemies.

9. Thou shall ask God to give you power to overcome them.

10. Thou shall believe that our relatives and friends, whose spirits have departed from the body, are within our own bodies to help us overcome all difficulties in life.[56]

In some of the ritual traditions of the Universal Spiritual Hagar's Churches, androcentric elements are especially obvious. One such tradition is Hurley's Feast, a celebration that occurs annually for one week from February 11 to February 17. The Hagar's churches do not celebrate Christmas, because Father Hurley taught them Christmas was introduced by whites. Instead, Father Hurley instituted Hurley's Feast. This is a time when church members have feast trees, which are loaded with gifts. The final feast day, February 17, is especially festive because it is the day when Father Hurley was born. Baer provides a vivid description of the celebration of this day:

> Hurleyites are to assemble at 6:00 A.M. for a "sunrise prayer session" to commemorate the birth of their God [Father Hurley] in 1884 to a humble black family in the racist climate of the post-civil war South. At 7:00 A.M.—the hour of Father Hurley's birth—all Hurleyites are to go down on [their] knees and meditate on the significance of this momentous event. Each member of the church should make a concerted effort to take the day off from work and remain at a Hagar's temple during the course of the day in order to celebrate Hurley's Feast with other saints. February 17 is meant to be a day of joy and relaxation, filled with ban-

quets, the exchange of gifts, socializing, playing cards or other forms of pleasure. The Hurleyite New Year occurs a week after the birth of Father Hurley and is called the Day of New Progression.[57]

There are also ritual observances in the Universal Hagar's Spiritual Churches, which make women the subject of the celebration. The seven-day memorial service held each year commemorates the passage of Mother and Father Hurley to the spiritual realm. Then there is Homegathering on the first Sunday in June, which celebrates Mother Hurley's return from the trip she took to Europe. Mother's Day in May is also dedicated to the honor of Mother Hurley.[58] Baer's description of the Mother's Day celebration at one of the Hagar's churches demonstrates the strong identification members have with Mother Hurley, an identification that rivals the closeness some Christians feel with the Virgin Mary. According to Baer,

> On Mother's Day, a bless service was conducted. For a five-dollar donation, individuals could obtain a "blessing" from Mother Hurley. During the Service, a large picture of Mother Hurley was placed on a "throne" covered with a white sheet that symbolized the "hem of Mother Hurley's garment." Each person received a blessing, knelt before the picture and held the cloth in both hands while asking Mother Hurley for a favor. The ritual was ended by making the sign of the cross three times. According to the pastor of the temple, Hurleyites feel the same way about Mother Hurley as some people feel about Mary, the mother of Jesus.[59]

Though male Christs are lifted up by Hurley as the saviors in the four astrological periods (Taurean, Arian, Piscean and Aquarian), and the most important ritual in the church commemorates the male founder, Hurley taught that the spirit of God abides in both men and women. And even though androcentric language appears in some of the faith statements of the church, the visibility of women in the major leadership roles of this and other African-American spiritual churches far surpasses the visibility of women in the highest leadership roles in mainstream African-American denominational churches. To date, the African Methodist Episcopal Church has not elected a black woman as bishop. (The United Methodist Church and the Episcopal Churches [white denominational churches] have elected black women bishops.)

My visits to the worship services at two Universal Hagar's Spiritual Churches on the East Coast provided me with the opinion that women are in charge at the highest levels in some of the churches. In both churches the congregations were predominantly female. The ministers in the churches were female. They performed a healing ritual in both churches. There were no bibles in either church. Nor were there images of Jesus or of saints. Rather, there were two large portraits: one of Father Hurley and one of Mother Hurley. When the congregations prayed, led by the female pastor, the members faced the East and directed their prayers to "Christ Hurley" and to "Mother Hurley." They also prayed in the name of other faithful members (female and male) who had passed into the spirit realm.[60] The musical instruments accompanying the singing were all percussion. During the singing, some women did a holy dance as the music swelled to a crescendo. In both churches, in all aspects of the worship, women were in charge. My conversations with some of the women leaders informed me that many women in the Universal Hagar's Spiritual Churches do not understand themselves to be oppressed in the church, even though some male language and a male figure (Father Hurley) dominate in the liturgy.

As far as women's roles are concerned, the Universal Hagar's Spiritual Churches are leading African-American christendom in providing major leadership opportunities for women. Many of the mainstream African-American denominational churches are dominated so completely by the preacher's ego needs and by the androcentric language and liturgy that black women in the church unconsciously participate in their own oppression and that of other women.

But large numbers of black women are answering God's call to ministry. As the Reverend Prathia Hall Wynn has reminded the church, the messages of these called women preachers "are forged in the crucible of their experience of blackness, femaleness, and the liberation of God in Jesus Christ. Their response to the call of God has often been the product of protracted struggle. Yet when 'yes' finally issued from the center of their being, they knew that it had been there all the time and that before they were even formed in the womb they were called and anointed. . . . They learned that to refuse to preach is to experience a fire in one's bones that can be quenched by nothing less than faithful, obedient preaching."[61]

The African-American denominational churches are learning that these women's obedience to God does not mean passive acceptance of women's oppression. It does not mean that women preachers will be uncritical of the sources for liturgy and ritual prevailing in the African-American denominational churches. It does not mean that black women will hesitate to question

the patriarchy in the Bible. Black women's obedient preaching will tear away
the masks of contentment that the churches would prefer black women to
wear. Rather, with God's help, black women in the churches will do what
they so often do in their communities; they will make a way out of no way.
They will make a way in the community for the black church to emerge as
God-filled presence, quickening the heart, measuring the soul and bathing
life with the spirit.

# Afterword

Having come to the end of this book, I feel inclined to do as Alice Walker did after finishing writing *The Color Purple*. She thanked "everybody [in the book] for coming." And she signed the final page "A.W., author and medium."[1] This last word, *medium,* suggests that she felt herself to be merely the instrument through which other voices were enabled. There is something of the spirit in this last stroke of Walker's pen. Something sacred.

I too felt thankful for what came as I wrote *Sisters in the Wilderness*. I was especially thankful for Hagar's coming. Through her, I learned that when one probes into African-American women's experience and tries to present it with some attention given to the religion and the God-filled faith coursing through black women's experience, a sense of sacredness emerges. I too felt like a medium through whom representation, analysis and critique were speaking. I discovered that "mediumship" provides what Hagar got: new vision.

I saw things about the African-American community and church history that I had not seen before—things that are not readily apparent because of the years and layers of androcentric veneer covering cultural history in the black community. For instance, the uncanny resilience of the mothering/nurturing/caring/enduring and resistance capacities of Hagar and black women has birthed a spirit of hope in the community. Historically, this spirit has kept the community alive as black women's spirituality and politics came together to design resistance strategies benefiting the entire community.

Like Hagar when she and her child were thrown out of Abraham's house into the wilderness, black women in the "wilderness" of America had to learn how to survive. Neither Hagar nor African-American women, in freedom, had enough resources for the survival of themselves and their families. Yet many black women, by the help of God, became very skilled at surviving. I suppose Hagar did too.

Reflection upon black women's sources revealed to me the survival strategies they have used to keep the community alive and hopeful. The strategies I saw were: 1) an art of cunning; 2) an art of encounter; 3) an art of care; and 4) an art of connecting. I use the word *art* here to indicate the high level of skill many black women developed as they created and adapted strategies to ensure their survival and that of their families. (However, some of this high-level female skill is exploited in the black community and in the churches.)

The art of cunning does not mean proficiency in deception and craftiness (lying and cheating) in order to accomplish personal goals. Rather, the art of cunning means "knowledge combined with manual skill and dexterity."[2] In relation to oppression, it means black women exercising a wholesome shrewdness that assures the survival of themselves and the entire community. Chapter 2 of this book points to Vyry, in Margaret Walker's *Jubilee,* who learned how to gather and properly name the herbs in the field. The cruel overseer could not deliver her up to death as had happened to one slave woman whose lack of knowledge of the proper herbs led to the death of her master. For Vyry, the art of cunning meant knowing how to be accessible to her slave holders while simultaneously staying out of the way of the slave master's cruel wife. The art of cunning meant using women's imagination and skill to devise economic strategies that fostered the economic well-being of the black family. Vyry's economic strategies after the Civil War brought her family a measure of prosperity. Many of the black mammies perfected the art of cunning so well that their work for slave masters actually (and subtly) benefited the slaves on many occasions. A case in point was Mammy Pleasant who, as Chapter 4 of *Sisters in the Wilderness* points out, is reported to have provided the finances for John Brown's raid. If we go with the idea that Hagar might in some way have been related to the founding and/or leading of the Hagarite Tribe, she surely would have developed this art of cunning as she dealt with other tribes—many no doubt led by males.

As a survival strategy, the art of encounter involved two movements: resistance and endurance. Timing was important. It seems as if black women knew when to exercise resistance strategies in relation to their and the community's oppression and when to endure. They tended to know when mass movements against oppression could be inaugurated effectively. It was no accident that a black woman, Ida B. Wells, birthed the modern civil rights movement in the late nineteenth century, and that another black woman, Rosa Parks, birthed the civil rights movement in the late twentieth century. Neither was it an accident that black women have encouraged black people to endure when, as Professor Eric Lincoln says, "endurance gave no promise."

During these times, in the face of genocidal white oppression, endurance was an act of defiance, a revolutionary act. The same can be said of Hagar. Though she demonstrated a serious act of resistance, she had to exercise endurance so that she and her son could survive. She had to endure more oppression from her slave owner Sarah.

Yet there is a negative side to black women's endurance. As Chapter 8 in *Sisters in the Wilderness* reveals, black women—the principal financial and spiritual supporters of the African-American denominational churches— have often helped male preachers shape these institutions into unproductive "endurance structures." That is, the theology and the community life in the institutions have been organized to support black women's endurance of sexist oppression *within* the African-American denominational churches and within the African-American community. Nevertheless, when "the black church" is at work arousing the African-American denominational churches to true liberation and survival/quality-of-life action, black women are in both forefront and background, making sure the efforts succeed. This is so because black Christian women collectively seem to be the medium through which "the black church" emerges in the black community.

The art of care, as a survival strategy of black women, manifested itself in commitment and charity. Without a doubt black women's sources reveal the commitment, devotion and love black women have had for their children, for the lovers in their lives, for their extended families, for their communities and for their churches. But black women's commitment and charity have been exploited both within and beyond the African-American community. As far as black women's commitment and charity are concerned, Zora Neale Hurston describes the problem well. In *Their Eyes Were Watching God,* the character Granny tells her granddaughter Janie that "it is this love business that's got black women working from can't see in the morning till can't see at night." "There ain't nothing wrong with love," she says. "It just makes you sweat." Be that as it may, it is this female care, commitment and charity that have preserved the life of the African-American community.

No survival strategy is more developed among many black religious women than the art of connecting. Harriet Tubman, Milla Granson and Mammy Pleasant knew with whom and how to connect in order to liberate slaves. Tubman connected with free blacks, with white abolitionists and with slaves in order to effect political liberation. Milla Granson connected with a slave holder who taught her to read. Then she connected with other slaves, taught them to read and thereby effected their educational liberation. Because they learned to read, many of these slaves forged passes and escaped into Canada. Mammy Pleasant was advisor to wealthy white men in California, increased her fortune considerably and used much of her money to secure the political and educational liberation of black people. In our own time black women like Mary McLeod Bethune, Fannie Lou Hamer and Patricia Reeberg perfected the art of connecting with the people and with the relevant social, political and religious structures that could contribute to the educational, political and spiritual wellbeing of African-American people: women, men and children. Sources used in this study reveal that many black women, especially church women, have the talent to connect immediately across differences in the black community in order to take care of crises that emerge. There is a lot of truth in the black folk saying that black men may be the head of the liberation struggle, but black women are the feet that keep the movement going; they know what it takes to keep something alive.

The greatest truth of black women's survival and quality-of-life struggle is that they have worked without hesitation and with all the energy they could muster. Many of them, like Hagar, have demonstrated great courage as they resisted oppression and as they went into the wide, wide world to make a living for themselves and their children. They depended upon their strength and upon each other. But in the final analysis the message is clear: they trusted the end to God. Every important event in the stories of Hagar and black women turns on this trust.

# NOTES

## Preface

1. By ordinary, I mean those black women who are not in the limelight like Harriet Tubman, Sojourner Truth and Mary McLeod Bethune. Ordinary black women are day-workers, factory workers, teachers, etc. (usually church women) who do their bit day by day contributing to black women's way of resisting and rising above the brutalities in the society that oppress black women and their children, male and female.

2. It is significant that Alice Walker dedicates her book *The Third Life of Grange Copeland* to her mother (an ordinary black woman) who, Walker claims, "made a way out of no way."

3. My coined concept, "colonization of female mind and culture," is based on the meaning of the concept *colonization* grounded in imperialism. Colonization involves taking over one culture by another, often by violent means. According to *The Columbia Encyclopedia,* colonization is the expansion of political, economic and cultural control "over an area by a state whose nationals have occupied it and connotes the settlement of a district by a people whose military might is greater than that of the native population." Colonization means that the dominating, intruding culture attempts either to wipe out or to assimilate the native culture into the dominating culture so that control and often exploitation of the natives' resources can take place. As *The Columbia Encyclopedia* maintains, "Before colonization can be effected, the indigenous population may be annihilated, confined to reservations, assimilated or converted to the culture of the colonists. Colonization has been an effective means of spreading culture." Analogous to the meaning of colonization above, colonization of female mind and culture means that male culture—emphasizing, mystifying, sacralizing and perpetuating the male figure and male thought—long ago invaded and subjugated the female figure and the continuity of female thought processes and accomplishments so that women's culture could neither take holistic form nor be visible and perpetuated. Thus female thought and culture were "converted

**213**

to the culture of the [male] colonists," and the cultural symbols of the male colonists imperialistically controlled the thought and behavior of women. Just as the colonization of geographical territories and populations has been affected by religious subterfuge and violent aggression on the part of the colonizers, so has the colonization of the female mind and culture been affected by the same agency of male colonizers, that is, religious subterfuge and violent aggression. Thus it is no wonder that Christian feminist theologians are questioning the core symbolism of the Christian religion for its part in supporting and reinforcing the oppression of women. Neither is it puzzling why women have had to undergo "consciousness raising" before their feminist-womanist consciousness could come to the surface and take shape.

4.  There are several ways in which the African-American denominational churches have acted as colonizing agents with regard to the minds and culture of African-American females. First, for the validity of its theological articulation (mostly done by males) it relies heavily and *uncritically* upon a thoroughly patriarchical and androcentrically biased text: the Bible. Black women in the church have been conditioned by the church to regard this patriarchical and androcentric bias as sacred, reaching its highest point of sacred power in male divinity. Second, in its proclamation and teaching offices, the African-American denominational churches have paid little or no consistent attention to the ancient cultural way African-American slaves created an oral canon from the canon. This oral canon was apparently quite egalitarian with regard to male and female. Strands of it can be detected in spiritual songs. Also, this oral canon is suggested by the way slaves appropriated certain biblical figures and stories and passed them along from generation to generation. These stories were thought to say something important about God's positive relation to both black male and black female experience. Without knowledge of this, contemporary black women have no way of knowing how the black community historically has understood the character of black women's experience in relation to God and the community. Third, though a black female culture also supports community life in the churches (since 80 percent of the members are female), the social and theological assessments of this life by male scholars and preachers do not reflect this cultural foundation. Neither the images/stories illustrating the sermons, nor the Christian education materials, nor the sociological and theological texts about the church reflect the female culture in the church. Rather this culture is submerged and its patterns are unnamed. Many black church women have been conditioned to adore black male preachers, to praise white male Jesus and faithfully to "serve" master Jesus. They are not encouraged to think seriously about *their* own lives shaping the questions the church answers. They are not encouraged to think seriously about *their* oppression and to use the symbolism of black female culture to shape questions and design strategies to challenge sexist oppression in the church. Rather,

many black church women ingest male culture through scripture, sermon and liturgy. They then become dependent upon aspects of the church's male culture to meet some of the most urgent emotional needs in their lives.

5.  The term *womanist* was coined by black, female, Pulitzer prize winner Alice Walker. She gives the following definition of a womanist:

    > 1. From womanish (Opp. of "girlish," i.e., frivolous, irresponsible, not serious.) A black feminist or feminist of color. From the black folk expression of mothers to female children, "You acting womanish," i.e., like a woman. Usually referring to outrageous, audacious, courageous or willful behavior. Wanting to know more and in greater depth than is considered "good" for one. Interested in grown-up doings. Acting grown up. Being grown up. Interchangeable with another black folk expression: "You trying to be grown." Responsible. In charge. Serious. 2. Also: A woman who loves other women, sexually and/or nonsexually. Appreciates and prefers women's culture, women's emotional flexibility (values tears as natural counter-balance of laughter) and women's strength. Sometimes loves individual men, sexually and/or nonsexually. Committed to survival and wholeness of entire people, male and female. Not a separatist, except periodically, for health. Traditionally universalist, as in: "Mamma, why are we brown, pink, and yellow, and our cousins are white, beige, and black?" Ans.: "Well, you know the colored race is just like a flower garden, with every color flower represented." Traditionally capable, as in: "Mamma, I'm walking to Canada and I'm taking you and a bunch of other slaves with me." Reply: "It wouldn't be the first time." 3. Loves music. Loves dance. Loves the moon. Loves the Spirit. Loves love and food and roundness. Loves struggle. Loves the Folk. Loves herself. Regardless. 4. Womanist is to feminist as purple to lavender (see Walker's *In Search of Our Mother's Gardens: Womanist Prose* [San Diego: Harcourt Brace Jovanovich, 1983], p. xi).

6.  The names associated with the development of womanist thought in theology, ethics, biblical studies, sociology of religion and ministry are Jacqueline Grant, Kelly Brown, Delores S. Williams, Katie Cannon, Marcia Riggs, Emily Townes, Joan Speaks, Renita Weems, Clarise J. Martin, Cheryl Townsend Gilkes, Imani Sheila Newsome, Joan Martin and Toinette M. Eugene. Additional womanist voices are emerging every day—for instance, Shawn Copeland, Karen Baker-Fletcher, Jacqueline Carr-Hamilton, Anne Elliott, JoAnne Terrell and Annie Ruth Powell.

7.  I indicate caste along with class as an oppression to be fought against because I recognize a caste system operating in North America. And caste assignment, determined by white males with great economic power, is based on biology. That is, "female" is a caste, and "color darker than white" is a caste. While all people

darker than white are in the "color caste," "black color" is the lowest in the color caste category and is analogous to the old "untouchable" caste in India.

When I was a little girl I heard the late black educator and minister Benjamin Mays describe a trip to India. The Indian person introducing him, in an effort to help his audience understand black people's situation in North America, described Mays as an "American untouchable."

While all women have been assigned to the oppressed caste "female," there are different degrees of privilege within this caste assignment. Therefore we can speak of all white women as oppressed (because of caste) and also privileged because of whiteness and, in some cases, because of considerable financial means. Black women, like all other black people, are assigned to the "black color" out/caste. But black women and other black people within the caste may belong to different socioeconomic classes; thus some blacks are privileged over other blacks. Black women are also assigned to the caste "female." This means that black women and white women can speak of a common oppression when they discourse about their "female caste" affiliation. Various white women and black women in this caste may also be able to speak of commonalities when they discuss similar values because they belong to similar socioeconomic classes. However, black women's assignment to the "lowest color caste" brings a different experience, which no white woman or any other woman of color is able to experience. Only black men are able to share this experience with black women. What is suggested here with respect to caste in America is that hierarchies exist within the caste arrangements. Some groups of color rank higher than others, depending upon which one is more useful to the function and maintenance of the white male-dominated social, economic, political and religious systems and which one is farthest removed from black color. The darker the color, the more inherent inferiority is assigned to the group by the social myths and ideologies constructed by white power in American society.

8. Feminist theologian Rosemary Radford Ruether identifies *sin* as anything that denies the full humanity of women. She assigns hermeneutical significance to this concept. See Ruether's book *Sexism and God-talk* (Boston: Beacon Press, 1983).

9. Womanist theologians have the double task of giving attention simultaneously to sexist oppression affecting black women and racial oppression affecting the entire African-American community. In her article "Womanist Consciousness: Maggie Lena Walker and the Independent Order of Saint Luke," sociologist Elsa Barkley Brown says that "woman experience" for many black women activists includes both women's struggle and race struggle. She chides white feminists for allowing "belatedly, black women to make history as women or as Negroes but not as 'Negro women.' What they [white feminists] fail to consider is that women's issues may be race issues, and race issues may be women's issues." See

Brown's article in *Black Women in America: Social Science Perspectives*, ed. Micheline R. Malson, Elizabeth Mudimbe-Boyi, Jean F. O'Barr and Mary Wyer (Chicago: University of Chicago Press, 1988), p. 174.

## *Introduction*

1.  The phrase *tradition(s) of African-American biblical appropriation* refers to the black community's way of appropriating texts, stories, images and personalities from the Bible and using these for generations to remind the community of some condition of its life and to illustrate how God has related to the condition.

2.  Edmonia Lewis, a nineteenth-century African-American sculptress, who finally worked in Italy, carved a famous statue named "Hagar in the Wilderness." Information about Lewis and her art are contained in Michaele Clift, "Object into Subject: Some Thoughts on the Work of Black Women Artists," in *Heresies: A Feminist Publication on Art and Politics* (vol. 4, no. 3, issue 15).

    A black woman, Susie King Taylor, writing her narrative in 1907, tells of her grandmother, who married in 1833 and later had two children, James and Hagar Ann. See Susie King Taylor, "Reminiscences of My Life in Camp," in *Collected Black Women's Narratives*, ed. Henry Louis Gates, Jr. (New York: Oxford University Press, 1988), pp. 1–76.

    In her novel *Iola Leroy*, first published in 1892, Frances Harper describes an ex-slave mother who "like Hagar of old, went out into the wide world to seek a living for herself and her child."

    The black American poet Paul Lawrence Dunbar, whose writing career extended from 1889 to 1906, wrote about "the members of the Afro-American Sons of Hagar Social Club." See Jay Martin and Gossie H. Hudson, eds., *The Paul Lawrence Dunbar Reader* (New York: Dodd, Mead & Company, 1971), p. 65.

    Novelist Richard Wright referred to the African-American family as Hagar's children.

    When he wrote *The Negro Family in the United States*, sociologist E. Franklin Frazier titled one chapter "Hagar and Her Children."

    Francis P. Reid's book of poetry *Given to Time* contains a long poem entitled "Hagar."

    In Toni Morrison's novel *Song of Solomon* there is a female character named Hagar.

    African-American anthropologist John Langston Gwaltney dedicated his collection of urban narratives *Drylongso* to "Lucy and all the other flowers in Aunt Hagar's garden." In the glossary to this book, Gwaltney describes Aunt Hagar as a "mythical apical figure of the core black American nation."

    Maya Angelou's poem "The Mothering Blackness" alludes to the woman as "black yet as Hagar's daughter." See Maya Angelou, "The Mothering Blackness," in *Poems* (New York: Bantam Books, 1981), p. 19.

Black preachers have also participated in the community's tradition of appropriating the biblical Hagar and her story. At a conference entitled "Black Women in Ministry" held at Princeton Seminary in the early 1980s, the Reverend Arlene Churn preached a sermon "Hagar, What Ailest Thee?" It is not unusual on any Sunday morning to hear a black preacher allude in his or her sermon to Hagar and Ishmael. Professor Henry Young at Garrett Theological Seminary edited a book of sermons by black preachers. One of these sermons is about Ishmael and makes reference to Hagar.

3. See Lawrence Levine, *Slave Culture and Slave Consciousness* (New York: Oxford University Press, 1977), pp. 23–38.

4. It should be pointed out here that the contexts in which Hagar appears in the deposits of black American culture suggest that African Americans primarily appropriated the Hagar who appeared in the Hebrew testament. I imagine that is because a story is associated with the Hebrew testament rendition of Hagar. Her story parallels black women's story (or history). In my research I found no African-American sources that connect Hagar with Paul or with events in the Christian testament.

5. To indicate the extent to which "making a way out of no way" affects black women's (and the black community's) consciousness and characterizes their understanding of their work in the world, I point to The National Black Sisters, Clergy and Seminarians Conference held August 2–7, 1982, at St. John's Provincial Seminary in Plymouth, Michigan. The name of this conference was "Making a Way Out of No Way."

6. The term *quality of life* used throughout this book refers to persons, families and/or communities attempting to arrive at well-being through the use of, search for and/or creation of supportive spiritual, economic, political, legal or educational resources. Whether quality of life involves positive or negative pursuit depends upon the nature of the moral attitudes and ethical commitments guiding a person's, a family's or a community's survival struggle toward well-being—well-being indicating a peaceful, balanced, upright, spiritual existence. In the context of much black American religious faith, survival struggle and quality of life struggle are inseparable and are associated with God's presence with the community. However, the reader should be aware that the term *quality of life* is much used today in the world of medical science. James J. Walter and Thomas A. Shannon have provided an enlightening discursus about the variety of meanings the term can have in different contexts. See their foreword to the book *Quality of Life: The New Medical Dilemma,* ed. Walter and Shannon (New York: Paulist Press, 1990). This interesting book purports "to present an overview of many aspects of the quality of life debate vis-à-vis medical decision making." Thus philosophical, theological and ethical perspectives on the subject are presented.

7. John S. Blassingame, *The Slave Community* (New York: Oxford University Press, 1972), p. 206.

8. Gayraud S. Wilmore, *Black Religion and Black Radicalism,* 2d ed. (Maryknoll, New York: Orbis Books, 1984), p. 223.

9. God-talk in this book assumes, as most black scholars do, that black consciousness does not make a dichotomy between the sacred and the secular. Therefore, even when the language about black women's lives in this book does not mention the word *God,* it is still god-talk in the sacred-secular sense. The god-talk is womanist because it, like Alice Walker's definition, lifts up women's mothering efforts in behalf of their children, emphasizes women's resistance and liberation efforts, advocates women connecting with women, affirms women's desire to know more than is thought good for women to know and applauds women's commitment to "survival and wholeness of entire people, male and female."

10 For an illustration of this Latin American feminist way of rereading see John S. Pobee and Barbel von Wartenberg-Potter, eds., *New Eyes for Reading* (World Council of Churches, 1986; Oak Park, Illinois: Meyer-Stone, 1987). Especially see Elsa Tamez's article, "The Woman Who Complicated the History of Salvation."

11. For an example of theorizing about additional characters in the Hagar-Sarah stories and reconstruing the order of the texts see Savina J. Teubal, *Hagar the Egyptian: The Lost Tradition of the Matriarchs* (San Francisco: Harper & Row, 1990).

12. Cornel West has done a brilliant work showing the genealogy of white supremacy beginning in European intellectual discourse. He shows how what he calls a "normative gaze" characterized this discourse and aided and abetted the rise of white supremacy. The normative gaze of modern European intellection was structured by the normative status it gave Greek aesthetic and intellectual standards and the inferior status it assigned to black beauty and intellection. This normative gaze, now endemic to Western culture, assures the reign of white supremacy in Western intellectual discourse. *Sisters in the Wilderness* affirms West's analysis here but moves in a more narrow vein to North American perspectives on color based on English rather than European cultural foundations. See Cornel West, "A Genealogy of Modern Racism," in *Prophesy Deliverance* (Philadelphia: Westminster Press, 1982).

## Chapter 1: Hagar's Story: a Route to Black Women's Issues

1. Genesis 16:1–16 comes primarily from J, although 16:3, 15–16 are from P. Genesis 21:9–21 comes from E. J, or the Yahwist tradition, is believed to have been written down in the tenth century B.C. while E is believed to have been written down in about the eighth century B.C. See Gerhard von Rad, *Genesis,* trans. John

H. Marks (Philadelphia: Westminster Press, 1956), p. 23; also see E. A. Speiser, *Genesis,* Anchor Bible (Garden City, New York: Doubleday & Company, 1964); also S. R. Driver, *The Book of Genesis* (New York: Edwin S. Gorhan, 1904).

2. In the Genesis 16 account the name of the slave owners are Sarai and Abram. But in Genesis, chapter 17, God changes the names of Sarai and Abram to Sarah and Abraham. Therefore, in my use of the Genesis 21 episode, I refer to the slave holders as Sarah and Abraham.

3. Gerhard von Rad, *Genesis,* p. 186.

4. Ibid.

5. Ibid., p. 179.

6. See Gerhard von Rad, *Genesis,* p. 186; also see Phyllis Trible, *Texts of Terror,* p. 12; also Claus Westermann, *The Promise to the Fathers,* trans. David E. Green (Philadelphia: Fortress Press, 1980), pp. 63–64; also Bruce Vawter, *On Genesis: A New Reading* (Garden City, New York: Doubleday Company, 1977), pp. 214–15. Trible and Westermann present interesting approaches to the strife in this passage between Hagar and Sarai. Departing from the harshness of several interpretations, Trible says, "Many translators alter the syntax to make Hagar the subject of the verb. They also attribute the verb (*qll*) the legitimate, though not necessary, meaning of contempt or disdain. Accordingly, one reads 'when she knew she was with child, she despised her mistress'; or 'when she saw that she had conceived, she looked with contempt on her mistress.' Yet the verb with its correct subject also offers the less harsh reading that is present in the translation, 'her mistress was lowered in her esteem.' " Apparently in accord with the feminist tendency to temper disputes between women, Trible concentrates upon the hierarchical relation between the women. This is a valuable approach because it reminds the reader that both women's lives are controlled by the social and legal structures created by patriarchy. Westermann's interpretation is significant because he identifies the social structure in which the argument occurs, that is, the family. He sees the first sections of chapters 16 and 21 as "belonging to a group of family narratives dealing with social struggle," but their unique characteristic is that they show women to be the real protagonists (p. 64). Westermann agrees with those biblical scholars (such as Elsa Tamez and von Rad) who do not see the etiologies in the texts as the primary issues.

7. Elsa Tamez, "The Woman Who Complicated the History of Salvation," in Pobee and Von Wartenberg-Potter, *New Eyes for Reading,* p. 8.

8. Trible, *Texts of Terror,* p. 30.

9. For a full discussion of the work of the redactors in this instance, see Gary A. Rensburg, *The Redaction of Genesis* (Winona Lake, Indiana: Eisenbrauns, 1986), pp. 28–52.

10. See the discussion of oral transmission in Norman K. Gottwald, *A Light to the Nations* (New York: Harper & Row, 1959), pp. 93–101.

11. Von Rad, *Genesis*, p. 187.

12. Trible, *Texts of Terror*, p. 13.

13. Von Rad, *Genesis*, p. 187.

14. See Trible's discussion of this in *Texts of Terror*, p. 13. Also see Exodus 1:11–12.

15. John Marshall Holt, *The Patriarchs of Israel* (Nashville: Vanderbilt University Press, 1964), p. 92.

16. *The New Jerusalem Bible* (Garden City, New York: Doubleday & Company, 1985), p. 35, note 16c.

17. Von Rad, *Genesis*, p. 188.

18. James Hastings et al., eds., *Dictionary of the Bible* (New York: Charles Scribner's Sons, 1909), p. 852.

19. Elsa Tamez, "The Woman Who Complicated the History of Salvation," p. 14.

20. Among the ancient Hebrews foreign slaves often fared worse than Hebrew and native slaves. "In the case of the maid-servant no release was permitted under ordinary circumstances, for it is assumed that the slave-girl is at the same time a concubine, and hence release would be against the best interest both of herself and of the home." See "Slave and Slavery" in the *Dictionary of the Bible*, pp. 864–66.

21. For other birth announcement formulas in the Bible see Genesis 17:19; Judges 13:5; Luke 1:31–33 and Luke 1:13–20.

22. It can be suggested here that promise and covenant in the Hebrew Testament contain God's assurance of survival for persons through their posterity. When Yahweh gives promise and makes covenant with Abram, survival is promised as well as economic resources (land) to sustain survival. (Survival meaning survival of one's family line.) Also associated with promise and covenant are intimations toward quality of life often involving transforming identity (Abram's and Sarai's names are changed to Abraham and Sarah) or defining it (as in Ishmael's, Samson's, John's and Jesus' birth announcements). Once the promise is given or the covenant is sealed, quality of life—mindful of the promise or covenant—involves the human search for, use and/or creation of economic, political, educational and spiritual resources for well-being. It seems to me that this connection among promise, covenant, survival and quality of life runs through both the Hebrew and Christian testaments. Therefore, it may be possible to identify a survival tradition in the scripture, just as one can identify a liberation and a prophetic tradition. What this suggests, of course, is that many biblical narratives can constitute this biblical survival tradition. In this book the Hagar narratives are highlighted because they are the particular survival stories the African-American community has passed along for generations. The Babylonian captivity of the Israelites may also provide narratives for this survival tradition.

23. Trible, *Texts of Terror*, p. 18.

24. Helmer Ringgren, *Israelite Religion*, trans. Davie E. Green (Philadelphia: Fortress Press, 1966), pp. 21, 22.

25. Ibid., p. 22.

26. Roland de Vaux, *Ancient Israel: Its Life and Institutions,* trans. John McHugh (London: Darton, Longman & Todd, 1961), p. 45.

27. Joseph Kaster, trans. and ed., *Wings of the Falcon: Life and Thought of Ancient Egypt* (New York: Holt, Rinehart and Winston, 1968), p. 50.

28. Ibid., pp. 67–68.

29. Adolph Erman, *Life in Ancient Egypt,* trans. H. M. Tirad (London: Macmillan and Co., 1894), p. 162.

30. De Vaux, *Ancient Israel: Its Life and Institutions,* p. 53.

31. It must be remembered that Abram in chapter 16 follows Sarah's suggestion about having a child by Hagar because God has told Abram in chapter 15 that a child will be born of his seed, and Sarai is barren. (Furthermore, the law prescribes certain rights for Sarai in this case of barrenness, so Abram is also following the law.) Abram will not have to adopt a slave of his household (not of Abram's seed) to inherit his (Abram's) goods and blessings. And in chapter 21, Abraham does not expel Hagar and Ishmael because Sarah has demanded it. From the text, the sense is that if God had not agreed with Sarah, the expulsion would not have happened since Abram loved his son Ishmael. (This does not, however, relieve Sarah from her chosen role of "wicked stepmother" as far as Ishmael is concerned.)

32. De Vaux, *Ancient Israel: Its Life and Institutions*, p. 53.

33. Ibid., p. 40.

34. Von Rad says, "Doubtless the narrator considered Ishmael a small child whom Hagar had to carry, then put down, etc. By Priestly computation, however, Ishmael must have been sixteen or seventeen years old at this time" (*Genesis,* p. 228).

35. De Vaux, *Ancient Israel: Its Life and Institutions,* p. 20.

36. Ibid., p. 85

37. Abraham dug a well here, and he and King Abimelech made a covenant not to aggravate each other over their herdsmen's use of the well. Jacob began his journey to Haran from this location (Genesis 28:10), and he made a sacrifice there on his way to Egypt (Genesis 46:1–5). Beersheba was a sacred place where several theophanies took place. Hagar, Isaac, Jacob and Elijah experienced the theophanies.

38. De Vaux, p. 10.

39. Ibid.

40. Von Rad makes an interesting point in reference to the absence of Ishmael's name in the Genesis 21 narrative. "The name Ishmael has been completely deleted . . . apparently to lift the event even more than it was in J into the realm of the universally human, since the narrator's age no longer knew any Ishmaelites." See von Rad, *Genesis,* p. 229. The question might emerge as to whether the disappearance of the Ishmaelites at this time could have been the result of the merger

of tribes that de Vaux describes in *Ancient Israel: Its Life and Institutions* in his treatment of nomadism. Could the Ishmaelites have become weak and merged with the Hagarites, who W. M. Nesbit says appear "only in very late passages" of the Hebrew Testament? See Hastings et al., *Dictionary of the Bible,* p. 325.

41. De Vaux, *Ancient Israel: Its Life and Institutions,* pp. 8, 9.

42. John D. Davis, *The Westminster Dictionary of the Bible,* rev. Henry Snyder Gehman (Philadelphia: Westminster Press, 1944; first published by the Trustees of the Presbyterian Board of Publication and Sabbath-School Work, 1898), p. 451.

43. Anna Starr, *The Bible Status of Woman* (New York and London: Fleming H. Revell Company, 1926), p. 62.

44. Ibid., pp. 66–68.

45. Ibid., p. 67. (Of course modern biblical scholarship would question Starr's observations.)

## Chapter 2: Tensions in Motherhood: from Slavery to Freedom

1   In the South after the Civil War, black women were very much a part of the redefining process. Much activity centered on "improving the morals" of black women. This was a misnaming of the situation, for actually the problem was not the black woman but the white men who forced their "affections" upon her. This fact is mentioned in Mrs. E. C. Hobson's "A Report Concerning the Colored Women of the South," in the John F. Slater Fund Occasional Papers (Baltimore: The Fund Trustees, 1986), occasional paper no. 9. The same book carries a report of black women's participation in the redefining work taking place in the Booker T. Washington endeavors at Tuskegee Institute. See John Q. Johnson, "Report on the Fifth Tuskegee Negro Conference," occasional paper no. 8. Also see Gerda Lerner, "Black Women in the Reconstruction South," in *Black Women in White America* (New York: Pantheon Books, 1972), p. 168. In Lerner's book see the following narratives: "The Breeder Woman" and "The Slaveholder's Mistress," pp. 152, 158. To understand the exploitation of black women's roles, see Toni Cade, ed., "On the Issue of Roles," *The Black Woman* (New York: New American Library, 1970), pp. 101f. For a discussion of black male/female crises see the following articles in Cade's book: "Motherhood" by Joanna Clark and "Dear Black Man" by Fran Sanders.

2.   For a discussion of black literature's way of presenting the vocational aspects of motherhood roles see Trudier Harris, *From Mammies to Militants* (Philadelphia: Temple University Press, 1982).

3.   Dr. Cheryl T. Gilkes, in her article "Institutional Motherhood in Black Churches and Communities: Ambivalent Sexism or Fragmented Familyhood?" explores the authority this emphasis upon motherhood in the church and community affords black women. Gilkes gives special attention to the meaning of this phenomena in the black sanctified churches.

4. Linda Brent, *Incidents in the Life of a Slave Girl* (Boston: By the author, Boston Stereotype Foundry, 1861), p. 87.

5. Lerner, *Black Women in White America*, p. 152.

6. Ibid., pp. 150–51.

7. William F. Allen, Charles P. Ware and Lucy McKim Garrison, *Slave Songs of the United States* (New York: P. Smith, 1929), p. 72.

8. This spiritual song has been sung by many church choirs. It was sung to me when I was a child by my grandmother whose mother, a slave, sang it to her.

9. Allen, Ware and Garrison, *Slave Songs of the United States*, p. 23.

10. Brent, *Incidents in the Life of a Slave Girl*, p. 36.

11. Ibid., p. 129.

12. Lerner, *Black Women in White America*, p. 69.

13. Philip S. Foner, ed., *The Voice of Black America* (New York: Simon and Schuster, 1972), p. 103. Also see Gates, *Collected Black Women's Narratives*.

14. The slave mother was often left with the care of slave children. Some fathers lived on different plantations. Lerner cites incidents showing how slave women schemed to keep their families together. See *Black Women in White America*, pp. 12, 13.

15. See Sarah Bradford, ed., *Harriet Tubman: The "Moses" of Her People* (by the author, 1869; reprinted, New York: Corinth Books, 1961).

16. Lerner, *Black Women in White America,* pp. 34–35.

17. Ibid., p. xxiii.

18. This is not to suggest that the antebellum black mother chose religion as an alternative to choosing the black man. Often she was forced to find other emotional support than black men because of the sudden and cruel manner in which males and females were separated from each other and sold. Moses Gandy's narrative cites such an incident. See Lerner, *Black Women in White America*, pp. 8–9. There are also narratives in which slaves speak of their love for their fathers. See Clifton H. Johnson, ed., *God Struck Me Dead* (Philadelphia: Pilgrim Press, 1969), p. 80. However, in a work by a twentieth-century artist, a black woman chooses religion rather than the black man. See James Baldwin, *The Amen Corner* (New York: Dial Press, 1968). Also see Rosemary Radford Ruether, "Black Theology vs. Feminist Theology," in *Christianity and Crisis* (April 15, 1974), pp. 69–74. In this article Ruether sketches a diagram of the racist-sexist system of classical southern society in which the black male is the lowest in authority in the scheme:

white (elite) male

—— *over* ——

white (elite) female

—— *over* ——

black female

—— *over* ——

X (black male)

19. Mary McLeod Bethune, at a Chicago Women's Federation in 1933, spoke of the black woman's invaluable historic contribution to the development of black religion in America. She said:

> In no field of modern social relationship has the hand of service and the influence of the Negro woman been felt more distinctly than in the Negro orthodox church. . . . It may be safely said that the chief sustaining force in support of the pulpit and the various phases of missionary enterprise has been the feminine element of the membership. . . . Throughout its growth, the untiring effort, the unflagging enthusiasm, the sacrificial contribution of time, effort and cash of the black woman have been the most significant factors, without which the modern Negro church would have no history worth the writing (Lerner, Black Women in White America, p. 583).

20. Lawrence Levine, "Slave Songs and Slave Consciousness," in *American Negro Slavery,* 2d ed., ed. Allen Weinstein and Frank Cattell (New York: Oxford University Press, 1983), p. 167.

21. Bert James Loewenberg and Ruth Bogin, *Black Women in Nineteenth-Century American Life* (University Park: Pennsylvania State University Press, 1976), p. 9.

22. Ibid., p. 128.

23. Jarena Lee, "Religious Experience and Journal," in Henry Louis Gates, Jr., *Spiritual Narratives* (New York: Oxford University Press, 1988; first published by Jarena Lee, 1849), pp. 3, 4.

24. Mrs. Maria Stewart, "Productions of Mrs. Maria W. Stewart," in Gates, *Spiritual Narratives* (originally published in Boston: Friends of Freedom and Virtue, 1835), pp. 75–77.

25. Old Elizabeth, "Memoir of Old Elizabeth: A Colored Woman," in Henry Louis Gates, Jr., ed., *Six Women's Slave Narratives* (New York: Oxford University Press, 1988; first published in Philadelphia: Collins, Printer, 1863), pp. 12, 14–15.

26 Samuel Charters, *The Bluesman* (New York: Oak Publications, 1967), p. 77.

27. Samuel Charters, *The Poetry of the Blues* (New York: Oak Publications, 1963), p. 173.

28. W. D. Handy, *Blues: An Anthology* (New York: Albert and Charles Bone, 1926; Collier Books of New York, 1972).

29. Langston Hughes, "Sylvester's Dying Bed," in *Selected Poems* (New York: Alfred A. Knopf, 1970), p. 38.

30. That the nurturing role of the black woman was exploited within the postbellum black community is evidenced by a statement a black woman made at the Fifth Tuskegee Negro Conference in 1896. She said, "Some of you men just want to put us in white folks kitchen and feed you while you walk up an' down the road." See Johnson, "Report on the Fifth Tuskegee Negro Conference," in The John F. Slater Fund Occasional Papers, occasional paper no. 8.

31. Any analysis of James Baldwin's literature must be cognizant of the major theme that runs through all his work—that white oppression of black people has gotten in the way of black people's free and open expression of their love for each other and for other people. Thus Ida (*Another Country*) does not dare express her love for Valvado because she fears this love will be made to destroy her. Rufus (*Another Country*) can only relate destructively to his partner because oppression and exploitation of him have already destroyed his ability to care. In *Go Tell It on the Mountain* Elizabeth's first true love destroys himself when police brutality brings dishonor to his love relationship with Elizabeth. In Baldwin's novel *If Beale Street Could Talk*, members of a black family are able to love each other only because they have already rejected most American values that oppress and prohibit mutual love relationships. The Christian religion is rejected. Baldwin's *The Amen Corner* also reflects this theme of oppression destroying black people's love relationships.

32. See James Baldwin, *Go Tell It on the Mountain* (New York: Alfred A. Knopf, 1953), p. 175.

33. Richard Wright, *The Long Dream* (New York: Harper & Brothers Publishers, 1950), p. 81.

34. Ibid., p. 82.

35. Richard Wright, *Native Son* (New York: Harper & Brothers Publishers, 1940), p. 241.

36. Ibid.

37. Ibid.

38. Ibid., p. 242.

39. Ibid., p. 246.

40. Mary Burgher, "Images of Self and Race in the Autobiographies of Black Women," in *Sturdy Black Bridges: Visions of Black Women in Literature,* ed. Roseann P. Bell, Bettye J. Parker and Beverly Guy-Sheftall (Garden City, New York: Doubleday & Company, 1979), p. 116.

41. Ibid., p. 117.

42. Ibid., p. 116.

43. See the discussion of this problem in Daryl C. Dance, "Black Eve or Madonna? A Study of the Antithetical Views of the Mother in Black American Literature," in Bell et al., *Sturdy Black Bridges,* pp. 123–32.

44. Carolyn M. Rodgers, *How I Got Ovah* (Garden City, New York: Doubleday & Company, 1976), pp. 11–12.

45. Margaret Walker, *Jubilee* (Boston: Houghton Mifflin, 1966), p. 407.

46. Among this cadre of writers and their works are Gwendolyn Brooks, "Maud Martha" in *The World of Gwendolyn Brooks* (New York: Harper & Row, 1971); Paule Marshall, *Browngirl, Brownstones* (New York: Knopf, 1974).

47. Barbara Christian, "An Angle of Seeing Motherhood," in *Black Feminist Criticism* (New York: Pergamon Press, 1985), pp. 211–52.

48. Alice Walker, *The Color Purple* (New York: Harcourt Brace Jovanovich, 1982), p. 34.

49. Ibid., p. 84.

50. Ibid., p. 165.

51. Ibid., p. 170.

52. Ibid., p. 18.

53. Celie's transcendent relation to her own experience is demonstrated in her statement about the beatings she receives from her husband. She says, "I make myself wood. I say to myself, Celie, you a tree."

54. Alice Walker, *The Color Purple,* p. 168.

55. Ntozake Shange, *For Colored Girls Who Have Considered Suicide When the Rainbow Is Enuf* (New York: Macmillan, 1975), p. 63.

56. Alice Walker, *The Color Purple,* p. 218.

57. The following quotations by black sociologist Barbara Rodes illustrate a traditional black understanding of black women's roles as mothers and nurturers: "The relationship between mother and child...is extremely important for Black people.... Black children...must be conditioned by a black mother, to the realities of this society." See Barbara Rodes, "The Changing Role of the Black Woman," in *The Black Family,* ed. Robert Staples (Belmont, California: Wadsworth Publishing Company, Inc., 1971), pp. 145–49. Also see Langston Hughes, *The Negro Mother and Other Dramatic Recitations* (Freeport, New York: Book for Libraries Press, 1971; first published in 1931). Hughes also portrays the black mother's role as complete self-sacrifice for the advancement of her children and of the race. Alice Walker's *The Color Purple* challenges these perspectives.

58. Margaret Walker, *Jubilee,* p. 135.

59. Alice Walker, *The Color Purple,* p. 168.

60. Ibid., p. 18.

61. Benjamin Brawley, *A Social History of the American Negro* (London: Collier-Macmillan Ltd., 1970; first published by the Macmillan Company in 1921), p. 218.

62 H. Mattison, ed., *Louisa Picquet, the Octoroon: A Tale of Southern Slave Life* (first published in New York by Reverend Mattison, 1861), in Gates, *Collected Black Women's Narratives,* p. 6.

63. Brawley, *A Social History of the American Negro,* p. 245.

64. Deborah Gray White, *Ar'n't I a Woman?* (New York: W. W. Norton & Company, 1985), pp. 119–20.

### Chapter 3: Social-Role Surrogacy: Naming Black Women's Oppression

1. Frederick Law Olmsted, *Journeys and Explorations in the Cotton Kingdom,* ed. David Freeman Hawke (New York: Bobbs-Merrill, 1971; first published in 1861), p. 63.

2. White, *Ar'n't I a Woman?*, p. 41.

3. In our time a most graphic portrayal of this particular kind of pressured surrogacy was in the motion picture *Clara's Heart* starring Whoopi Goldberg. In this movie Clara (Goldberg) is the domestic for a wealthy white couple whose young son is caught in the middle of their journey toward divorce. Both parents neglect the child to pursue their own fulfillment. Clara steps in and provides the mothering-nurturing care for the young son. More fact than fiction, this movie is illustrative of the kind of surrogacy roles domestics often assume beyond the black community in the homes of their (usually) white employers.

4. For a discussion of the legal and moral issues surrounding contemporary surrogate motherhood see Thomas A. Shannon, *Surrogate Motherhood: The Ethics of Using Human Beings* (New York: Crossroad, 1988).

5. Thomas Shannon provides a summary of the concepts of coercion and "undue influence" as these may influence women's decisions about surrogacy in our time and as they (the concepts) are used in the current discussion about surrogate motherhood. See *Surrogate Motherhood: The Ethics of Using Human Beings*, chap. 3.

6. White, *Ar'n't I a Woman?*, p. 47.

7. Ibid.

8. Ibid.

9. This and other slave testimony regarding mammies is contained in White, *Ar'n't I a Woman?*, pp. 49f.

10. Ibid.

11. Eugene Genovese, *Roll, Jordan, Roll: The World the Slaves Made* (New York: Random House, 1974), pp. 360–61.

12. W. E. B. Du Bois, *The Gift of Black Folk* (New York: Washington Square Press, 1970). There are different reports about her birthplace. Some scholars say Georgia. Others say Virginia. She herself said she was born on August 19, 1814, in Philadelphia. The various accounts of Mammy Pleasant's background conflict. For a most recent account see the entry "Pleasant, Mary Ellen," by Lynn Hudson, in Darlene Clark Hine, *Black Women in America: An Historical Encyclopedia*, vol. 2 (New York: Carlson Publishing, Inc., 1993), pp. 932–33. (Hudson also provides several bibliographical sources about Mammy Pleasant.)

13. According to Du Bois, "When she first heard of the project of John Brown she was determined to help him, and April 5, 1858, when John Brown was captured at Harper's Ferry, they found upon him a letter reading: 'The ax is laid at the foot of the tree; when the first blow is struck there will be more money to help.' This was signed by three initials which the authorities thought were 'W.E.P.'—in fact they were 'M.E.P.' and stood for Mammy Pleasant. She had come East in the spring before with a $30,000 United States draft which she changed into coin and meeting with John Brown in Chatham or Windsor, Canada, had turned this money over to him. It was agreed, however, that he was not to strike his blow

until she had helped to arouse the slaves. Disguised as a jockey, she went South and while there heard of Brown's raid and capture at Harper's Ferry. She fled to New York and finally reached California on a ship that came around Cape Horn sailing in the steerage under an assumed name" (Du Bois, *The Gift of Black Folk*, pp. 141–42).

14. Ibid.

15. White, *Ar'n't I a Woman?*, p. 56.

16. Ibid., pp. 54–55.

17. This is not to suggest that such empowerment led to autonomy for slave women. Quite to the contrary, slave women, like slave men, were always subject to the control of the slave owners. And as Deborah Gray White's description of mammy reveals, the empowerment of mammy was directly related to the attempt of pro-slavery advocates to provide an image of black women that proved the institution of slavery was vital for molding some black women in accord with the maternal ideals of the Victorian understanding of true womanhood.

18. Some scholars estimate that about 80 percent of slave women worked in the fields. The other 20 percent worked as house servants. See Robert Fogel and Stanley L. Engerman, *Time on the Cross* (Boston: Little, Brown and Company, 1974), pp. 39–58.

19. Bell Hooks, *Ain't I a Woman?* (Boston: South End Press, 1981), p. 23.

20. Ibid., p. 22.

21. Henry Louis Gates, Jr., ed., "The Narrative of Bethany Veney, a Slave Woman," in *Collected Black Women's Narratives* (Veney's narrative first published in Worcester, Massachusetts, 1889).

22. Mattison, *Louisa Picquet, the Octoroon: A Tale of Southern Slave Life*, p. 17.

23. Mary Prince, *The History of Mary Prince, a West Indian Slave*, in Gates, *Six Women's Slave Narratives* (first published in London, England, by F. Westley and A. H. Davis, 1831), p. 6.

24. Ibid., p. 7.

25. Allen, Ware and Garrison, *Slave Songs of the United States*, p. 5.

26. J. F. Bayliss, ed., *Black Slave Narratives* (London: Collier-Macmillan Ltd., 1970), p. 122.

27. Tubman, in this role, was called Moses by the slaves, and she assumed this role voluntarily. Inasmuch as this role extended into the Civil War, where she served as scout, led troops and even served as a nurse for Union soldiers when called upon, she can be said to be one of the few female slaves in antebellum America who participated in voluntary surrogacy rather than coerced surrogacy. Clearly, she exercised choice in the roles she filled.

28. Mattison, *Louisa Picquet, the Octoroon: A Tale of Southern Slave Life*, pp. 18–21.

29. William Wells Brown, "Narrative of William Wells Brown," in *Puttin' on Ole Massa*, ed. Gilbert Osofsky (New York: Harper & Row, 1969), pp. 194–95.

30. White, *Ar'n't I a Woman?*, pp. 37–38.
31. Ibid., p. 15.
32. Alice Walker, *The Color Purple*, p. 225.
33. George M. Fredrickson, *The Black Image in the White Mind*, 2d ed. (Middletown, Connecticut: Wesleyan University Press, 1987), p. 57.
34. White, *Ar'n't I a Woman?*, p. 29.
35. Hooks, *Ain't I a Woman?*; p. 52.
36. Paula Giddings, *When and Where I Enter* (New York: William Morrow & Company, 1984), p. 62.
37. Carter G. Woodson and Lorenzo Greene, *The Negro Wage Earner* (Washington D.C.: The Association for the Study of Negro Life and History, 1930), p. 31.
38. Paula Giddings, *When and Where I Enter*, p. 37.
39. Hooks, *Ain't I a Woman?*, p. 37.
40. Gwaltney, *Drylongso*, pp. 146–47.
41. Ibid., p. 151.
42. Ibid., p. 150.
43. Woodson and Greene, *The Negro Wage Earner*, p. 61.
44. Ibid., p. 59.
45. Philip S. Foner and Ronald L. Lewis, eds., *The Black Worker*, vol. 5 (Philadelphia: Temple University Press, 1980), p. 55.
46. Ibid., p. 55.
47. Ibid.
48. Paula Giddings, *When and Where I Enter*, p. 143.
49. June O. Patton, "Document: Moonlight and Magnolias in Southern Education: The Black Mammy Memorial Institute," in *The Journal of Negro History* 65 (2) (Spring 1980), p. 153.
50. Joel R. Williamson, "Black Self-Assertion Before and After Emancipation," in *Key Issues in the Afro-American Experience*, vol. 1, ed. Nathan I. Huggins, Martin Kilson and Daniel M. Fox (New York: Harcourt Brace Jovanovich, Inc., 1971), pp. 219–20.
51. Lee Guidon, quoted in B. A. Botkin, ed., *Lay My Burden Down* (Chicago: University of Chicago Press, 1945), p. 66.
52. Ibid.
53. Tines Kendricks, quoted in Botkin, *Lay My Burden Down*, p. 70.
54. Nicey Kinney, quoted in Botkin, *Lay My Burden Down*, p. 82.
55. Cuto, quoted in Botkin, *Lay My Burden Down*, p. 84.
56. Botkin, *Lay My Burden Down*, p. 148.
57. Williamson, "Black Self-Assertion Before and After Emancipation," p. 234.
58. Ibid., pp. 232–33.
59. Ibid.

60. For instance, see Botkin, *Lay My Burden Down,* pp. 70, 77, 79, 84, 99, 104, 118, 132, 134, 151, 159, 160. In all these references, black people refer to their mothers as Mammy.
61. Gwaltney, *Drylongso,* pp. 148, 154, 155.
62. Elizabeth Bettenhausen, "Hagar Revisited," *Christianity and Crisis* (May 4, 1987), pp. 157–59.

## Chapter 4: Color Struck: a State of Mind

1. For a discussion of narcissism see the definitions in the *Diagnostic and Statistical Manual of Mental Disorders* of the American Psychiatric Association. Also see C. Fred Alford, *Narcissism: Socrates, the Frankfurt School, and Psychoanalytic Theory* (New Haven: Yale University Press, 1988), pp. 2, 3. Also see Shirley Sugerman, *Sin and Madness: Studies in Narcissism* (Philadelphia: Westminster Press, 1976). Especially see Sugerman's chapter "Narcissus Re-considered: The Myth." She provides a good description of the Greek myth of Narcissus as it is contained in several sources. The most familiar version is that provided by Ovid in *Metamorphoses,* Book III. According to this version, Narcissus, son of the nymph Leiriope, was very beautiful. His mother asked Tiresias, the seer, about the future of Narcissus. Tiresias said that the lad would live to be very old, provided he did not get to know himself. Narcissus was hardhearted and rejected all the females who fell in love with him, including Echo, who faded away for love of Narcissus and only left her voice behind. One of the nymphs whom Narcissus rejected prayed that he would love someone and never gain what he loved. Nemesis heard the prayer and directed Narcissus to a stream to drink. As he knelt by the stream, Narcissus saw the reflection of his own image and immediately fell in love with it. All of his life, he was preoccupied with his own image. Finally he pined away, unable to realize union with what he loved, "for there was no other" (Sugerman, pp. 19–20).
2. For a discussion of narcissism also see the *Encyclopedia of Psychology* (New York: Wiley, 1984). The Rodney King case in Los Angeles, California, in 1992 is an example of the manifestation of white racist narcissism in action. The policemen's brutal beating of King and the jury's acquittal of them stem from the white, racist, narcissistic consciousness in this country.
3. Sociologist of religion Joseph R. Washington has shown that there was an anti-black strain in English religion that seriously affected English attitudes toward black people wherever they met them. See *Anti-Blackness in English Religion, 1500–1800* (Lewiston, New York: The Edwin Mellen Press, 1984). Also see Washington, *Race and Religion in Early Nineteenth Century America, 1800–1850,* vol. 2 (Lewiston, New York: The Edwin Mellen Press, 1988). Cornel West has shown how anti-black attitudes developed in European intellectual discourse and yielded white supremacy. See *Prophesy Deliverance!*

4. It is not being claimed here that Mather was guilty of racial arrogance. In *The Negro Christianized* Mather said: "Their complexion sometimes is made an argument why nothing should be done for them. . . . As if the great God went by the complexion of men in His favours to them! As if none but *whites* might hope to be favoured and accepted with God. . . . Away with such trifles! The God who looks on the heart, is not moved by the colour of the skin."

5. Quoted by Winthrop D. Jordan, "Unthinking Decision: The Enslavement of Negroes in America to 1700," in *American Negro Slavery,* ed. Allen Weinstein and Frank Otto Gattell (New York: Oxford University Press, 1973), p. 16.

6. Ibid.

7. Ibid., p. 39.

8. Cited in Winthrop Jordan, *White Over Black: American Attitudes Toward the Negro, 1550–1812* (New York: W. W. Norton & Company, 1977), p. 7.

9. Ibid.

10. See Shakespeare's "Dark Lady" pictured in his sonnets numbered 127, 130, 131, 132 in any standard collection of his complete works. Shakespearean critic Hallet Smith has this to say about Shakespeare's sonnets to the "Dark Lady:" "They involve a mistress of the poet's, a mysterious 'Dark Lady'—i.e., not blonde, as the current fashion in beauty preferred—who is sensual, promiscuous and irresistible. . . . The poet's attitude toward her is frankly lustful, with occasional pangs of conscience and feelings of revulsion" (Hallet Smith, "Sonnets," in G. Blakemore Evans, ed., *The Riverside Shakespeare* [Boston: Houghton Mifflin Company, 1974], p. 146). The tension in the sonnets to the "Dark Lady" derive from the conflict between the prevailing standards of beauty in a society preferring whiteness and the poet's struggle to acknowledge beauty in darkness.

11. Jordan, *White Over Black*, p. 7.

12. T. H. Green and T. H. Grose, eds., *David Hume, Essays: Moral, Political and Literary,* vol. 1 (London, 1875), p. 252. Hume's statement is not to obscure the fact that John Locke had earlier implanted in the English mind the idea of the equality of all men. But the fact that many of these Englishmen, especially many of the American colonists, saw the African as subhuman meant that these black people were not in the category of full humanity and therefore the idea of black men equal to white men was out of the question.

13. See George M. Fredrickson's discussion of this in *The Black Image in the White Mind,* 2d ed. (Middletown, Connecticut: Wesleyan University Press, 1987), pp. 1–42.

14. Jordan, *White Over Black,* p. 258.

15. Ibid., p. 96.

16. Ibid.

17. Leslie Howard Owens, *This Species of Property: Slave Life and Culture in the Old South* (New York: Oxford University Press, 1976), p. 10.

18. *The Apostolic Fathers,* 2 vols., trans. Kirsopp Lake (New York: G. P. Putnam's Sons, 1919), vol. 1, p. 407.

19. Discussion of the use and appropriation of the Noah-Ham story to validate the enslavement of Africans is contained in Jordan, *White Over Black,* pp. 17–20; Fredrickson, *The Black Image in the White Mind,* pp. 60–61; Leslie Howard Owens, *This. Species of Property,* p. 14; Thomas Virgil Peterson, *Ham and Japheth* (Metuchen, New Jersey: The Scarecrow Press and The American Theological Library Association, 1978).

20. Charles Nichols, *Many Thousand Gone* (Leiden: E. J. Brill, 1963), p. 12.

21. Ibid., p. 12.

22. Edmund L. Drago, *Broke by the War: Letters of a Slave Trader* (South Carolina: University of South Carolina Press, 1991), p. 17.

23. Ibid., pp. 16–17.

24. Jordan, *White Over Black,* pp. 77, 78.

25. Ibid., p. 77.

26. Ibid.

27. This census of 1840 was the first census to record the number of mentally ill and feebleminded, the "insane and idiots as they were classified." See William Stanton, *The Leopard's Spots: Scientific Attitudes Toward Race in America, 1815–1859* (Chicago: University of Chicago Press, 1960), p. 58. This shows how the federal government has used dishonest strategies to keep the American public believing that black people were intellectually inferior to whites.

28. Stanton, *The Leopard's Spots,* p. 65.

29. Charles Francis Adams, ed., *Memoirs of John Quincy Adams, Comprising Portions of His Diary From 1795–1848* (Philadelphia: J. B. Lippincott & Co., 1874–77), vol. 12, pp. 61–62.

30. Stanton, *The Leopard's Spots,* p. 71.

31. Ibid., p. 62–63.

32. The disdain upper-class white northerners had for some poor southern whites is revealed in the arrogant manner in which they referred to the poor whites. A case in point is Whitelaw Reid's reference to a North Carolina poor white as "the cracker." See Whitelaw Reid, *After the War: A Southern Tour May 1, 1865, May 1, 1866* (Cincinnati: Moore, Wilstach & Baldwin, 1866), p. 26.

33. Gerald David Jaynes, *Branches Without Roots: Genesis of the Black Working Class in the American South, 1862–1882* (New York: Oxford University Press, 1986), p. 255.

34. Ibid., p. 259.

35. Ibid., p. 255.

36. Consider the degraded opinion wealthy whites (the employers) had of poor white people. According to Jaynes, "Poor whites were invariably described as 'ignorant' and 'unreliable'—'lazy and dissolute plebeians, in short' (as a tobacco planter characterized them), 'the most offensive class of society.' Even the slaves, and their progeny were wont to sing, 'I'd rather be a nigger than a poor white man' " (Jaynes, *Branches Without Roots,* p. 253).

37. Jaynes, *Branches Without Roots,* p. 256.

38. Ibid.

39. Botkin, *Lay My Burden Down,* p. 256.

40. Ibid., p. 258.

41. Ibid., p. 242.

42. Jaynes, *Branches Without Roots*, p. 256.

43. August Meier, *Negro Thought in America, 1880–1915* (Ann Arbor, Michigan: University of Michigan Press, 1968), p. 21.

44. Ibid., p. 20.

45. See Stanton, *The Leopard's Spots.*

46. Richard Lowitt and Maurine Beasley, eds., *One Third a Nation: Lorena Hickok Report on the Great Depression* (Urbana, Illinois: University of Illinois Press, 1981), p. 148. Hickok was commissioned by Harry Hopkins, head of the Federal Emergency Relief Administration, "to prepare confidential reports on conditions in the United States, as the administration of Franklin D. Roosevelt grappled with the problems associated with providing relief to the victims of the Great Depression" (Preface to *One Third a Nation*). For a year (1934–35) Hickok interviewed victims, employers and others.

47. Ibid., pp. 151–52.

48. Ibid., p. 152.

49. Ibid., p. 121.

50. Ibid., p. 195.

51. For other studies that treat causes and effects of the Great Depression of 1929–39 see John Kenneth Galbaith, *The Great Crash* (Boston: Houghton Mifflin Company, 1954); John A. Garrity, *The Great Depression* (New York: Harcourt Brace Jovanovich, 1986); Charles P. Kindleberger, *The World in Depression, 1929–1939* (Los Angeles: University of California Press, 1973).

52. Daniel J. Kevles, *In the Name of Eugenics* (New York: Alfred A. Knopf, 1985), p. ix.

53. See W. E. Castle, *Genetics and Eugenics* (Cambridge: Harvard University Press, 1921), pp. 265–312.

54. Kevles, *In the Name of Eugenics,* p. 58.

55. Ibid.

56. Ibid., p. 59.

57. Ibid., p. 61.

58. Ibid.
59. Ibid.
60. Ibid., p. 62.
61. Ibid.
62. During this time of economic crisis in other parts of the Western world, white racist narcissism expressed itself in a deadly form of eugenics politics. Nazi Germany rendered millions of Jews homeless and poor and exterminated them. The frightening part of this for me, an American black, is that Hitler's eugenics was not his original creation but finds its parents in the eugenics ideas about racial superiority that were alive in many sections of the world, especially in the United States, in the early part of the twentieth century. Hitler's eugenics politics were a logical consequence of what was created and first perpetuated by England and America under the name of eugenics.
63. Elizabeth Allen, Barbara Beckwith, Jon Beckwith, Steven Chorover, "Against Sociobiology," *New York Review of Books* (November 13, 1975).
64. Ibid.
65. See the critique, "Sociobiology—Another Biological Determinism," in *Bioscience* 26:5 (April 1976): 182–86. Also see Edward O. Wilson's response, "Academic Vigilantism and the Political Significance of Sociobiology," in the same issue of *Bioscience*.

### Chapter 5: Sisters In The Wilderness And Community Meanings

1. Old Elizabeth, "Memoir of Old Elizabeth, A Colored Woman," p. 7.
2. Ibid., p. 4.
3. Most scholars have regarded as useless any attempt to date the spiritual songs. Some songs could have been created in the seventeenth, eighteenth or nineteenth centuries. Nobody knows when the earliest of these songs were created and sung by the slaves. While most of the collecting of the songs for publication was done after the Civil War during the late nineteenth century, there is no evidence to suggest that most of the songs were created during the nineteenth century. Therefore, it can be assumed that eighteenth, nineteenth (and perhaps even seventeenth) century Euro-American ideas about the wilderness were backgrounds upon which slave notions of the wilderness and wilderness experience also developed.
4. From Allen, Ware and Garrison, *Slave Songs of the United States,* p. 14.
5. This song was sung in the black Baptist church when I was a child. According to *Slave Songs of the United States,* similar versions were sung in the Methodist camp meetings in the late nineteenth century.
6. Allen, Ware and Garrison, *Slave Songs of the United States,* p. xii.
7. Ibid.
8. Ibid.

9. Roderick Nash, *Wilderness and the American Mind* (New Haven: Yale University Press, 1967), p. 24.

10. Ibid., p. 25.

11. Ibid., p. 32.

12. See Nash's discussion of the way that the Bible, Puritanism and notions of progress influenced the pioneers' idea of nature as hostile and their determination to conquer it and thereby to regard the entire effort as progress and as ordained by God (*Wilderness and the American Mind,* pp. 34–43). Also see Perry Miller, *Errand into the Wilderness* (New York: Harper Torchbooks 1964; originally published by The Belknap Press of Harvard University Press in 1956); also Peter N. Carroll, *Puritanism and the Wilderness* (New York: Columbia University Press, 1969); also Charles Berryman, *From Wilderness to Wasteland: The Trial of the Puritan God in the American Imagination* (Port Washington, New York: Kennikat Press, 1979).

13. Ibid., p. 46.

14. Ibid., p. 47.

15. Ibid.

16. Ibid., p. 65.

17. Ibid., p. 67.

18. Ibid.

19. Ibid.

20. Ibid., p. 108.

21. Kate Drumgoold, "A Slave Girl's Story," in Gates, *Six Women's Slave Narratives,* p. 3.

22. To get a sense of the flux in the world of the newly emancipated slave see Ira Berlin, Steven F. Miller, Leslie S. Rowland, "Afro-American Families in the Transition from Slavery to Freedom," in Darlene Clark Hine, ed., *Black Women in United States History,* vol. 1 (New York: Carlson Publishing Inc., 1990), pp. 84–117.

23. Hagar, like African-American women and the African-American community, experienced bondage, freedom without the necessary resources for survival, and faith in the promise of God to be with her child as it grew. Many women and African-American religious people believe in this same kind of promise as far as their children's future is concerned.

24. Since Hagar functions symbolically in this development of African-American thought about the wilderness, Ishmael—an extension of Hagar—figures into this symbolic configuration. His economic plight very much resembles the black American male economic plight. The casting out of Ishmael by his father Abraham aborts Ishmael's right to inherit the resources that would ultimately make him head of the household. African-American men have for generations been cast out of the economic system in America. And their deprivation of adequate

economic resources often prevents them from becoming heads of black house-holds. A case in point is the way the Aid to Dependent Children system works in America. Since the father's income is not adequate fully to support his family, mothers who receive this aid must make sure that the father of the children is not in the household. She thus becomes head of the household.

25. There is enough evidence in the lyrics of the antebellum spiritual songs to show that the religious life of the slaves was characterized by a melding of the spiritual and the political. See Allen, Ware and Garrison, *Slave Songs in the United States.*

26. In Hagar's story the political and the spiritual interconnect in the wilderness when the angel of the Lord asks Hagar the question of her destination, and Hagar's response brings into the scene words about her political act of running away from slavery. Hagar's act is political, because it challenges the authority of the governing forces in this Hebraic tribe. And since slaves were property, this act threatens to lessen the economic resources of the tribe. The spiritual connects with the political reality as the angel of the Lord promises survival to Hagar's posterity, names Hagar's unborn child Ishmael (God who hears) and finally as Hagar names the angel of the Lord—"Thou art a God of seeing" (Genesis 16:13). Hagar's response to all of this is radical obedience to the angel of the Lord, who tells her to return to her "mistress and submit to her" (Genesis 16:9). Spiritual, in this sense, means human encounter with a divine source so that the human is, in some way, empowered. Hagar is empowered to name, and she names God.

27. Evelyn Brooks, "Religion, Politics and Gender: The Leadership of Nannie Helen Burroughs," in Hine, *Black Women in United States History,* vol. 1, p. 155.

28. Benjamin Quarles, "Harriet Tubman's Unlikely Leadership," in Hine, *Black Women in United States History,* vol. 16, p. 1132.

29. Ibid., p. 1134.

30. Ibid., p. 1135.

31. Ibid., p. 1137.

32. Gwaltney, *Drylongso,* p. xv.

33. Though there are many models of black womanhood in the black community, sociologist Joyce Ladner reveals that the most persistent and pervasive model is of an economically independent, strong, self-sufficient, hardworking woman inside and outside the home who exerts a strong and often dominant role in the family. See Joyce A. Ladner, *Tomorrow's Tomorrow* (Garden City, New York: Doubleday & Co., 1971).

34. Justin Dewey, *The True Woman: A Series of Discourses* (Boston: Lee and Shepard, 1869), p. 1.

35. W. Cunningham, *True Womanhood* (New York: Thomas Y. Crowell & Company, 18–), p. 11.

36. Rev. S. G. Anderson, *Woman's Sphere and Influence* (Toledo, Ohio: Franklin Printing and Engraving Co., 1898), p. 7.

37. Cunningham, p. 10.

38. Claudia Tate, Introduction, in *The Works of Katherine Davis Chapman Tillman,* The Schomburg Library of Nineteenth-Century Black Women Writers (New York: Oxford University Press, 1991), pp. 3–62.

39. See Linda M. Perkins, "The Impact of the 'Cult of True Womanhood' on the Education of Black Women," in Hine, *Black Women in United States History,* vol. 3, pp. 1065–76 (originally published in *Journal of Social Issues* 39, no. 3 [1983], pp. 17–28).

40. For a discussion of late-nineteenth-century educated Black Baptist women's use of biblical women to model African-American womanhood see Evelyn Brooks, "The Feminist Theology of the Black Baptist Church, 1880–1900 (1980)," in Hine, *Black Women in United States History,* vol. 1, pp. 167–95. For a church woman's account of the work for Baptist women in the late nineteenth century see Mary Cook, "The Work For Baptist Women," in *The Negro Baptist Pulpit,* ed. Edward Brawley (Philadelphia: American Baptist Publication Society, 1890), pp. 271–86.

41. Anna Julia Cooper, *A Voice From the South,* The Schomburg Library of Nineteenth-Century Black Women Writers (New York: Oxford University Press, 1988), p. 11.

42. Ibid., p. 12.

43. Ibid., p. 13.

44. Ibid., p. 59.

45. Ibid., p. 60.

46. Ibid.

47. Tate, Introduction, p. 7.

48. Cooper, *A Voice From the South,* p. 32.

49. Mary Helen Washington, Introduction, to Cooper, *A Voice From the South,* p. xxx.

50. Ibid. Washington is careful to cite many reasons why Cooper, in her work, seems to maintain a distance between herself and the masses of black women. Three of these reasons are 1) to communicate to the public that there are black women who possess "refinement, intelligence and training"; 2) "As a woman, Cooper had to fight against both black and white men who posed tremendous obstacles to her own education"; and 3) "As a passionate and committed feminist, she had to struggle against the masculinist bias in black intellectual circles and against racism among white feminists." Washington's account of Cooper's biography reveals that Anna Julia Cooper was a courageous teacher committed to the education of black young people—as Cooper's outstanding service as principal at Washington, D.C.'s M Street School demonstrated. White racism on the Wash-

ington school board caused Cooper's dismissal from this post primarily because she was successfully preparing black students to enter Ivy League schools.

51. Perkins, "The Impact of the 'Cult of True Womanhood' on the Education of Black Women," in Hine, *Black Women in United States History*, p. 1072.

52. Brooks, "Religion, Politics, and Gender," p. 181.

53. Ibid., p. 181.

54. Ibid., p. 171.

55. Dolores Janiewski, "Sisters Under Their Skins: Southern Working Women, 1880–1950," in Hine, *Black Women in United States History*, vol. 3, pp. 779–801.

56. Ibid., p. 792.

57. Ibid.

58. Ibid.

59. Brooks, "Religion, Politics, and Gender," p. 169.

60. Janiewski, "Sisters Under Their Skins," pp. 787–88.

61. As reported in Beverly O. Ford, "Case Studies in Black Female Heads of Households in the Welfare System: Socialization and Survival," in Hine, *Black Women in United States History*, vol. 2, p. 369.

62. Ibid., p. 373.

63. Abby Lincoln's article "Who Will Revere the Black Woman?" speaks to this tension. Lincoln says, "When a white man 'likes colored girls,' his woman (the white woman) is the last one he wants to know about it. Yet . . . when a Negro 'likes white girls' his woman (the Black woman) is the first he wants to know about it. . . . White female[s] . . . are flagrantly flaunted in our faces as the ultimate in feminine pulchritude. Our women are encouraged by our own men to strive to look and act as much like the white female image as possible. . . . At best we are made to feel that we are poor imitations and excuses for white women." See Lincoln's article in Cade, *The Black Woman*, pp. 80–84. Other articles in Cade's book that touch on this tension are Fran Sanders, "Dear Black Man," pp. 73–79; Joyce Green, "Black Romanticism," pp. 137–42.

64. Dance, "Black Eve or Madonna? A Study of the Antithetical Views of the Mother in Black American Literature," pp. 123–32.

65. Ibid., p. 126.

66. Frank Chalk and Kurt Jonassohn, *The History and Sociology of Genocide* (New Haven: Yale University Press, 1990), pp. 8–9.

67. The text of this petition is contained in William L. Patterson, ed., *We Charge Genocide* (New York: International Publishers Co., 1970).

68. Ibid., p. 10.

69. Ibid., pp. vii, 48.

70. Ida B. Wells-Barnett, *A Red Record: Tabulated Statistics and Alleged Causes of Lynching in the United States, 1892–1893–1894,* in Henry Louis Gates, Jr., ed. *Selected Works of Ida B. Wells Barnett,* in The Schomburg Library of Nineteenth-

Century Black Women Writers, p. 141. For more about lynching see the following: Jacqueline Dowd Hall, *Revolt Against Chivalry: Jessie Daniel Ames and the Women's Campaign Against Lynching* (New York: Columbia University Press, 1979); Trudier Harris, *Exorcising Blackness: Historical and Literary Lynching and Burning Rituals* (Bloomington: Indiana University Press, 1984); NAACP, *Thirty Years of Lynching in the United States, 1889–1918* (New York: Arno Press and the New York Times, 1969); Walter White, *Rope and Faggot: A Biography of Judge Lynch* (New York: Knopf, 1929); Donald L. Grant, *The Anti-Lynching Movement: 1883–1932* (San Francisco: R and E Research Associates, 1975); James R. McGovern, *Anatomy of a Lynching: The Killing of Claude Neal* (Baton Rouge: Louisiana State University Press, 1982); James Elbert Cutler, *Lynch-Law: An Investigation into the History of Lynching in the United States* (Montclair, New Jersey: Patterson Smith, 1969; originally published 1905); and Howard Smead, *Blood Justice: The Lynching of Mack Charles Parker* (New York: Oxford University Press, 1986).

71. By the time the petition "We Charge Genocide" was submitted to the United Nations in 1951, hate groups had proliferated in America. The petition identifies twenty groups operating out of Georgia, Florida, Alabama, Virginia, Tennessee, Pennsylvania, Texas, Kentucky and Michigan. See Patterson, *We Charge Genocide*, p. 158.

72. See sociologist Joyce Ladner's discussion of the attempt of slave masters to destroy the African culture of slaves in her article "Racism and Tradition: Black Women in Historical Perspective," in Hine, *Black Women in United States History*, vol. 9, pp. 269–81.

73. Maude White Katz, "She Who Would Be Free—Resistance," in Hine, *Black Women in United States History*, vol. 9, p. 321.

74. Ibid., pp. 321–22.

75. David Hatchett, "Harassment of Black Politicians," *Crisis* 100, no. 5 (June–July 1992), pp. 49–50, 54–56.

76. Ibid., p. 49.

77. Katz, "She Who Would Be Free—Resistance," p. 324.

78. John Winston Coleman, *Slavery Times in Kentucky*, as quoted by Katz, "She Who Would Be Free—Resistance," p. 324.

79. Katz, "She Who Would Be Free—Resistance," p. 375.

80. Ibid.

81. Ibid., pp. 324–25.

82. Ibid., p. 325.

83. Ibid., p. 326.

84. Ibid., p. 327.

85. Ibid.

86. Ibid. p. 329.

87. Charles Payne, "Men Led, But Women Organized: Movement Participation of Women in the Mississippi Delta," in Hine, *Black Women in United States History,* vol. 16, pp. 1–2, 13.
88. Ibid., p. 5.

### *Chapter 6: Womanist God-Talk nd Black Liberation Theology*

1. James Cone, *A Black Theology of Liberation,* 2d ed. (Maryknoll, New York: Orbis Books, 1990).
2. Naim Stifan Ateek, *Justice and Only Justice* (Maryknoll, New York: Orbis Books, 1989), p. 77.
3. All biblical quotations in this chapter are from the Revised Standard Version.
4. See footnote to Leviticus 19:20–22, The New Oxford Annotated Bible, pp. 146–47.
5. James Cone, *A Black Theology of Liberation,* p. 2.
6. There is evidence in the Christian testament to support the claim that Jesus was not biased toward the Samaritans as a people, though he may have been biased against their traditions. The parable of the Good Samaritan in Luke 10:29ff shows Jesus teaching that there were people outside of Israel who, in their relationships with their fellow humans, pleased God more than people inside Israel like the priest and the Levite. And the incident of Jesus meeting the Samaritan woman at Jacob's well (John 4:7ff) illustrates Jesus' willingness to communicate with people who traditionally were not regarded highly by Jews. But Jesus, showing bias, does not hesitate to tell the Samaritan woman, "You worship what you do not know; we worship what we know, for salvation is from the Jews" (John 4:22). This statement suggests superiority of Jewish traditions. It also denies the efficacy of salvation for Samaritans on the basis of their own faith and practices resting upon the Pentateuch; the Samaritans rejected the remaining sections of the Hebrew testament. But Jesus does not exclude the Samaritans from the gospel. He stayed among them for two days at their request, and many Samaritans were converted. It should be indicated here that Matthew wrote of Jesus' life in terms of Jesus' commitment to the salvation of the nation of Israel. The book of Luke (the only place where the parable of the compassionate Samaritan appears in the Bible) emphasizes the universality of Jesus' message and makes it available for all people. We could judge Matthew 10:5 to be an insert by the writer of the book and probably not the words of Jesus. But if we do that we can doubt the authenticity of all the reported words of Jesus contained in the Christian testament—since Jesus did not write anything. The point is that the Hebrew and Christian testaments are often ambiguous when confronted with the issue of the equality of non-Jewish people and their values. The testaments are silent about the abolition of the institution of slavery in the ancient world. Womanist theologians might ask: Can the liberation norm in black theology be completely

validated today by the Bible, which sends out equivocal messages about the liberation of slaves, especially about the liberation of female slaves?

7. James Cone, *A Black Theology of Liberation*, p. 31.

8. Ibid., p. 36.

9. Inasmuch as several Christian liberation theologians are beginning to try to understand the God of the scriptures also from the perspective of the non-Hebrew victims in the Bible, tensions are bound to emerge within the ranks of liberation theology over the issue of how the theologian uses the Bible. Palestinian liberation theologians and Native American liberation theologians identify with the Canaanites in the Hebrew testament rather than with the ancient Israelites. Many womanist theologians and African-American people identify with Hagar instead of with Sarah and Abraham. Palestinian liberation theologian Naim Ateek states the problem clearly: "Liberation theologians have seen the Bible as a dynamic source for their understanding of liberation, but if some parts of it are applied literally to our situation today the Bible appears to offer to the Palestinians slavery rather than freedom, injustice rather than justice, and death to their national and political life. . . . No Palestinian Christian theology can avoid tackling the issue of the Bible: How can the Bible, which has apparently become part of the problem of the Arab-Israeli conflict, become part of its solution? How can the Bible, which has been used to bring a curse to the national aspirations of a whole people, again offer them a blessing? How can the Bible, through which many have been led to salvation, be itself saved and redeemed?" (Ateek, *Justice and Only Justice*, pp. 75, 77). Native Americans and African Americans can ask similar questions given their histories of having been robbed of their land (Native Americans) and enslaved (African Americans). For a Native American position on this issue of liberation theology's use of the Bible see Robert Allen Warrior, "Canaanites and Conquerors," *Christianity and Crisis* 49:12 (September 11, 1989).

10. For instance, it is most alarming that Cain Hope Felder, in his critique of biblical scholars' failure to give attention to the significant role of Africa and Africans in the Bible, gives *very little* attention to the African Hagar. Felder, a Christian testament scholar, does not allude to Hagar in the Christian testament. Though he cites countless references from the book of Galatians, he never alludes to Hagar's inferior place in that book. This is a clear instance of the invisibility of "the oppressed of the oppressed" (for example, the non-ruling class women and female slaves of African descent) in scholarship by black males. See Cain Hope Felder, *Troubling Biblical Waters: Race, Class, and Family* (Maryknoll, New York: Orbis Books, 1989).

11. Cecil Cone, *The Identity Crisis in Black Theology* (Nashville: The African Methodist Episcopal Church, 1975), p. 23.

12. Ibid., p. 39.

13. Ibid., p. 36.

14. The explication of black experience appearing in this section comes from my own published work. See Delores S. Williams, "Black Theology's Contribution to Theological Methodology," *Reflections* (New Haven: Yale University Divinity School, April–June 1983), pp. 12–16.

15. James Cone's identification of Jesus as black tends to associate blackness with sacredness.

16. James Cone, *A Black Theology of Liberation,* 1st ed. (Philadelphia and New York: J. B. Lippincott Co., 1970), p. 55.

17. Ibid.

18. James Cone, *God of the Oppressed* (New York: Seabury Press, 1975), p. 23.

19. James Deotis Roberts, *Liberation and Reconciliation* (Philadelphia: Westminster Press, 1971), p. 9.

20. Cecil Cone, *The Identity Crisis in Black Theology,* pp. 43, 45.

21. Roberts, *Liberation and Reconciliation,* p. 14.

22. James Cone, *God of the Oppressed,* p. 52.

23. Ibid., p. 8.

24. Cecil Cone, *The Identity Crisis in Black Theology,* p. 18.

25. However, it should be noted here that in the last printing of his book, *A Black Theology of Liberation,* James Cone included a new introduction that owns the sexist character of his early work. In the new printing, Cone uses inclusive language. But Cone does not use the heritage of black female intellection to shape his ideas in this most recent issue of the book.

26. Jacqueline Grant, "Black Theology and Black Women," in *Black Theology: A Documentary History, 1966–1979,* ed. James Cone and Gayraud Wilmore (Maryknoll, New York: Orbis Books, 1979), pp. 418–33.

27. Hagar's encounter with God in Genesis 21 results in her receiving new vision that allowed her to see the resources for saving the life of her nearly dead child Ishmael. Time and again, African-American women have testified that God gave them the insight they needed to make a way out of no way.

28. For a long time some folk wisdom in the black community has claimed that in relation to the community's survival and liberation, "the brothers dream dreams," but "the sisters have the vision."

29. Thus it is no wonder that black women have initiated many black civil rights movements, have been the prime knowers and movers of the black church movement in America and have led in economic advancement in the African-American community.

30. If Rosa Parks had not sat down, Martin Luther King, Jr., could not have stood up. If Ida Wells Barnett had not monitored the lynching of black people in this country, there would not have been such a complete record.

31. Jürgen Moltmann, "The Crucified God: God and the Trinity Today," in *New Questions of God,* ed. Johannes B. Metz (New York: Herder & Herder, 1972), pp. 33–35.

32. A discussion of certain classical emphases precedes the consideration of these issues in relation to black liberation theology because this study assumes, as does James Cone, that classical theological traditions laid the foundations for much of what we believe doctrinally. See Cone's treatment of the classical responses to the question of the historical Jesus in James Cone, *A Black Theology of Liberation,* 2d ed., pp. 110–28.

33. For a concise treatment of the development of classical Christian ideas about the atonement, see Alan Richardson, *Creeds in the Making* (London: Student Christian Movement Press, 1951), pp. 96–113; for an old but thorough treatment of the biblical roots of the sacrificial notions of atonement see Alfred Cave, *The Scriptural Doctrine of Sacrifice* (Edinburgh: T. & T. Clark, 1877); also see Hastings Rashdall, *The Idea of Atonement in Christian Theology* (London: Macmillan and Company, Limited, 1920); also see Gustaf Aulen, *Christus Victor* (New York: The Macmillan Company, 1951).

34. Richardson, *Creeds in the Making,* p. 21.

35. Ibid.

36. Ibid.

37. This notion of the significance of the death of identity has come to me through conversations with Yalini Senathirajah, a Tamil immigrant living in New York City.

38. The inference here is both individual and collective—body, mind and spirit in terms of the individual and body, mind and spirit in terms of the community.

39. Olin P. Moyd, *Redemption in Black Theology* (Valley Forge, Pennsylvania: Judson Press, 1979), p. 134.

40. Ibid. I disagree with Moyd. Black religion has grown out of one of the most complex expressions of faith in America.

41. Ibid.

42. Roberts, *Liberation and Reconciliation,* p. 144.

43. Ibid., pp. 153–54.

44. The term *revaluing value* has to do with reassessing and/or renaming social principles, goals, standards, values of a group and/or society. Revaluing value may also have to do with rendering visible what has been invisible and then naming and assigning value to what is rendered visible. This is especially true of women's experience.

45. Roberts, *Liberation and Reconciliation,* pp. 176–77.

46. Ibid., p. 177.

47. Ibid., pp. 178–79.

48. Ibid., pp. 183–84.

49. J. Cone, *God of the Oppressed,* p. 196.

50. Ibid., p. 198.

51. Ibid., p. 207.
52. Ibid., pp. 207, 208.
53. Ibid., pp. 208–9.
54. Ibid., pp. 212, 213.
55. Ibid., p. 217.
56. Ibid.

## Chapter 7: Womanist-Feminist Dialogue: Differences And Commonalities

1. This term comes from Asian feminist theologian Chung Hyun Kyung's book *Struggle to Be the Sun Again: Introducing Asian Women's Theology* (Maryknoll, New York: Orbis Books, 1990), p. 76.
2. Ibid., p. 76.
3. Ibid.
4. Ibid., p. 77.
5. Ibid.
6. Ibid.
7. Ibid., p. 79, emphasis added.
8. See the African feminist Awa Thiam's discussion of this in her chapter "Skin Whitening," in *Black Sisters, Speak Out: Feminism and Oppression in Black Africa* (London, England: Pluto Press, 1986).
9. See Rosemary Radford Ruether's discussion "Anthropology: Humanity as Male and Female" in *Sexism and God-talk* (Boston: Beacon Press, 1983), pp. 94–99.
10. A notable exception to this is Barbara Hilkert Andolsen, *Daughters of Jefferson, Daughters of Boot Blacks* (Macon, Georgia: Mercer University Press, 1986).
11. For a full discussion of the limitation of the *patriarchy* nomenclature and a new naming for African-American women, see Delores S. Williams, "The Color of Feminism or Speaking the Black Woman's Tongue," *Journal of Religious Thought* (Spring–Summer 1986), pp. 42–58.
12. Quoted by Elizabeth Hoon, "Black Woman, White Woman: Separate Paths to Liberation," *The Black Scholar* 4, no. 7 (April 1978), p. 49.
13. Renita Weems, "A Mistress, A Maid and No Mercy," in *Just a Sister Away: A Womanist Vision of Women's Relationships in the Bible* (San Diego, California: LuraMedia, 1988), p. 11.
14. Ibid.
15. Some examples of this important work include Elisabeth Schüssler Fiorenza, *Bread Not Stones* (Boston: Beacon Press, 1984), *In Memory of Her* (New York: Crossroad, 1983), and *But She Said* (Boston: Beacon Press, 1991); Letty Russell, ed., *Feminist Interpretation of the Bible* (Philadelphia: Westminster Press, 1985); Phyllis Trible, *God and the Rhetoric of Sexuality* (Philadelphia: Fortress Press, 1978) and *Texts of Terror.*

16. See Letty Russell, ed., *The Liberating Word: A Guide to Nonsexist Interpretation of the Bible* (Westminster Press, 1981).
17. Cheryl Townsend Gilkes also refers to a hermeneutic of affirmation as she describes what she terms an "Afro-Centric Biblical Tradition." See Gilkes, "Mother to the Motherless, Father to the Fatherless: Power, Gender and Community in an Afro-Centric Biblical Tradition," *Semeia* 47 (1989).
18. Oral text, or what Cheryl Townsend Gilkes calls creating an African-American biblical tradition, means black people taking from the written text what the community considered to be normative for its life and what they took to be the true word of God in the Bible. This is often passed along in fragments.
19. Gilkes, "Mother to the Motherless, Father to the Fatherless," p. 58.
20. Ibid.
21. Ibid.
22. Ibid.
23. See Mercy Amba Oduyoye and Musimbi B. A. Kanyoro, eds., *The Will to Arise: Women, Tradition and the Church in Africa* (Maryknoll, New York: Orbis Books, 1992).
24. Rosemary N. Edet, "Christianity and African Women's Rituals," in Oduyoye, *The Will to Arise*, pp. 25–39.
25. Jacqueline Olagunju, quoted by Judith Ann Diers, "Freeing Liberation Theology," in *MS* 3, no. 1 (July/August 1992).
26. Gilkes, "Mother to the Motherless, Father to the Fatherless," p. 77.
27. See Lee's and Old Elizabeth's testimony quoted in Chapter 2 above.
28. In her treatment of African women theologians' work of freeing liberation theology, Judith Ann Diers reports that in parts of Africa "the widowhood ritual reflects a wider traditional belief that a woman is a person only if she is married and has children; a childless woman is considered cursed and the marriage often ends in divorce." See Diers, "Freeing Liberation Theology."
29. Hispanic feminist theologians and ethicists Ada Maria Isasi-Diaz and Yolanda Tarango mention the importance of survival to Hispanic women. See Isasi-Diaz and Tarango, *Hispanic Women: Prophetic Voice in the Church*.
30. Tamez, "The Woman Who Complicated the History of Salvation," pp. 5–17.
31. Ibid., p. 14.
32. Speiser, *Genesis*, p. 156.
33. Tamez, "The Woman Who Complicated the History of Salvation," p. 14.
34. Ibid., p. 11.
35. Joanne Carlson Brown and Rebecca Parker, "For God So Loved the World?" in Joanne Carlson Brown and Carole R. Bohn, eds., *Christianity, Patriarchy and Abuse* (New York: The Pilgrim Press, 1989), pp. 1–30.
36. For instance, I do not propose that black women leave the church. Brown and Parker advocate women leaving the church lest they participate in perpetuating

the destructive and oppressive ideas in Christian notions of atonement. The African-American denominational church is basically a women's community composed of about 85 percent women. It can indeed be transformed from within if the sisters decide to do so, since they control the purse strings in the church. Also, black Christians have not always believed what the white Christian theological tradition advocates, though most of them do believe in redemption through Jesus' death on the cross. Today, there may or may not be high value placed upon suffering by black church people. But strong identification with Jesus on the cross could suggest that black church women do see certain kinds of suffering as redemptive. We do not have enough scientific studies of what black women believe doctrinally to answer the question of what black Christian women believe about suffering. We will just have to wait until more evidence is in to say, with any degree of certainty, what black women in the churches believe today.

37. Brown and Parker, "For God So Loved the World?" p. 2.
38. Martin Luther King, Jr., quoted in Brown and Parker, "For God So Loved the World?" p. 20; their source is the compilation of Martin Luther King, Jr.'s, writings edited by James Washington, *A Testament of Hope* (New York: Harper & Row, 1986), p. 47.
39. Ibid., p. 20.
40. For a discussion of the historical and theological use of moral suasion among African-American theologians, see Robert C. Williams, "Moral Suasion and Militant Aggression in the Theological Perspective of Black Religion," *Journal of Religious Thought* 30, no. 2 (Fall–Winter 1973–74), pp. 27–50.
41. For instance, the young black female activist Sister Souljah expressed this view on a 1992 special about racism on public TV in New York City. Phil Donahue was master of ceremonies of the show, which featured among others, Tony Brown, Cornel West and John Silber, president of Boston University.
42. While I would not go as far as some young black people in saying the nation is without a moral conscience, I would say that moral suasion is now an antiquated strategy; it was useful during slavery when there was a strong abolitionist movement in America. When the issue was chattel slavery, this strategy seemed to have effectively prodded white moral conscience in some quarters of the nation. Today, when the African-American issues are white supremacy, black genocide through drugs, white privilege and the need for a redistribution of the economic resources in this country, moral suasion as a civil rights strategy is about as effective as a cup of water on a forest fire. White America seems moved more by the loss of money than by any working of its moral conscience. This is perhaps the reason why the boycott has proven to be a more effective tool in the civil rights struggle. It affects the pocketbook and does not appeal to moral conscience.

43. Brown and Parker, "For God So Loved the World?" p. 27.

44. Ibid., pp. 27–28.

45. Kelly Delaine Brown, "God Is As Christ Does: Toward a Womanist Theology," *Journal of Religious Thought* 46, no. 1 (Summer–Fall 1989), pp. 7–16.

46. Ibid., p. 14.

47. Ibid., p. 16.

48. Ibid.

## Chapter 8: Womanist Reflections On "The Black Church," the African-American Denominational Churches and the Universal Hagar's Spiritual Church

1.  For sociological attempts to define the black church, see C. Eric Lincoln and Lawrence Mamiya, *The Black Church in the African American Experience* (Durham, North Carolina: Duke University Press, 1991); W. E. B. Du Bois, *The Negro Church* (Atlanta: Atlanta University Press, 1903); E. Franklin Frazier, *The Negro Church in America* (Chicago: University of Chicago Press, 1969); E. Franklin Frazier and C. Eric Lincoln, *The Negro Church in America: The Black Church Since Frazier* (New York: Schocken Books, 1974). Also see Hart M. Nelson and Anne Kusener Nelson, *Black Church in the Sixties* (Lexington: University of Kentucky Press, 1975); see Peter Paris, *Social Teaching of the Black Churches* (Philadelphia: Fortress Press, 1985). For theological responses to the black church see James Cone, *For My People: Black Theology and the Black Church* (Maryknoll, New York: Orbis Books, 1984); James Deotis Roberts, *Roots of a Black Future: Family and Church* (Philadelphia: Westminster Press, 1980). For historical perspectives on the black church, see Albert Raboteau, *Slave Religion: The "Invisible Institution" in the Antebellum South* (New York: Oxford University Press, 1978); Gayraud Wilmore, *Black Religion and Black Radicalism,* 2d ed. (Maryknoll, New York: Orbis Books, 1983); James M. Washington, *Frustrated Fellowship: The Black Baptist Quest for Social Power* (Macon, Georgia: Mercer University Press, 1986). For pastoral perspectives on the black church, see Wyatt T. Walker, Harold A. Carter and William Jones, *The Black Church Looks at the Bicentennial: A Minority Report* (Elgin, Illinois: Progressive National Baptist Publishing House, 1976).

2.  See Jarena Lee, "The Life and Religious Experience of Jarena Lee, A Coloured Lady, Giving an Account of Her Call To Preach The Gospel," in William L. Andrews, ed., *Sisters of the Spirit* (Bloomington, Indiana: Indiana University Press, 1986), pp. 25–48. Also see Old Elizabeth, "Memoir of Old Elizabeth, A Colored Woman."

3.  Immorality here refers to preachers exploiting the financial resources and emotional needs of black women in order to increase the preacher's personal financial resources and to build a strong power base for himself so that he becomes a pow-

er broker in the community. He uses this power primarily for self-advancement and not to advance the survival, liberation and struggle for a positive, productive quality of life for the black community.

4. See her letter to Booker T. Washington dated November 30, 1890, contained in *The Booker T. Washington Papers,* vol. 3, ed. Raymond Smock, Louis Harlan and Stuart Kaufman (Urbana, Illinois: University of Illinois Press, 1974).

5. There are serious questions black people must ask about the American national political forces (for example, political parties and surveillance forces like CIA) and the African-American denominational churches which are purported to be the only viable institutions in the African-American community. Why have the oppressive white power structures allowed these church groups to exist in the black community for over a hundred years while they (the white power structures) consistently destroyed other black groups that have the ability to become powerful and long-lasting in the black community? A case in point here is the Black Panther Party, which was consistently harassed and finally all but destroyed. Another case was Marcus Garvey's Universal Negro Improvement Association. I cannot help but wonder if Martin Luther King, Jr., and Malcolm X were, in part, assassinated because they were fast becoming institutions in the African-American community supported by the organizations they were founding. These organizations were operating beyond the power range of either the denominational churches or the black Muslim movement. Yet the organizations of Martin and Malcolm were based on spiritual foundations deriving from the religious ethos of African Americans, and these organizations together had one insistent political intent: the full liberation of African-American people. We black people have bought into the idea (fostered by white politicians, media and power structures) that the black denominational churches are the only viable "institutions" in the black community. We are indoctrinated to believe that they alone determine the way black people think and vote. Thus black preachers easily become the power brokers between the black community and white power and just as easily can become corrupted by the "tid-bits" offered to them by oppressive white power structures. The liberation interests of the black community become highly compromised as the preacher's personal ambitions are rewarded by the collusive white power structures. (I suppose one of our problems as African-American people is that we depend so much upon white definitions for the meaning we assign to our cultural realities. We do not see, name appropriately or emphasize other avenues through which black culture is transmitted. Therefore we think the word *institution,* as defined by white sociologists, aptly identifies our cultural realities. What if black people began to identify beauty shops, barber shops, street corners and other non-church places as also major "funnels" through which black culture was transmitted—instead of thinking in "institutional" terms as defined by white sociologists? Would

we not get an expanded sense of the interconnectedness of our cultural "funnels" and see more clearly how our communities could be organized to foster a consistent culture of survival, resistance and liberation? And if our cultural ideas become thoroughly non-sexist, non-homophobic and Afrocentric, would it not be to our advantage to have all of these places—the denominational churches, the beauty shops, the barber shops, the street corners—as the "funnels" for African-American culture?)

6.  Consider where sexual exploitation of a woman led in the following account: Some years ago, when I lived in a Tennessee town, a black man there killed his wife. When the reasons for this husband's actions surfaced, it was learned that the wife, a leading usher in one of the black denominational churches, had become sexually involved with the preacher. The preacher convinced the woman to take her and her husband's savings out of the bank and give the money to the church. The husband had worked a long time at a rather stable job and had, for many years, diligently put aside most of the money that was in savings. When he learned what the wife had done, he tried to get the money back but could not. In a fit of rage he killed the wife. The preacher left town until the husband's trial was held. The husband was convicted and put in prison. Then the preacher came back to town and resumed his pastorate.

    There is also the case of the denominational church in Massachusetts where the preacher's girlfriend came into the church to fight the preacher's wife, and the preacher ran out the back door of the church. Many, many instances exist of the sexual exploitation of black women in these churches. Black women and entire congregations have kept silent about these matters and have not often disciplined the preachers for their actions. In too many cases business in the church went on as usual. This sets a terrible example for young black people who need moral models of responsible and honest leadership guiding our people. I am convinced that this kind of activity in the denominational churches will only stop when black women open their mouths and tell their stories. We black women need to quit thinking about how good or bad white people will think we are if we tell the stories about our abuse and exploitation. White people and white churches hardly have the moral rectitude and moral fitness that would allow them to be judges of anybody's morality. Centuries and centuries of slave holding and their continuing racism have forfeited the right of white people to make moral judgments about black people. We black women must tell our stories of sexual and financial exploitation within the denominational churches *for the benefit of black people, so that the churches can be cleaned up within, so that the salvation and liberation of black women in the churches can occur.* God will surely judge the African-American denominational churches for oppressing women just as some of our black theology insists that God's judges the white churches for practicing and affirming racism.

7. When I visited the Edgecombe Correctional Facility in New York City in 1991, I saw the woeful failure of the African-American denominations to have meaningful ministry among the prisoners who were about 98 percent black and Hispanic—more black than Hispanic. All male, these prisoners: had been brought down to the Edgecombe facility from Rikers Island, a full-fledged prison. These men were eligible to be released from Rikers Island *if they could find a job on the outside.* The prison system gave these men fifteen days to find a job in New York. Many of the men had been in prison for some time. There was no assistance program to help the men in the job-finding process. They were to do it all on their own. If they could not find a job in fifteen days, they were sent back to Rikers Island. It seems to me that this is an area in which the African-American denominations, through a well-planned and well-supported ecumenical effort, could work to help prisoners. As I talked with these men, I learned that they had not given up on the denominational churches, but they were highly critical of them. Several talked about the way the preachers had exploited their mothers by encouraging the mothers to give their money to the denominational church, even when there was no food on the women's tables at home. Others talked about the need of denominational members and ministry to come from behind denominational walls and bring an effective ministry into the streets and territories beyond the church grounds.

8. Lincoln and Mamiya, *The Black Church in the African American Experience,* chap. 13, "The Black Church and the Twenty-First Century: Challenges to the Black Church," pp. 382–404.

9. The black church emerges from the soul of community memory when community is centered by the inseparable inter-connected struggles for survival, liberation and positive quality of life formation for poor and oppressed peoples.

10. See Lincoln's and Mamiya's discussion of the mutual aid societies in *The Black Church in the African American Experience,* chap. 9, "The American Dream and the American Dilemma: The Black Church and Economics," pp. 236–73. Also see treatments of mutual societies in August Meier and Elliott Rudwick, *From Plantation to Ghetto* (New York: Hill and Wang, 1970).

11. In this context the term *Americanized* refers to the transformation of patterns of slave culture and sanctioned ways of behaving to patterns of dominant American culture and ways of behaving sanctioned by the Anglo-American status quo.

12. *Mainline* here means the same as it does among whites, that is, Baptist, Methodist, Episcopal, Presbyterian, Lutheran. Catholicism can also be considered mainline.

13. Patricia Reeberg, "The African-American Church and the Community, Part I," an interview in *Routes* 2, no. 9 (September 7–20, 1992), p. 4.

14. Ibid.

15. Ibid.

16. One of the key proponents of Afrocentricity, Dr. Molefi Asante, describes it as a transformation of African-American people's world-view from Europe-centered to Africa-centered. Thus he speaks of Afrocentricity as "a transforming agent in which all things that were old become new and a transformation of attitudes, beliefs, values and behavior results. . . . A new reality is invoked; a new vision is introduced. . . . It is the first and only reality for an African people; it is simply rediscovery." See Molefi Asante, *Afrocentricity* (Trenton, New Jersey: African World Press, 1988), p. 2. Also see Asante's *The Afrocentric Idea* (Philadelphia: Temple University Press, 1987).

17. W. E. B. Du Bois, "The Work of Negro Women in Society." in *W. E. B. Du Bois: Writings in Periodicals Edited by Others,* ed. Herbert Aptheker (Millwood, New York: Kraus-Thomson Organization, 1980).

18. Brown, "God Is As Christ Does," p. 14.

19. Ibid.

20. See Jacqueline Grant, *White Women's Christ, Black Women's Jesus: Feminist Christology and Womanist Response* (Atlanta: Scholars Press, 1989). Also see Brown, "God Is As Christ Does."

21. I know it is difficult to separate the person of Jesus from the work of Jesus. But I contend here that the question of the work of Jesus belongs more properly to the issue of salvation and the discussion of atonement.

22. See Cain Hope Felder, *Troubling Biblical Waters: Race, Class, and Family* (Maryknoll, New York: Orbis Books, 1989).

23. See Joseph R. Washington, Jr., *Black Sects and Cults* (Garden City, New York: Doubleday/Anchor, 1973).

24. See these works on the black spiritual tradition in North America: Hans A. Baer, *The Black Spiritual Movement: A Religious Response to Racism* (Knoxville, Tennessee: The University of Tennessee Press, 1984); Baer, "An Anthropological View of Black Spiritual Churches in Nashville, Tennessee," *Central Issues in Anthropology* 2, no. 2 (1980), pp. 53–58; Baer, "Prophets and Advisors in Black Spiritual Churches: Therapy, Palliative or Opiate?" *Culture, Medicine and Psychiatry,* vol. 5 (1981), pp. 145–70; Baer, "Black Spiritual Churches: A Neglected Socio-Religious Institution," *Phylon: Atlanta University Journal of Race and Culture* 42 (1981), pp. 207–23. As Baer indicates, much more scholarship needs to be devoted to the study of the spiritual movement among African Americans. It would certainly add to our knowledge if scholars in women's studies would do further, in-depth research on the roles and contributions of black women to the development of the theology and religious practices in the black spiritual churches.

25. Baer indicates that there is some dispute among scholars about the exact date when the first spiritual church was established among African Americans. See his discussion of this in *The Black Spiritual Movement,* p. 18.

26. Ibid., p. 18.

27. Ibid.

28. Ibid., p. 28.

29. See Baer, *The Black Spiritual Movement,* pp. 110–59.

30. Ibid., p. 117.

31. See Gordon Melton's discussion of this connection in *The Encyclopedia of American Religions,* vols. 1 and 2 (Wilmington, North Carolina: McGrath Publishers, 1978).

32. Baer, *The Black Spiritual Movement,* p. 123.

33. Ibid., p. 132.

34. Ibid., p. 119. Also see Robert Tallant, *Voodoo in New Orleans* (New York: Collier, 1946).

35. Baer, *The Black Spiritual Movement,* p. 8.

36. Ibid., p. 47.

37. Ibid., p. 84.

38. Hans Baer makes the point that very little research attention has been given to the Universal Hagar's Spiritual Churches. His chapter on this group in *The Black Spiritual Movement* is the most extensive study of the Hagar's churches that I have discovered.

39. While these particular spiritual churches are named after Hagar, there do not seem to be any religious practices within the churches devoted to Hagar. Neither are there commemorative moments devoted to Hagar. I assume that the Hagar in the names of these churches functions in a way similar to that of "St. John," "St. James," and "St. Paul's" in the names of other African-American Protestant churches. I suggest that these proper biblical names mirror the model of faith and religious experience the particular congregation wants to implant in the community's memory.

   The name of Father Hurley's group—Hagar—does model the kind of faith and experience that correlates with African-American women's (and the black family's) faith, history and ongoing experience. Given Hurley's strong religio-nationalistic and family emphases, the name of Hagar in these churches reinforces the sense of Africa, bondage, resistance and final autonomy.

40. See Baer, *The Black Spiritual Movement,* p. 84.

41. Ibid., pp. 86–89.

42. Ibid., p. 86.

43. Ibid., p. 88.

44. Ibid.

45. Ibid.

46. Ibid.

47. As quoted by Baer from the newspaper of the Universal Hagar's Spiritual Church, called the *Aquarian Age.* This particular quotation came from the May 1939 issue of the paper.

48. Baer, *The Black Spiritual Movement,* p. 89.

49. Ibid.

50. Written in 1907 by Eva S. and Levi Dowling, *The Aquarian Gospel of Jesus Christ* attempted to relate the essentials of Jesus' life during his childhood before his ministry—a part of Jesus' story not contained in the Christian testament.

51. See Baer, *The Black Spiritual Movement,* pp. 91–93.

52. Ibid., p. 92.

53. Ibid.

54. See *The Aquarian Age,* October 1938; April 1969; February 1975. Baer also uses these references in his discussion of Father Hurley's response to racial stratification. See Baer, *The Black Spiritual Movement,* pp. 189f.

55. For a full rendering of Father Hurley's teachings about Christ, about the inauguration of the Aquarian Age, and about his view of the problems of Protestantism for black people, see *The Aquarian Age,* 1938–75. Also see Baer, *The Black Spiritual Movement,* pp. 91–96.

56. Quoted by Baer, *The Black Spiritual Movement,* pp. 107–8.

57. Ibid., pp. 105–6.

58. Ibid., p. 107.

59. Ibid.

60. To me, these prayers were reminiscent of some of the ancestor worship important for some traditional African religions.

61. Prathia Hall Wynn, Foreword, to *Those Preachin' Women,* ed. Ella Pearson Mitchell (Valley Forge, Pennsylvania: Judson Press, 1985), pp. 9–10.

### Afterword

1. Walker, *The Color Purple,* p. 245.

2. This is the second definition of *cunning* in Funk & Wagnalls Standard Desk Dictionary.

# INDEX